CO CED 361

AMERICAN SOCIOLOGICAL ASSOCIATION

THE AMERICAN SOCIOLOGICAL ASSOCIATION

CAREER PUBLICATIONS SERIES

PEER REVIEW OF TEACHING: LESSONS FROM AND FOR DEPARTMENTS OF SOCIOLOGY

Edited by

Thomas L. Van Valey
Western Michigan University

American Sociological Association
1430 K St NW Suite 600
Washington DC 20005
202-383-9005
www.asanet.org

Copyright © 2011 by the American Sociological Association

All rights reserved. No part of this book may be reproduced or utilized in any form or by any means, electronic or mechanical including photocopying, recording, or by any information storage or retrieval systems, without permission in writing from the publisher.

To order on-line go to: www.asanet.org for additional information on this or other ASA publications, contact:

American Sociological Association
1430 K Street NW, Suite 600
Washington DC 20005

Tel (202) 383 9005
Fax (202) 638 0882
TTY (202) 638 0981
Email: apap@asanet.org
ISBN: 9780912764450

Library of Congress Control Number: 2011911373

This volume is lovingly dedicated to Carla Beth Howery (1950-2009). It was her idea, and she was the driving force behind it until she was no longer able to do so. Every one of the people responsible for completing this volume owes a debt to Carla - both professional and personal - far greater than this simple volume can represent.

Hopefully, in its own small way, it will help to continue her vision and hopes for the future of the American Sociological Association and of Sociology.

Contents

Foreword and Acknowledgements

Some explanation is obviously necessary, since the co-editor of this volume, Carla Howery, to whom it is dedicated, is no longer with us except in spirit. The idea for this volume, which was hers, originated in work she did with the American Association for Higher Education back in the 1990's. She invited a number of sociologists to join her at an AAHE conference in Albuquerque to learn about and discuss the notion of peer review. I was one of those people. Following that conference, she put together an agenda and materials for several workshops that she organized for regional professional meetings. Several of us participated in those workshops with her. In addition, she asked a number of us to write essays on issues related to the peer review of teaching which were to be published in a volume by the ASA.

Some essays were written, submitted, and Carla sent them out for review. Others were drafted but not completed. Still others were never written. For a variety of personal and professional reasons, the project languished for a several years. Then, a couple of years before she retired, Carla asked me to help her finally put together the volume that she had conceived so many years before. However, because of her personal health situation, she asked me to take the lead on the volume. During the interim, a fair number of pieces had been completed. I had written a couple, Ted Wagenaar had written a couple, Keith Roberts and Mike Brooks each had finished one and several others were in draft form. Carla was also planning on writing several. Therefore, just before she retired from the ASA, I went to Washington so we could decide on the table of contents and divide up the various pieces that either had been drafted and needed editing or still needed to be written. Unfortunately, after she retired, the cancer that Carla so valiantly fought further limited her ability to work on the project, and she was unable to complete several of her assigned essays. Therefore, after she died, I asked several people if they would write those essays so the volume could be completed.

The volume is divided into five major segments. The first, "The Context for Peer Review" contains three essays, and sets the stage for the discussion of the peer review of teaching. Ted Wagenaar's essay lays the groundwork for why peer review is important. Vaneeta D'Andrea's essay further locates it in the work of the AAHE and the ASA. Finally, Beth Rushing's essay elaborates on the argument that teaching, like research and publications, should be a public rather than a private activity.

The second major segment describes some of the "Modes of Peer Review." There are many ways that peers can review and evaluate their own teaching and the teaching of their colleagues. Ted Wagenaar discusses one of the more promising approaches, the teaching portfolio, where an instructor collects, organizes, and presents materials relevant to his/her teaching. Carol Bailey initially drafted the next essay on the use of teaching circles as a mechanism for opening the conversation about teaching in a department. I edited and revised her essay for this volume. This is followed by an essay that John DeLamater initially drafted on the use of interviews with students as a mechanism for getting feedback about teaching. I also edited and revised John's essay for this volume. Keith Roberts' essay on an instrument for observing teaching not only provides an example format, but also offers a perspective on what is probably the most common approach to the peer review of teaching. Closing out the segment is the previously unpublished essay by Vaneeta D'Andrea and Hans Mauksch on the use of video feedback as a supplement in peer observation. Vaneeta graciously agreed to update it for this volume.

The third segment, "Preparing, Identifying, and Appropriate Use of Peers," examines a variety of issues that are related to the peer review of teaching. The first essay, coauthored by Brent Bruton, focuses on beginning teachers - graduate students - and suggests how they might be trained not only to do research, but to teach and to expect their teaching to be evaluated publicly. Maxine Atkinson and Andrea Hunt then turn to the other extreme – experienced, tenured faculty – and look at the issue of the peer review of teaching from the perspective of those relatively few institutions where a policy of post tenure review has been implemented. Finally, I finish the segment with some concerns about how to accomplish the process of peer review in an ethical manner and some ideas about responding to them.

The third segment and this fourth segment, "Implementation Strategies," recognize that some departments and some faculty will have difficulty with the notion of the peer review of teaching. This segment offers some ways to begin the conversation about the peer review of teaching and also to get it started. The first essay, by Ed Kain, offers a number of ways to get faculty involved in the conversation about peer review. This is followed by Mike Brooks' essay focusing on the important role that the chair of a department can make in both initiating the conversation and implementing a departmental strategy. The last essay is a compilation that I put together of Carla Howery's writings on the pedagogical colloquium and how it can be used to sensitize a department to the importance of teaching.

The final segment, "Resources," is just that. It contains the bibliography on the peer review of teaching that Carla Howery initially put together and that I updated, largely based on the resources provided in the various chapters of this volume.

I do want to take this opportunity to recognize the many people who have made this volume possible. It begins with Chick Goldsmid and Everitt Wilson who first introduced me to the importance of good teaching so many years ago when I was a graduate student at the University of North Carolina. It must also include Amos Hawley, Tad Blalock, and Gerry Lenski who were the models to which I have always aspired. And, of course, it must include Carla Howery, since she did so much more than just come up with the idea for the volume and then hand it over to me to finish. I am particularly grateful to Margaret Weigers-Vitullo and the staff of the ASA's Professional and Academic Affairs Program for their guidance and assistance as the volume has moved forward, one baby step after another. Finally, I owe much to the patience of the early contributors to this volume whose work took so long to see fruition, and the willingness of the colleagues who stepped in to help finish it. The end product of all those efforts is before you. While it is not the same as it would have been with Carla at the helm, I and all the contributors hope that it will continue the work that Carla held so dear – the teaching of Sociology and the improvement of the profession.

January 25, 2011
Thomas L. Van Valey
Western Michigan University

I

THE CONTEXT FOR PEER REVIEW

1

The Peer Review of Teaching

Theodore C. Wagenaar, Miami University

Budget crises exist in almost all states. Strategic priorities committees exist on most campuses and some programs and departments have been closed. The proportion of contingent faculty members has climbed dramatically while the proportion of tenure-track positions has declined. Increases in the cost of college have far outstripped increases in the Consumer Price Index. Accreditation agencies, legislatures, and citizens alike ask questions about the value of a college education and how learning outcomes can be assessed. Trustees and other groups seek to weigh in on areas that have traditionally been the domain of professors. Tenure has come under fire (Hacker and Dreifus, 2010; Taylor, 2010), and attacks on "liberal" professors have been on the rise. (Gaff, 2009).

There has been a shift in values from a faculty focus to a student and learning focus. A big part of this shift in thinking about learning has been in terms of greater collaboration with students. Alternative educational models have emerged - interdisciplinary study, an emphasis on critical thinking, finding practical uses of knowledge, and the role of community and global engagement.

These and other developments in higher education have called attention to the role of the professor and the social contract that the academic profession has with the public. That contract reassures the public that professors can and will govern themselves, and thus can be granted academic freedom as an inherent part of the social contract. Most typically, the interest of professors in academic freedom has centered on their job rights and job security. Yet, academic responsibility is an important corollary of academic freedom. Faculty members have an ethical responsibility to perform well, to uphold the ideals of the profession, and to hold their peers accountable (Hamilton, 2009), particularly in the face of the changes noted above.

Peer review lies at the heart of the responsibilities of professors in the social contract they hold with the public. It also contributes substantially to the maintenance of academic freedom by upholding professional competence. However, socialization into the role of a responsible peer has been neglected, and it appears that academics have largely abdicated the responsibility for teaching graduate students and new faculty members about the essential ingredients of an ethical professional identity. Similarly, socialization into the role of an effective instructor has also been neglected at many institutions. As a result, many faculty members take a rather narrow view of academic freedom (protect my job) and are only minimally aware of and dedicated to the role of peer review and shared governance (Hamilton, 2009). This is especially true for contingent faculty, who experience what Rice (2006) calls the "unbundling of faculty roles." Therefore, contingent faculty receive even less of the professional and pedagogical socialization necessary for success.

Hamilton (2009) and Gaff (2009) and other recent critics skimp on specific strategies for implementing and improving peer review. In this article I wish to help fill the voids in socialization and knowledge by examining the peer review of teaching and offering advice for its successful completion. I join Bernstein and Edwards and others in saying that "We Need Objective, Rigorous Peer Review of Teaching" (Bernstein and Edwards, 2001).

WHAT IS PEER REVIEW?

Peer review underlies the assessment process in higher education. Almost all schools require some type of internal peer review of candidates for promotion and tenure; many also require external peer reviews. Faculty members routinely receive reviews of grant proposals and journal articles. In short, peer review has long been a hallmark of higher education as part of the social contract that highlights the professional status of professors.

The role of peers in evaluating teaching has become more systematic (Seldin, 2006). Until recently, the peer review of teaching primarily involved reviewing student evaluation scores. Relatively few schools have engaged faculty members in direct observation of teaching and in reviews of teaching materials. Academic freedom debates often precluded direct observation due to uncertainty (and even disputes) over whose definition of effective teaching would be used. The fact that relatively few faculty members have explicitly learned how to teach and how to review teaching has also hindered a more systematic and comprehensive examination of teaching (Hamilton, 2009).

The turning point for more systematic peer review occurred in 1994 when the American Association for Higher

Education developed a Teaching Initiative Project on the peer review of teaching (Hutchings, 1994). This project highlighted the need for greater peer collaboration. Effective peer review depends on comprehensive collaborative thinking about teaching, which involves: how faculty members teach their subjects; how each course fits in with the overall goals of the program; how different faculty members teaching the same course can assume more joint responsibility for a course and learn from each other; how instructors can learn teaching strategies from their peers; how they can actually teach a course together; and how they can nurture a departmental culture that puts teaching center stage. Departments that work collaboratively will usually approach the various forms of peer review more effectively. Massy, Wilger, and Colbeck (1994) observed that several features characterize collaborative departments that support teaching: frequent faculty interaction, tolerance of differences, generational equity, workload equity, course rotation, comprehensive student and peer evaluations, balanced incentives, consensus decision-making, and most importantly, effective chairs. A collaborative department is not necessarily a prerequisite for effective peer review, but such a style greatly facilitates effective peer review.

Peer review more generally involves reviews of both research and teaching. The peer review of research has its own problems, which this essay does not address, but it usually focuses on the end product of the research process. The peer review of teaching generally involves the entire process, going beyond classroom observation and including a professor's role in curriculum development, advising, and other teaching related issues. It also frequently involves reviews of teaching materials, such as syllabi, assignments, and exams and even student products.

"Peer Review" does require some consideration of the two terms. First, who is a "peer?" Generally, peers are those at a similar level in the institutional hierarchy and with similar duties. So, full-time administrators would generally not be considered peers. This presents a role ambiguity for administrators, which is complicated because they are held accountable for student learning (Gaff, 2009). Of course, colleagues in one's department generally would be considered peers. Less clear is the role of chairs -- they serve both as faculty peers and as administrators. These dual roles may generate role conflict, which may hamper chairs' contributions to effective peer review.

Also less clear is the role of colleagues in other disciplines -- can someone be a peer who knows little or nothing about one's discipline? On the one hand, one might argue that lack of familiarity with disciplinary content may make such a reviewer more attuned to teaching issues (Millis, 1999). On the other hand, one might argue that only a peer in the same discipline can fully place teaching behaviors in proper context. For example, a same-discipline reviewer could provide specific examples that a different-discipline reviewer could not. Muchinsky (1995) suggests that same-discipline reviews should focus on content as well as process, but that different-discipline reviews should focus only on process. Gaff (2009) notes that peer review across disciplines does not work very well because recent educational ventures (such as interdisciplinary programs) are organized horizontally whereas universities are organized vertically.

Is an instructional specialist or someone in a teaching and learning center a peer? Perhaps more so, if such a person holds faculty rank and is at least somewhat familiar with the discipline of the instructor. Perhaps less so, if such a person has observational skills but lacks faculty experience (although such a person could still provide valuable insights). In this essay I will consider a peer to be someone whose primary responsibilities currently include or previously included teaching. Thus, I do not see a peer outside one's discipline as less of a peer but rather a different type of peer. The important point is to clarify the definition and role of peers at the local level in a way that enhances the overall goals of the peer review program.

The second element of "Peer Review" raises the issue of what constitutes "review?" Review can include everything from a casual review of student evaluations to the most rigorous and analytical assessment of both teaching materials and in-class teaching. For this essay, I will consider a review as reflecting both information gathering and information processing. Information gathering, at minimum, includes relevant teaching materials (syllabi, assignments, exams, samples of student work) and in-class observations. Interviews with those reviewed also yield information. Something must be done with the information so that the person being reviewed benefits as well the school, which reflects the information processing stage.

WHY THE INTEREST IN PEER REVIEW?

In addition to the AAHE project noted above, the seminal work on this topic is Boyer's (1990). He stressed both the scholarship of teaching and the need for greater recognition and support of the teaching role. Also at work have been public and media perceptions that universities overemphasize research at the expense of teaching (Hacker and Driefus, 2010). As a result, many universities and colleges have strengthened the emphasis on teaching in their promotion and tenure decisions and have also provided more support for improving teaching. Fairweather (2002) suggests, however, that the personnel review process has had little apparent effect on teaching improvement. Still, greater sensitivity to the competing demands of universities' bureaucratic and professional spheres (as well as other contradictions) has yielded renewed interest in teaching and its assessment (Rau and Baker, 1989). New instructional modes, such as online learning, have also heightened interest in teaching assessment, particularly peer review (Bennett and Santy, 2009). Similarly, sites such as "ratemyprofessor.com" and the widespread and sometimes exclusive use of student evaluations of teaching have led to rising skepticism about the utility of student evaluations as a form of review. Critics note that student evaluations overemphasize in-class teaching behaviors and require caution when used in (El Hassan, 2009; Wagenaar, 1995).

These trends have promoted interest in peer review. The renewed interest in the teaching role has generated increased attention to assessing and developing performance in that role, and critical reviews of student evaluations have generated interest in alternative approaches. Peer review also provides another mechanism for faculty and schools to address accountability concerns. In fact, many states have begun requiring peer review as part of the tenure, promotion, and merit processes. Indeed, Seldin (2006) documented the growing use of peer review of teaching, along with a decline in the over reliance on student evaluations.

WHY USE PEER REVIEW?

Peer review can provide a deeper and more comprehensive analysis of teaching than other forms of evaluating teaching, by providing expert review of both teaching materials and classroom teaching. Peers are better qualified than students, for example, to assess an instructor's mastery and selection of course content, the course organization, the appropriateness of course objectives and materials, the appropriateness of evaluative strategies, and the appropriateness of methodology used to teach specific content areas (Bernstein, 2008). Peers may also have more information about an instructor's commitment to teaching and concern for student learning, and may also have more information about an instructor's contributions to departmental, campus-wide, and disciplinary efforts to improve teaching. Given the important role of student learning in assessing teaching, peers may also be better able to make assessments about student learning by reviewing student products (Keig and Waggoner 1994).

From a sociological viewpoint, teaching has traditionally been viewed as a private activity (Palmer, 1998). Instructors typically close their doors when they teach, both figuratively and literally. Peer review can help open those doors by making teaching more public and more shared. Peer review can help to raise teaching to the status of research -- worthy of review by colleagues, worthy of our best efforts because our work will be displayed, and worthy of professional rewards. Peer review carries prestige and nurtures a growing culture of evidence in teaching akin to the culture of evidence that we have long experienced in research (cf. Halpern, 1994). In addition, peer review often yields greater peer collaboration because peer review can help move teaching to a more collaborative responsibility for quality teaching across a department and for student learning across the curriculum (Gaff, 2009; Hutchings, 1996).

Of course, peer review can also occur without collaboration. Moreover, when it does, the causal order is not entirely clear -- peer review helps generate a collaborative climate and a collaborative climate serves as a precursor for successful peer review. Regardless, promoting both requires trust, an effective chair (see Chapter 13 in this volume), a structure that promotes interaction (such as regularly scheduled meetings on teaching issues – see Chapter 5 in this volume), and a supportive institutional climate. Quinlan (1996) provided descriptions of the various forms collaboration can take: individual and team mentoring, reciprocal class visits, teaching circles, departmental teaching libraries, pedagogical colloquia, teaching portfolios, course portfolios, and departmental reviews. As with the peer review of research, the peer review of teaching yields professional rewards for the reviewer as well as the recipient. The reviewer may encounter alternative forms and strategies of teaching, which may help strengthen the reviewer's teaching (Kohut, Burnap, and Yon, 2007). Done on a broad scale, peer review helps build a culture of teaching excellence.

The public display of teaching also encourages self appraisals among both the persons being reviewed and the reviewers. Peer review often encourages instructors to reassess what they are doing and why. The process inevitably involves instructors in a reflective self dialogue about their teaching. It encourages a self critique of one's efforts, an introspection regarding why we made the choices that we did, and how successful they have been. In the process, peer review encourages a reassessment of our presentation of teaching self as well as a reassessment of our teaching. For example, Austin (1992) found that peer collaboration results in a deeper interest in and commitment to teaching excellence as well as a more humanistic approach to students, one that is reflected in instructors' increased sensitivity to student differences.

Peer review also affords triangulation -- the use of multiple data sources to improve teaching. As is true in many research ventures, multiple data sources provide a more complete and more accurate view of the social reality we wish to describe. Peer review helps round out a comprehensive examination of teaching when used with student evaluations, teaching portfolios, and self reviews, and helps counterbalance the weaknesses inherent in each of these sources of data (Brinko, 1993). Student evaluations, for example, reflect primarily students' perceptions about in-class performance dimensions, and they refer to the entire course instead of a particular class session. Centra (1994) found that ratings given by peers correlated only modestly with scores on a commercial student evaluation form. This finding suggests that different criteria may be applied by the two audiences and underscores the need for triangulation.

Peer review helps to generate a public dialogue about teaching -- our own teaching experiences, teaching sociology, and teaching in general. Such shared analyses generate ideas for change and possibly improvement, and help construct a dialogue about teaching that in and of itself puts teaching center stage. As a result, teachers become more comfortable sharing what they do and learning from others. In the end, the social climate of teaching takes on greater collective involvement and representation when peer review becomes institutionalized.

Finally, peer review has multiple beneficiaries. Instructors obviously benefit from suggestions for improved teaching, and the suggestions also bolster their teaching portfolios. Students benefit from the improved instruction and from the greater sense of a learning community that results from their involvement in the review process (Kumaravadivelu, 1995). Peers benefit by assessing their own teaching while observing others. For example, Nordstrom (1995) includes items in his worksheets requiring the observer to note how his or her teaching may benefit from what has been observed. Programs benefit from the data provided by uncovering strategies for improving both the program and the collective teaching enterprise. Again, Nordstrom (1995) provides items that assess the role of a course in the overall curriculum. Finally, departments and schools benefit from more comprehensive personnel reviews and from the potential impact on organizational goals and their attainment (Toth and McKey, 2010).

WHAT NEEDS TO OCCUR BEFORE THE REVIEW?

In a word... planning. Clearly, the most successful peer review programs are part of an institutionalized program. A culture that is supportive of teaching both within the department and the school is most useful for implementing successful peer review (Lomas and Nicholls, 2005). However, effective peer review inevitably requires considerable planning regarding the format, processes, and outcomes of a program. Isolated and individually organized, single-visit peer reviews (which do not require much planning) are helpful on a personal level but have little impact on the teaching culture in a department. In contrast, Sullivan (1995) described how her department developed a four-step approach to the peer review of instructors and professors. Doing so required some difficult discussions and decisions about teaching in general, teaching sociology in particular, how teaching could and should be assessed, and who should be reviewed. Nordstrom (1995) also described the development of a peer review program, and stresses the linkages such a program must have with other ways of assessing teaching as well as with the multiple uses of the program. Given the widespread use of contingent faculty, Gaff (2009) argues that peer review must include such faculty members. However, completing comprehensive reviews of everyone in a large department could be extremely time consuming.

The reward system must incorporate peer review. In a formative way, it helps if the institutional reward system recognizes the interest and willingness of faculty members to submit to peer review. In a summative way, the institutional reward structure is even more important because it sets the stage both for the process and the outcomes of the reviews. Summative peer review generally fails when it is merely suggested, or even when it is required but is done so without a solid connection to the reward system. Both the process and the outcomes of the peer review process must be closely connected with reviews for promotion, tenure, and merit at both the departmental level and at levels above (Fairweather, 2002).

Will the process be only one directional, with the reviewer sharing perceptions with the instructor regarding observable behavior only? Or, will it incorporate the teacher's and students' perspectives as well, and also cover non-observable teacher behavior (such as syllabi and assignments) in the process?

Kumaravadivelu (1995) argues for a multidimensional model of peer evaluation. This model incorporates the perceptions of the teacher, the learners, and the observer in a review of a particular classroom session. Incorporating the teacher's intentions and perceptions helps the observer understand the teacher's definition of the situation. Kumaravadivelu also provides useful generic instruments for gathering self observation reports both before and after the class session, as well as learner and peer observation reports. He notes that his forms can and should be adapted to various disciplines. Clearly, he argues that triangulation *within* the peer review process strengthens the validity of peer review by broadening the perspective on this slice of a teacher's social reality.

Which rating scales will be used? There is some merit to the argument that schools (and perhaps even departments) should develop their own scales to be responsive to local issues and local definitions of effective teaching. Self-developed scales also increase faculty ownership of both the process and content of the peer review plan. On the other hand, using established scales takes advantage of the pre-testing and implementation efforts already expended by other faculties. Berk, Naumann, and Appling (2004) describe a five-step process for creating peer observation scales. My own favorite is a lengthy form developed by Helling (1988), who reviewed numerous articles on peer review and identified specific teaching behaviors for each of three approaches: teaching by presentation, teaching through discussion, and teaching through discovery. At first, the form looks imposing and difficult to implement, given the number of teaching behaviors listed. But the reviewer as well as the instructor can identify those behaviors most relevant for a particular class. The important point is to use a form that best suits both the process and the class.

Training must occur. Training at the departmental level will help focus peer review on the particular needs of faculty and may generate discipline-specific discussions about enhancing teaching. Still, peers are very generous -- most assign ratings of "very good" or "excellent" (Root, 1987). In fact, faculty members are less confident rating teaching than research, and tend to give high ratings as a result. This lack of confidence may result from lack of training, inexperience, insufficient socialization into the peer reviewer role, or an exchange assumption that if good ratings are given good ratings will be received. However, faculty members have more confidence rating teaching materials than actual teaching (Braskamp and Ory, 1994). Thus, without training and without a culture of systematic inquiry into teaching, peer review may revert to mutual back scratching. Centra (1994) found discrepancies among ratings from three sources: peers selected by a faculty member, peers selected by a dean, and deans. These discrepancies may again reflect a lack of training, but they may also reflect the use of different criteria by different raters. Training improves reliability, as well as contributes to a common framework of understanding and increased skills in differentiating levels of teaching competence. A school culture that promotes inquiry into teaching also helps – this can be promoted through seminars, support for attendance at teaching conferences, and competent support personnel.

The actual details of the review process should be outlined before a review takes place. A pre-observation conference should occur, and the goals should be clarified (Carter, 2008). For example, is the review to be summative or formative? Generally, it is best to begin the process with a formative approach, to focus the review on diagnosis and feedback, to reduce the threat factor, and to help institutionalize the process. Only with experience and institutionalization is peer review likely to be useful for summative and evaluative purposes. Morehead and Shedd (1997) provide an argument for using external reviewers for summative purposes. Webb and McEnerney (1995) described how a formative peer review program developed, summarized the outcomes, made recommendations, and provide sample forms. Kell and Annetts (2009) provide a description of a similar program at a different school.

How many peers will be involved, and how many visits will occur? Formative reviews can be done with just one reviewer and a single visit, but summative and evaluative reviews should be done with at least two reviewers and multiple visits (at least two) to enhance reliability and validity. Prezas, et al (2009) explain their experience with multiple reviewers.

Will the visit occur in the regular classroom or in a special classroom set up for video recording? (8 in this volume.) Especially in the initial stages, people feel more comfortable in their regular environments. Video recording can intrude in the normal classroom atmosphere, although those who have experienced it have indicated that most people become oblivious to the recording about ten minutes into the review. However, video recording has unique advantages. For example, it enables the reviewer and the teacher to replay the teaching behaviors that led the reviewer to make specific comments. Video recording can also address reliability and validity concerns because the same teaching session can be reviewed by multiple reviewers. Similarly, video recording can help validate other sources of information about teaching. Tips for successful use include encouraging a faculty member to try it before the actual peer review recording, reviewing recordings of other faculty and soliciting their feedback, soliciting feedback from instructional experts on recordings of other faculty, explaining the process to students before the recording day, discussing ownership of the recordings, and discussing the rating forms that will be used. If video recording poses problems, you might consider the LiveScribe pen, which records audio at the point where you are writing, so that you can listen to and share the audio at the point you made a particular note. Online peer review is also possible (Bennett and Santy, 2009).

When in the term will the review occur? It is probably best to wait until at least half of the term is over in order to better assess the relationship between the instructor and the students. It is also best to avoid the last few weeks in the term because both instructors and students typically feel stressed. Will the visit be a surprise or will the faculty member know beforehand? Opinions are mixed on this issue. Some think that instructors will choreograph an unusually effective session if they know when the visit will occur. Others feel that it is difficult to mask basic teaching skills with "extra" preparation. Still others feel that informing the instructor beforehand establishes an atmosphere of trust. I feel that instructors should be informed because it is important to do everything possible to help them succeed.

There several other questions that should be considered. Which teaching materials will be reviewed? Focusing on the total teaching and learning experience helps develop a more comprehensive view of teaching and learning. Hence, I recommend a review of at least the syllabus and some assignments and exams. It also helps to develop the criteria to be used in such reviews and to share these with faculty members before they are reviewed. For example, sample student papers help reviewers better understand the faculty member's responsiveness to student learning needs. Student ratings should also be peer reviewed so that they can be placed in context. Will a conference occur before the visit so the reviewer can be informed about the class thus far? Such a conference helps the reviewer place the day's review in context and also helps foster communication on teaching with the instructor being reviewed. Should students be told about the review? Those who argue "yes" do so based on the belief that students have a right to know what is occurring in their classroom and that socializing students into the review process will encourage them to take student evaluations more seriously. Those who argue "no" feel that the instructor may coax students into being model students for a day. My recommendation is to inform the students of the review and to socialize students into how the review process works, their role in the process, and the potential outcomes.

Who will control the information that is produced? In formative peer reviews, I recommend that all notes and information remain with the person reviewed. This practice fosters willingness to engage in peer review and meets the formative goal of helping someone better understand his/her teaching. In summative reviews, it should be made clear who will see the observation reports and through which hierarchical channels the information will pass. Checks on the veracity and appropriateness of information should be implemented, such as giving the person reviewed the opportunity to comment on the reports and incorporating a group review when more than one reviewer is involved, to minimize the potential biases of any one reviewer.

Finally, sociological variables such as gender and race may introduce biases in peer reviews. Unfortunately, little research has been done on these factors in peer review. As sociologists, we can begin to identify possible sources of bias and strategies for alleviating them.

WHAT HAPPENS DURING AND AFTER THE REVIEW?

Preliminary discussions will help clarify the goals and expected outcomes of peer review and will help determine which observation forms will be used during the review and how they will be used (Hammersley-Fletcher and Orsmond, 2004). What type of notes should the reviewer take? When an observation is not going to be video recorded, my preference is to use the "double entry" method. With this approach, the reviewer divides note paper in half vertically, and on the one side takes notes about the presentation as a student might, and on the other side makes comments for the instructor. This approach enables the instructor to see exactly where in the presentation the reviewer noted a particular comment or made a suggestion. This contextual reminder helps the instructor make specific changes based on the comments. However, the approach should be explained before the review lest the instructor worry about the volume of notes the reviewer takes.

A consultation session should occur soon after the review. This session enables the reviewer to explain and expand upon notes taken, and gives the instructor an opportunity to ask for clarification or further information. This session can also contribute to developing a teaching culture in the department by promoting discussions about teaching. Feedback should be descriptive rather than evaluative to reduce the threat factor and to enhance the utility of the comments (e.g., "some students seemed to miss your transition point" versus "your transition point failed"). The reviewer should be careful to clearly distinguish descriptions of teaching behaviors from suggestions for improvement. Descriptions of teaching behaviors (e.g., "the instructor looked down at her notes when a student started talking") are more useful than only summary statements (e.g., "the instructor needs better relations with students"). Start out with strengths and gradually move into areas needing attention. Use "I" statements when describing weaknesses (e.g., "I wasn't clear about the example you used to support X theory") and "you" statements when describing strengths (e.g., "You effectively turned that student's question into an opportunity to illustrate critical thinking").

The reviewer should look for patterns rather than focusing exclusively on idiosyncratic teaching behaviors. This strategy also helps an instructor learn how to see patterns in his/her own teaching. Avoid judgments. Provide opportunities for the instructor to respond to the review, both formally and informally. If the review is summative and evaluative, the review should be written and shared with the instructor. If teaching materials are part of the review, be sure the review covers them as well. Also, include contextual factors, such as class size, time of day, attendance on the day of the review, and whether the course is an elective or a required course. These factors affect student evaluations and may also affect peer reviews. If multiple reviewers are involved, decide to present either a combined review or separate reviews. Brinko (1993) has an extensive list of literature-based effective feedback principles.

Finally, compare and connect the observer's perceptions with the teacher's and learners' perceptions, as indicated by such forms as provided by Kumaravadivelu (1995). Focus particularly on points of similarity and discrepancy, and engage the instructor in a discussion of possible reasons for discrepancies. Numerous suggestions and specific strategies for implementing the peer review process can be found in Hutchings (1995).

WHAT PROBLEMS MIGHT OCCUR?

The peer review of teaching has its own set of problems. Mutual back scratching can occur in a competitive environment. For this reason, it is best to begin peer review for formative and diagnostic reasons. Few reviewers receive training, which limits their objectivity and both the comprehensiveness and the utility of reviews. In addition, faculty should be familiar with some of the literature on teaching and learning. When questions emerge, a useful first response is, "What does the literature show?" Unless the goals and procedures have been carefully determined, reviewers may simply follow their own predilections and thereby compromise the utility of peer review (Courneya, Pratt, and Collins, 2008). Until the peer review of teaching becomes part of the institutionalized culture of the department and the school, agreed upon goals and definitions of effective teaching will be difficult to negotiate.

Too many schools have implemented the peer review of teaching without providing the requisite support staff. If a review indicates problem areas, the instructor should have a center for teaching and learning to consult for improvement strategies. An institutional support structure will enhance the utility of peer review. Sampling problems also exist. How can a "random" sampling of teaching occur? Should it occur? Reviewers should be sensitive to reliability and validity issues, but not at the risk of over-standardization. Some flexibility is necessary to respond effectively to each instructor's particular situation.

Peer review can be very time consuming. A multiple-visit, multiple-reviewer peer review can easily take over 12 hours, counting pre- and post-review discussions, report writing, and follow-up. Faculty members comment frequently and vociferously about all the extra work peer review involves, particularly in schools with an ethos of "doing more with less." One ameliorative strategy may be the use of peer coaching, in which pairs of faculty members voluntarily meet to discuss and improve their teaching (Huston and Weaver, 2008).

AFTER ALL, WHAT REALLY IS GOOD TEACHING?

Perhaps the most difficult problem in the peer review of teaching involves the potential for bias. Courneya, Pratt, and Collins (2008) for example, show that peer reviews of teaching are affected by the reviewers' preconceived definitions of effective teaching and by the propensity to look for their own teaching practices in the teaching of others. Moreover, peer review often becomes a political issue, one worthy of its own analysis. Our definition of effective teaching (even teaching itself) can become problematic because we often fail to see how such definitions are integrally connected to our political and social worlds. Can someone who favors one approach to explaining reality (say, a postmodernist or a Marxist) legitimately review and assess the teaching of someone who favors a different approach (say, a hard-core empiricist or a functionalist)? Who is to say what effective teaching "really" is? Is it possible to devise a single definition? With multiple definitions, whose definition should (and does) prevail? Do power imbalances influence which definition receives emphasis? Even if a single or multiple definitions emerge, what right do some reviewers have to impose such definitions on those who do not share these definitions? Does academic freedom protect the rights of a faculty member to teach how she or he wishes (Keig and Waggoner, 1995)? Or, should we, as Gaff (2009) advocates, begin to use peer review to underscore the academic responsibility aspect of academic freedom?

These are difficult issues, and they frequently derail progress toward peer review. Still, three thoughts come to mind. First, many aspects of effective teaching receive widespread agreement and empirical support. For example, effective teaching results in student learning. Active learning strategies are generally more effective than passive ones. Students indicating difficulty in understanding probably reflect in part the nature of the teaching. Teaching and learning at higher cognitive levels (such as analysis and synthesis) are generally more important (and more difficult) than teaching and learning at lower cognitive levels (such as memorizing). Centra (1994) categorizes teaching effectiveness into 13 categories of performance, grouped into three teaching skill areas: motivational skills, interpersonal skills, and intellectual skills. These and other aspects of teaching can be peer reviewed at some level (Smith and Walvoord, 1993).

Second, widespread agreement on particular theoretical approaches, on the exact core of a discipline to be stressed, or the best teaching method are probably not desirable, even if such agreement were possible. In fact, exposure to alternative views and teaching strategies strengthens students' understanding of the core issues and points of disagreement in a discipline. What is important is to review an individuals' teaching as it relates to the discipline's current theories and methods, as it relates to the department's curricular and course goals, how the teaching reflects widely supported features of effective teaching, and how it affects student learning.

Third, peer review generates public conversations about teaching in general and teaching one's discipline in particular. Such conversations, along with the alteration in the culture of teaching, yield a social context within which further discussions and questions emerge, the results of which often infuse the classrooms of all, or most of, the teachers in a department. In this way, teaching becomes a more collective process as faculty members own more of the entire teaching and learning process that students experience. The net result is improved teaching on multiple (and sometimes competing) dimensions. But at the least, improved teaching is likely to occur, which is probably the most important outcome of peer review (see Chism, McKeachie, and Chism, 2007, for ideas on how to connect peer review more directly to learning). The peer review of teaching will also enhance the academy by shoring up the role of academic freedom and shared governance.

REFERENCES

Austin, A.E. 1992. Supporting Junior Faculty Through a Teaching Fellows Program.@ In *Developing New and Junior Faculty*, edited by M.D. Sorcinelli and A.E. Austin. New Directions for Teaching and Learning No. 50. San Francisco: Jossey-Bass.

Bennett, S. and J. Santy. 2009. "A Window on Our Teaching Practice: Enhancing Individual Online Teaching Quality Through Online Peer Observation and Support. A UK Case Study." Nurse Education in Practice 9(6):403-406.

Berk, R.A., P.L. Naumann, and S.E. Appling. 2004. "Beyond Student Ratings: Peer Observation of Classroom and Clinical Teaching." *International Journal of Nursing Education Scholarship* 1(1):article 10.

Bernstein, D.J. 2008. "Peer Review and Evaluation of the Intellectual Work of Teaching." *Change: The Magazine of Higher Learning* 40(2):48-51.

_____, and R. Edwards. 2001. "We Need Objective, Rigorous Peer Review of Teaching. *The Chronicle of Higher Education* (January 5): B24.

Boyer, E. 1990. *Scholarship Reconsidered: New Priorities for the Professoriate.* Princeton: The Carnegie Foundation for the Advancement of Teaching.

Braskamp, L.A. and J.C. Ory. 1994. *Assessing Faculty Work.* San Francisco: Jossey-Bass.

Brinko, K.T. 1993. "The Practice of Giving Feedback to Improve Teaching: What is Effective?" *Journal of Higher Education* 64:574-593.

Carter, V.K. 2008. "Five Steps to Becoming a Better Peer Reviewer." *College Teaching* 56(2):85-88.

Centra, J.A.. 1994. "The Use of the Teaching Portfolio and Student Evaluations for Summative Evaluation." *Journal of Higher Education* 65 (5):555-570.

Chism, N.V.N, W.J. McKeachie, and G.W. Chism. 2007. *Peer Review of Teaching: A Sourcebook*. Bolton, MA: Anker.

Courneya, C., D.D. Pratt, and J. Collins. 2008. "Through What Perspective Do We Judge the Teaching of Peers?" *Teaching and Teacher Education: An International Journal of Research and Studies* 24(1):69-79.

El Hassan, K. 2009. "Investigating Substantive and Consequential Validity of Student Ratings of Instruction." *Higher Education Research & Development* 28(3):319-333.

Fairweather, J.S. 2002. "The Ultimate Faculty Evaluation: Promotion and Tenure Decisions." *New Directions for Institutional* Research 2002 (114):97-108.

Gaff, J.G. 2009. "Academic Freedom, Peer Review, and Shared Governance in the Face of New Realities." Pp. 19-36 in *The Future of the Professoriate: Academic Freedom, Peer Review, and Shared Governance*, edited by N.W. Hamilton and J.G. Gaff. Washington DC: Association of American Colleges and Universities.

Hacker, A. and C. Dreifus. 2010. Higher Education? *How Colleges are Wasting Our Money and Failing Our Kids—and What We Can Do About It.* New York: Times Books.

Halpern, D.F. 1994. "Rethinking College Instruction for a Changing World." Pp. 1-12 in *Changing College Classrooms*, edited by D.F. Halpern and associates. San Francisco: Jossey-Bass.

Hamilton, N.W. 2009. "Proactively Justifying the Academic Profession's Social Contract."Pp. 1-18 in *The Future of the Professoriate: Academic Freedom, Peer Review, and Shared Governance*, edited by N.W. Hamilton and J.G. Gaff. Washington DC: Association of American Colleges and Universities.

Hammersley-Fletcher, L. and P. Orsmond. 2004. "Evaluating Our Peers: Is Peer Observation a Meaningful Process?" *Studies in Higher Education* 29(4):489-503.

Helling, B.B. 1988. "Looking for Good Teaching: A Guide to Peer Observation." *Journal of Staff, Program, and Organizational Development* 6 (4):1-12.

Huston, T. and C.L. Weaver. 2008. "Peer Coaching: Professional Development for Experienced Faculty." *Innovative Higher Education* 33(1):5-20.

Hutchings, P. 1994. "Peer Review of Teaching: From Idea to Prototype." *AAHE Bulletin* 47 (3):3-7.

_____, editor. 1995. *From Idea to Prototype: The Peer Review of Teaching*. Washington, DC: American Association for Higher Education.

Keig, L.W. and M. Waggoner. 1994. *Collaborative Peer Review: The Role of Faculty in Improving College Teaching* (ASHE/ERIC Higher Education Report # 2). Washington: Association for the Study of Higher Education.

_____. 1995. "Peer Review of Teaching: Improving College Instruction Through Formative Assessment." *Journal on Excellence in College Teaching* 6 (3):51-83.

Kell, C. and S. Annetts. 2009. "Peer Review of Teaching: Embedded Practice or Policy-Holding Complacency?" *Innovations in Education and Teaching International* 46(1):61-70.

Kohut, G.F., C. Burnap, and M.G. Yon. 2007. "Peer Observation of Teaching: Perceptions of the Observer and the Observed." *College Teaching* 55(1):19-25.

Kumaravadivelu, B. 1995. "A Multidimensional Model for Peer Evaluation of Teaching Effectiveness." *Journal on Excellence in College Teaching* 6 (3):95-113.

Lomas, L. and G. Nicholls. 2005. "Enhancing Teaching Quality through Peer Review of Teaching." *Quality in Higher Education* 11(2):137-149.

Massy, W.F., A.K. Wilger, and C. Colbeck. 1994. "Overcoming Hollowed Collegiality: Departmental Culture and Teaching Quality." *Change* 26 (4):11-20.

Millis, B. 1999. "Three Practical Strategies for Peer Consultation." New Directions for Teaching and Learning 79 (Fall):19-28.

Morehead, J.W. and P.J. Shedd. 1997. "Utilizing Summative Evaluation Through External Peer Review of Teaching." *Innovative Higher Education* 22 (1):37-44.

Muchinsky, P.M. 1995. "Peer Review of Teaching: Lessons Learned from Military and Industrial Research on Peer Assessment." *Journal of Excellence in College Teaching* 6 (3):17-30.

Nordstrom, K.F. 1995. "Multiple-Purpose Use of A Peer Review of Course Instruction Program in a Multidisciplinary University Department." *Journal on Excellence in College Teaching* 6 (3):125-144.

Palmer, P. 1998. *The Courage to Teach: Exploring the Inner Landscape of a Teachers Life*. San Francisco: Jossey-Bass.

Prezas, R., M. Shaver, T. Carlson, J.S. Taylor, and R. Scudder. 2009. "Peer Review of Teaching: Multiple Raters." *Perspectives on Issues in Higher Education* 12:59-63.

Quinlan, K.M. 1996. "Involving Peers in the Evaluation and Improvement of Teaching: A Menu of Strategies." *Innovative Higher Education* 20 (4):299-307.

Rau, W. and P.J. Baker. 1989. "The Organized Contradictions of Academe: Barriers Facing the Next Academic Revolution." *Teaching Sociology* 17 (April):161-175.

Rice, R. E. 2006. "From Athens and Berlin to LA: Faculty Work and the New Academy." *Liberal Education* 92 (4):6]–13.

Root, L.S. 1987. "Faculty Evaluation: Reliability of Peer Assessments of Research, Teaching, and Service." *Research in Higher Education* 26:71-84.

Seldin, P. 2006. *Evaluating Faculty Performance: A Practical Guide to Assessing Teaching, Research, and Service*. Bolton, MA: Anker.

Smith, H.L. and B.E. Walvoord. 1993. "Certifying Teaching Excellence: An Alternative Paradigm to the Teaching Award." *AAHE Bulletin* 46 (2):3-5,12.

Sullivan, T.A. 1995. "Teaching Evaluation by Peers." *Teaching Sociology* 23 (January):61-63.

Taylor, M. 2010. *Crisis On Campus: A Bold Plan for Reforming Our Colleges and Universities*. New York: Knopf.

Toth, K.E. and C.A. McKey. 2010. "Identifying the Potential Organizational Impact of an Educational Peer Review Program." *International Journal for Academic Development* 15(1):73-83.

Wagenaar, T.C. 1995. "Student Evaluation of Teaching: Some Cautions and Suggestions." *Teaching Sociology* 23(1):64-68.

Webb, J. and K. McEnerney. 1995. "The View From the Back of the Classroom: A Faculty-Based Peer Observation Program." *Journal on Excellence in College Teaching* 6 (3):145-160.

2

Rewarding Teaching: Lessons from the Faculty Roles and Rewards Movement

Vaneeta-marie D'Andrea,
Global Higher Education Consulting

> *"...scholarship is a choice of how to live,*
> *as well as a choice of career"*
> (Mills, 1959: 196)

REWARDING TEACHING IN SOCIOLOGY

Since the mid-70s, sociologists have been at the forefront of improving undergraduate teaching. At first, it was through the American Sociological Association's (ASA) Teaching Projects, funded by the federal Fund for the Improvement of Postsecondary Education and the Lilly Foundation. Later, it was through the various programs the ASA took over once the external funding ran out. Some of these include the Departmental Resources Group (DRG) and the ASA catalog of teaching materials which were run so effectively by Carla Howery, Deputy Director of ASA until shortly before her untimely death in 2009. It is these materials that became the initial set of resources in what is now the ASA's online instructional resource center, called "TRAILS: Teaching Resources and Innovations Library for Sociology" (http://trails.asanet.org).

During her tenure at the ASA, Carla championed teaching and learning developments, and was also instrumental in establishing the ASA Task Force on "Recognizing and Rewarding the Scholarly and Professional Work of Sociologists", which she chaired. It was the work of that Task Force that began to challenge the thinking in the discipline about re-valuing teaching as a scholarly activity and establishing mechanisms to reward the work of teaching sociologists. The report of the Task Force was presented to ASA Council in 1998, and its recommendations are as follows:

Departments of Sociology are encouraged to:

1. *Review, enhance and enact the institution's mission statement and, to the extent possible, set department goals that support the statement in concrete and public ways. The department should communicate its mission to the administration, other departments, students, and all department members at the point of hiring as well as in guidelines for faculty review, promotion and tenure.*

2. *Identify new means to evaluate a wider range of professional and scholarly work.*

3. *Design and implement systems of peer review, or close approximations, for a greater range of professional work, particularly teaching.*

4. *Revise 'poor practices' or old habits by examining how the department and the institution articulate faculty work priorities, and evaluate and reward work.*

5. *Engage in collaborative work within the department and across departments to enact collaborative goals and nurture individual's talents and interests.*

6. *View the department as a unit with certain institutional obligations but those do not require each person to do exactly the same things; recognize the developmental potential for each faculty member across the career. (Howery, 1998:5)*

The balance of this chapter first considers the wider national context within which these recommendations are situated, and then proceeds to identify some lessons learned from their implementation.

BACKGROUND TO THE FACULTY ROLES AND REWARDS MOVEMENT

As Wagenaar discusses in Chapter 1 of this volume, and in his earlier work (1998), the focus on reexamining the reward structure for academics over the last decade has been led and supported by the *Faculty Roles and Rewards Project* of the former American Association of Higher Education (AAHE). Underlying this project was Boyer's (1990) challenge to re-think the teaching/research nexus. His work identified four major categories of what he called scholarship. In an earlier work (D'Andrea & Gosling, 2005), I summarized his four categories of scholarship. For this I drew heavily on Rice's (1992) further development of Boyer's work (see Figure 1). The four categories include:

- **scholarship of discovery**
finding new knowledge - *'what has traditionally been known as original research* (1992: 123).'

- **scholarship of integration**
finding new relationships among previous research outcomes

- **scholarship of practice (**also known as the scholarship of engagement)
connecting academic work with the needs of society

- **scholarship of teaching**
'draw(ing) the strands of a field together in a way that provides both coherence and meaning' to the teaching process and students' learning (Rice, 1992: 125)

Figure 1 An enlarged view of scholarly work

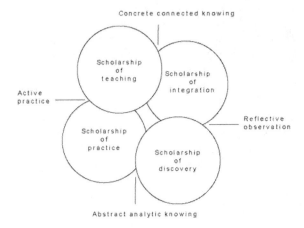

Rice, 1992: 122

Essentially, Boyer's major contribution to the debate on the teaching/research nexus was that teaching related activities also constituted a form of scholarship, and as such should be recognized and rewarded in the same way as the scholarship of discovery. The AAHE used Boyer's argument to support its initiative to address inequities in rewards for different types of academic work.

FACULTY ROLES & REWARDS PROJECT

The initial work of the AAHE to address faculty roles and rewards was framed around the notion of peer review, since most reward structures for academic work are embedded in departmental and institutional systems that involve peers in the process of deciding on promotion, tenure and other forms of professional recognition. The AAHE project was designed to address the issues surrounding the development of the peer review of teaching (Hutchings, 1994). The work of this project was initially campus-based and involved the participation of several disciplines within each participating institution.

> *The activities in the pilot campus peer review of teaching programmes were quite varied and directly linked to local needs and circumstances. They included: teaching circles, reciprocal classroom observation visits, and course and teaching portfolios. The aim of all the activities was to find strategies for extending peer review to teaching. This required the development of processes and procedures that could produce the evidence needed for these reviews. This meant finding ways to:*
> - *document the review of teaching*
> - *"go public" with the evidence*
> - *engage, collaboratively, with the teaching/learning processes on each campus*
> - *acknowledge this process as part of the scholarly work of academics.*
> (D'Andrea, 2002).

The second phase of the AAHE project focused on working with professional academic organizations in order to gain additional support from academics for the changes being promoted. By engaging directly with professional organizations, the peer review of teaching practices could be disseminated to a broader audience than that available on local campuses. Moreover, if professional organizations accepted this new view of scholarship, it would encourage teaching to be taken more seriously and rewarded accordingly.

It was at this point, in 1998, that the ASA became involved with the work of the AAHE on peer review. By this time, it had become known as the *Forum on Faculty Roles and Rewards* and was being led within the AAHE by Eugene Rice, a trained sociologist. However when funding for this work ended at the AAHE, the activities were taken on by the Carnegie Academy for the Scholarship of Teaching and Learning (CASTL) (Hutchings, 2001). CASTL divided the work into three major strands: 1) the Carnegie Scholars Program, 2) the Teaching Academy Campus Program and 3) and the Scholarly Societies Program. Sociologists were involved in all three strands, and each one was aimed at a different level of engagement: the individual, the institutional and the professional association.

1) The main goal of the Carnegie Scholars Program was to demonstrate that teaching and learning, as a scholarly activity, is worthy of the same forms of peer review as all other scholarship. Sociology was one of 20 disciplines selected to participate in the Carnegie Scholars program, and there were two cohorts of sociology Carnegie Scholars, one in 1999 and the other in 2000.

2) The ASA Task Force recommendations reflect the focus of the initial activities of the Teaching Academy Campus program -- to begin 'campus conversations' on teaching and learning, and to develop opportunities for cross-campus collaboration on improving student learning. A number of sociology departments were involved in the Teaching Academy Campus program, including Syracuse University and the University of Wyoming.

3) The principle underlying the Scholarly Societies Program was that academic life and faculty identities are powerfully shaped by scholarly societies. Based on this principle, these organizations were seen as critical to the process of broadening the conception of scholarly work [to include teaching and learning] (D'Andrea, 2002: 7). The ASA applied to the AAHE for one of the small grants available through this program in order to develop the recommendations of the ASA Task Force listed above. The ASA project had a two-pronged approach: the first focused on the development of departmental collaborative cultures around peer review; the second aimed to collect examples of lessons learned from departments.

LESSONS LEARNED FROM
THE FACULTY ROLES & REWARDS PROJECT

In this section, the focus is on lessons learned at each of the three levels of engagement where peer review or the scholarship of teaching and learning activities take place in the context of Sociology.

Lessons at the Individual Level

The two sociology cohorts of the Carnegie Scholars program have had influence on their own campuses and within the ASA as both role models for teaching scholarship and as catalysts for conversations on the scholarship of teaching and learning. In addition, these individuals have been joined by others to create an interest group within the International Society for the Scholarship of Teaching and Learning. The interest group *(ISSOTL; www.issotl.org)* enhances the impacts of their individual participation..

> *This group is the first ISSOTL discipline-based internal interest group.... In line with the mission of ISSOTL, the mission and objectives of the sociology interest group are to foster inquiry, encourage collaborations, share resources, disseminate findings, and establish applications on techniques to improves post-secondary learning and teaching in the discipline of sociology and closely related fields. More specific goals include the following:*

> - *Find and exchange resources for SoTL inquiry in sociology and closely related fields.*
> - *Form SoTL project collaborations including those that cross institutional and national boarders.*
> - *Propose and organize a session related to SoTL and sociology at the meetings of ISSOTL.*
> - *Help non-sociologists see the usefulness of the sociological imagination for understanding learning and teaching.*
> - *Work to enhance the status of SoTL in sociology including making connections between ISSOTL and various sociological professional organizations around the globe.*
> - *Co-author articles for the ISSOTL newsletter, The International Commons and the ASA Section on Teaching and Learning newsletter, Teaching/Learning Matters.* (McKinney, 2009)

Lessons at the Campus Level

One interesting example of changes at the campus level is from the Sociology Department at the University of Wyoming. They created a peer review program called *Partners in Pedagogy (PIP)*. The goal of PIP was to improve on the standard 'snapshot' visitation system to colleagues' classrooms by providing repeated visits by paired faculty partners to observe the full range of teaching by the other. This visitation system incorporated a wider range of information including: commenting on syllabi and teaching philosophies as well as classroom observation (sometimes via videotape). The system was designed to rotate the pairings over time, so eventually all members of the department would have the opportunity to observe and understand each other's approach to teaching. Initially, PIP was a response to dissatisfaction with the existing basis for evaluating teaching and the desire of faculty to create a collective commitment to teaching and learning. Thus, the goal for the department was a better informed and broader base of faculty, capable of carrying out teaching evaluations for personnel decisions and providing useful feedback to their peers on how to improve the learning experience of students. It was seen as another way to triangulate data from more traditional sources such as student teaching evaluations. The lessons learned thus far include:

- more occasions for serious discussions about ways to improve teaching need to be provided
- stimulate and experiment with ideas for new teaching practices
- reinforce the departmental value on the quality of teaching and learning

Lessons at the Scholarly Society Level

Changes to the reward structures for teaching sociologists have been supported by the American Sociological Association's Academic and Professional Affairs Program. The ASA's proposal to AAHE mentioned above outlined five specific developments that it planned to assist with the development of a culture of collaboration for the peer review of teaching within departments. These included:

1. setting up a biweekly electronic communication to chairs about peer collaboration (this is now in place in the form of Chairlink).
2. conducting an annual survey of chairs about the evaluation of teaching (this is now included in the ASA's survey of departments).

3. providing professional development workshops for departmental chairs and the Departmental Resources Group on peer collaboration(these are offered at the ASA's annual meeting, through the Chairs' Conference, the Graduate Directors' Conference, and the DRG training sessions).

4. producing a booklet of examples of "best practices" of peer collaboration and review collected from sociology departments and offered for sale through the ASA Teaching Resources Center (the current volume addresses some of this).

5. setting up a peer referral service for sociologists to work with each other as peer reviewers (such a service was announced in Footnotes, but never gained momentum).

SUMMARY

The peer review of teaching, advanced through the ASA Task Force on Faculty Roles and Rewards, has begun, through conversations on many campuses and the other tools designed to promote and evaluate the scholarship of teaching and learning. Overall, the purpose of the peer review of teaching, in its many forms, is to make the private act of teaching a public and collaborative process, provide multiple data sources for the evaluation of teaching and learning, provide a more complete and more accurate assessment of the teaching and learning enterprise, and encourage a dialogue about teaching.

Returning to the to the original goals of the ASA Task Force on "Recognizing and Rewarding the Scholarly and Professional Work of Sociologists, it is evident from this brief review that sociologists were at the forefront of early activities to enhance the learning experience of their students, and continue to work actively in this area. Some of the goals have been taken forward in systematic ways within departments and institutions, and others are being addressed by the ASA itself, as well as international interest groups committed to engaging the scholarship of teaching and learning. In the end, individual faculty, sociology departments and their students all benefit from this new emphasis on teaching and learning.

REFERENCES

AAHE Bulletin (1998) 'About AAHE's Peer Review of Teaching Project', (February): 12.

Boyer, E. (1990) *Scholarship Reconsidered: New Priorities for the Professoriate.* Princeton: The Carnegie Foundation for the Advancement of Teaching.

D'Andrea, V. (2002) *Peer Review of Teaching in the USA.* York, UK: LSTN Generic Centre.
www.heacademy.ac.uk/.../id29 Peer Review of Teaching in the USA.rtf

D'Andrea, V. & D. Gosling (2005) *Improving Teaching and Learning: a whole institution approach*, Buckinghamshire: McGraw Hill/Open University/SRHE Press.

Edgerton, R., P. Hutchings and K. Quinlan (1991) *The Teaching Portfolio: Capturing the Scholarship in Teaching.* Washington: American Association for Higher Education.

Howery, C., Van Valey, T. and T.C. Wagenaar (Eds) (1998) *Peer Review of Teaching: Departmental Resources Group Training Session Handbook.* Washington, D.C. American Sociological Association.

Howery, C. (1998) *Recognizing and Rewarding the Professional and Scholarly Work of Sociologists.* A report of the Task Force of the American Sociological Association. Washington, D.C.: American Sociological Association

Howery, C. (1997) *Enhancing Peer Collaboration in Teaching Sociology*: a proposal to the American Association for Higher Education. Washington, DC. American Sociological Association.

Hutchings, P. (2001) personal email communication, (hutchings@carnegiefoundation.org), 14 August.

Hutchings, P. (1996) *Making Teaching Community Property*. Washington, DC: American Association of Higher Education.

Hutchings, P. (1995) "Choosing from a Menu of Strategies", *From Idea to Prototype: the peer review of teaching.* Washington, D.C.: American Association for Higher Education, Tab 6: 1-9.

Hutchings, P. (1994). "Peer Review of Teaching: From Idea to Prototype: lessons from a current AAHE teaching initiative project." *AAHE Bulletin* 47 (3):3-7.

McKinney, K. (2009) "Sociology Internal Interest Group Approved by ISSOTL", *ASA Footnotes*, 37 (1) http://www.asanet.org/footnotes/jan09/issotl.html.

Mills, C.W. (1959) *Sociological Imagination*. New York: Oxford University Press.

Rice, R.E. (1992) 'Toward a Broader Conception of Scholarship: the American context', in Whiston, T.G. and Geiger, R.L. (eds), *Research and Higher Education: the United Kingdom and the United States*, Buckingham: Open University Press, 117-129.

Wagenaar, T.C. (1998) 'Peer Review of Teaching,' in C.B. Howery et al. *Departmental Resources Group Training Session Peer Review of Teaching*, American Sociological Association Meeting.

Wagenaar, T.C. (1998) "Teaching Portfolios" in C.B. Howery et al. *Departmental Resources Group Training Session Peer Review of Teaching*, American Sociological Association Meeting.

No author (1998) "Peer Partners Enhance Teaching at Wyoming", in Howery, C., Van Valey, T. and T.C. Wagenaar (eds) (1998) Peer *Review of Teaching: Departmental Resources Group Training Session Handbook*. Washington, D.C. American Sociological Association.

3

Making Teaching Public

Beth Rushing, University of Washington, Tacoma*

Teaching has been, and for most still is, the most private element of the faculty member's role. Even though there is always an audience in teaching – at least one learner – the teaching/learning interaction is typically hidden from colleagues except on special occasions and in scripted ways. This chapter argues that teaching should be made more public and more visible to colleagues, for the benefit of both faculty and students.

When teaching is public, it is open to examination by others. It becomes part of something larger than the individual professor in a particular classroom; it becomes part of a community, what Lee Shulman (1993) calls "community property." Parker Palmer further asserts that "good teaching is always and essentially communal" (1998, p. 115). As a communal phenomenon, then, good teaching belongs to the group (however that group is defined), and needs to be available for inspection and comment. Collegial review provides informed feedback and fosters further examination and discussion of teaching. Making teaching public, then, is necessary for enhancing teaching effectiveness.

Faculty members are already familiar and comfortable with the fact that research is public. Indeed, the very purpose of academic research is to make it public, for presentation to colleagues in campus colloquia, academic conferences, and journals. But even with our familiarity with taking *research* public, there is considerable resistance to making *teaching* public. Part of

---

* I am profoundly grateful to the University of Washington's Helen Riaboff Whiteley Center for providing the solitude and inspiring surroundings to write most of this chapter and to Maxine Atkinson and Tom Van Valey for helpful comments on prior versions.

this resistance is based in a lack of familiarity (and thus an associated fear) with making teaching public. Part is located in institutional practices that are built on that fear, such as guidelines about how teaching observations are scheduled and conducted. Finally, part of the resistance may also be due to uncertainty about how teaching would be evaluated.

So how do faculty members evaluate how well they are teaching? Too often, departments and universities assess teaching quality by relying solely or predominantly on standardized student evaluation course evaluation forms. These evaluations are notoriously problematic from the point of view of faculty members (Beran and Rokosh, 2009), yet it is clear that resistance to peer review as an alternative (or complement) has been strong.

Through the scholarship of teaching and learning, faculty members open their classrooms to engage with colleagues in a different way, and in a way that can still be controlled by the faculty member. Presentations and publications of research documenting the effectiveness of a particular approach to teaching a topic, or constructing a teaching portfolio (see Chapter 4 in this volume), or participation in teaching circles (see Chapter 5 in this volume) are indeed instances of opening the classroom. These and other activities contribute to the ongoing vitality of our understanding of effective teaching and learning, and allow us to develop a body of knowledge about effective teaching. Our understanding of what excellent teaching is, and how to document it, has expanded considerably as a result of the scholarship of teaching and learning. One consequence is that early career faculty at some institutions are increasingly noting that excellent teaching is becoming expected -- ratcheting up pre-tenure expectations, even while publication maintains its dominant place in the faculty reward system (Rice, 2002). Nevertheless, at other institutions, the "teacher-scholar" is increasingly the model for faculty excellence (Salmon, 2008).

While the scholarship of teaching and learning is a manifestation of making teaching public and professional, my argument here is not necessarily a call for all faculty to engage in it. The scholarship of teaching and learning is not simply teaching, but "teaching gone 'meta'" (Huber, 2001). It is but one way to put teaching and learning in the public sphere. Making teaching public is a more inclusive objective, one that asks faculty to think about and engage in discussions about teaching with one another and with students, to talk and write about and observe teaching, all with the purpose of improving teaching and student learning. While this kind of work might include the scholarship of teaching and learning, it is not *required* for it to be valuable in the improvement of teaching and learning.

In a nutshell, making teaching public is good for teaching, it is good for student learning, and it is good for all the individuals and the institutions involved in the teaching and learning enterprise. Some of the rewards of making teaching public are described in the next section.

WHY IS IT DESIRABLE FOR TEACHING TO BE PUBLIC?

Making teaching public is beneficial for individuals and institutions. For the individual faculty member, the benefits include personal and professional growth and greater confidence in the validity of peer or collegial evaluation. For the department (or division or school or university), making teaching public generates a more vital community of scholars and an enhanced ability to document the quality of work being done in the unit. Students gain from having faculty who have received feedback on teaching effectiveness and who are thus more likely to be effective. Disciplines benefit from the enhancements of knowledge about how teachers and students engage material, from better-prepared students who move into careers and successful lives (Atkinson, 2001).

There is also a personal reason some faculty share for making teaching public. Palmer (1993) says that the privatization of teaching is painful for faculty. It results in a loss of community, an evaluation system that is a "dangerous impostor" for identifying good teaching, and dissatisfying interactions with students and colleagues. For many faculty, teaching provides an important dimension of satisfaction at work (Lindholm, 2004, Solem and Foote, 2006). However, this pleasure is often tempered by the perception of many faculty that their colleagues do not care as much about the quality of teaching as they do (Wright, 2008). It is difficult to be motivated to improve something that others do not value. Furthermore, why expose one's potential vulnerabilities if the result is of no consequence? In response, faculty members who have made the effort to make their teaching public report a greater sense of shared purpose (Cameron et al, 2002), better collective understanding of the criteria for evaluating teaching (Wright, 2008), and a stronger sense of community (Briggs, 2007).

One major impetus for making teaching public is to increase our knowledge about what approaches or strategies might be effective. The population of students is changing -- the educational experiences they bring to the classroom, their expectations, and their level of preparation are all very different now compared to when most of their faculty were students. This is true across virtually all institutions. While diversity in the classroom is energizing and educationally beneficial, it requires a different type of work by the faculty member (Atkinson, 2000). Making teaching public can advance our knowledge about how best to meet these ever-changing learning needs of students (Sorcinelli et al, 2006).

Making teaching public generates documents and artifacts that can be "shared, discussed, critiqued, exchanged, built upon" (Shulman, 1993, p. 7). It thus helps to create a culture whereby teaching is taken seriously as scholarly work. It allows peer observation of teaching to be much broader than the traditional colleague visit to the classroom and memo to the faculty member's file. It helps to build a "teaching commons," a place where faculty can offer ideas and build upon the ideas of others (Huber and Hutchings, 2006). This teaching commons may be sited in journals, faculty development workshops, curriculum collaboration, disciplinary association conferences, and beyond. In the end, it results in a growing body of knowledge about effective teaching practice.

In a context of increasing corporatization of the university, institutions of higher education have their own reasons for making teaching public - demands for accountability from external sources, and a related need for faculty to participate in more authentic assessments of their effective teaching and learning. The external accountability pressures from accrediting bodies and states, are increasingly interested in seeing documented evidence of student learning. This is a reality of contemporary university life in the US, and even more so in Europe and Australia. It has significant implications for the work and daily life of faculty, especially when the reporting requirements and standards are not established in collaboration with them (Wright, et al, 2004).

To the extent that making teaching public also results in the kind of work that faculty (and institutions) value and reward, it can also enhance the quality of work for faculty. Teaching occupies a considerable portion of faculty time and effort, and as teaching becomes recognized as a more public, more scholarly enterprise, its value in the eyes of colleagues and administrators is raised (Shulman, 1993).

WHAT ARE THE BARRIERS TO MAKING TEACHING PUBLIC?

One barrier to making teaching public is also one of the defining features of the professoriate – autonomy. Faculty members enjoy a considerable degree of autonomy in their day to day work, and this autonomy is greatly valued. Lindholm's analysis of academic career aspirations at a large public research institution highlights this need for autonomy, or as one respondent stated it, "the ability to do *what* I want, *when* I want and *how* I want" (2004:611, italics in original). This is an important feature of the work of tenure-track and tenured faculty. Making teaching public does not have to threaten that autonomy. Inviting colleagues to observe one's teaching allows faculty to decide how to respond to feedback, but still may leave them feeling vulnerable to the potential biases of their colleagues. In contrast, a teaching circle, where faculty simply discuss their approaches to a particular topic or course is likely to be far less threatening. Similarly, presenting or publishing a paper on the efficacy of a particular case statement or lab exercise is also an instance of making teaching public, and this also has the advantage of looking like the other elements of work over which faculty do have control.

Another barrier to making teaching public is that teaching is often not perceived to be taken seriously. At nearly all universities and colleges, faculty roles are a combination of research, teaching, and service; it is the balance of the elements that varies considerably. Salmon (2008) argues that "many professors do not identify professionally as teachers." This is not a new problem – at the beginning of the last century, Abraham Flexner argued that the focus on research was detrimental to the education of students: "a college instructor is commissioned to teach boys by reason of a proficiency and interest that frequently unfit him to do that very thing" (1908, p. 183). Graduate programs do not always do a good job of preparing PhD students to be strong teachers. While some do provide more meaningful support for students to develop expertise in teaching, and some institutions are requesting evidence of teaching effectiveness for job candidates, much remains to be done to make it clear that universities (and the faculty who comprise them) value and reward teaching.

Fear is a considerable barrier to making teaching public. Palmer's title - *The Courage to Teach* - reflects the central role fear plays in teaching. Opening the classroom to other faculty opens the door to potentially negative consequences for the teacher. This point is illustrated by a recent essay in the *Chronicle of Higher Education*, which offered strategies for faculty facing a peer observation to generate "the best report you are capable of obtaining" (Schweizer, 2009). Among the strategies were: know who the observer will be, arrange the visit for a course and topic with which you are particularly strong, structure the course activity to be observed, and "prepare, prepare, prepare." The unambiguous message here is that while these peer visits may be seen as a necessary evil, the faculty member being observed can and should manipulate the situation so that the written report is more positive. Moreover, if the purpose of peer observation is simply to check off that part of the annual departmental responsibilities, or to have a report available for reappointment, tenure, promotion, or post-tenure review, then why do it any other way? Gaming one's peer observation report seems perfectly reasonable if the purpose of a peer observation is not to improve one's teaching.

Part of the difficulty with certain methods of making teaching public (such as mid course evaluations or peer observations of teaching) lies in the relationship between formative and summative evaluations. Summative evaluations have formal and significant consequences. They are experienced as annual merit evaluations and periodic reviews for reappointment, promotion, and tenure. Formative evaluations are for self-improvement and are not intended for other purposes. Nevertheless, faculty hesitate to develop formative assessments "for fear that the information gathered will be used for summative purposes" (Morehead and Shedd, 1997, p. 39). But even formative feedback is not truly private; at least one other person is privy to the information under review.

While the corporatization of higher education is one of the driving forces behind making teaching public, it is also a barrier. It is a barrier in the sense that there is perhaps greater fear on the part of faculty members to open the classroom to scrutiny, given the potential for capricious administrators to make judgments (Shortland, 2004; Meyer and Evans, 2003). The increasingly tenuous nature of faculty work – the growth in contingent faculty, a declining proportion of tenure track and tenured faculty – compounds the already-existing lack of trust between faculty and administrators. Thus, for a considerable portion of faculty, making teaching public may seem like a risky endeavour.

Schiller and her colleagues (2004) describe an effort by three faculty to create a teaching community. Even though they had developed clear ground rules to manage the potential risks associated with participation (based in Palmer's 1998 work), their invitations to involve other faculty members failed: "it was pointed out to us that our administrators could claim our teaching was weaker than desirable *because* we were seeking ways to improve it" (p. 170, emphasis in the original). This experience underscores the point made by Wright et al (2004) that a high level of mutual trust is a prerequisite for initiating and sustaining conversations about teaching.

Surely, we can make the peer review of teaching less risky. Making teaching public provides an opportunity for faculty to receive feedback on how to improve, to at least reassure themselves that they are doing a good job, or to address problems. The challenge, then, is to create a setting within which we can be more secure about the consequences of making teaching public, in which faculty jobs are not on the line. Asking questions about the quality of teaching, and soliciting feedback on one's teaching, should strengthen a faculty member's job security, not jeopardize it.

THE WAY FORWARD

Were universities consciously organized with the goal to promote student learning, they would have long ago made shared and effective teaching and learning experiences the norm, not the exception. Were we serious in our commitment to remake our colleges and universities into learning organizations that consciously promote student learning, we would not accept the current organization of our work (Tinto, 1997, 2, 4). So, how do we make the changes necessary to challenge the isolated, privatized model of teaching and learning? The changes are both formal and informal, and at both the individual and institutional levels.

Making teaching public should involve students. How are we to know if teaching is effective if we exclude students from the conversation? How might we move beyond the end-of-course student evaluations of teaching and begin to see students as informants or even collaborators with regard to the effectiveness of our teaching? Mid-course narrative evaluations, conducted by the instructor, are one example of a method that incorporates students. However, the introduction of a third party into this process extends further the wedging open of the classroom. That person may serve as a liaison between the faculty member teaching a course and the students in the course (per Schiller et al 2004). In some instances, a teaching assistant or lab coordinator might also serve such a liaison role in a more ongoing process of continual feedback (e.g., "students are confused about the last illustration - you may want to review that at the beginning of the next class"). Some institutions organize such mid-course evaluations so that they are, by default, formative in nature. The faculty member shares her/his goals and objectives with the third party, introduces the reviewer to the class, conducts the class, and leaves. The third party then engages students in a guided conversation, and then later has a conversation with the faculty member.

Students can be excellent informants on the effectiveness of teaching. However, they may need some guidance on how to carry out this role. Too often, they have been conditioned to be passive recipients of what happens in the classroom, and sometimes they prefer to be passive (Cox, 2009). Faculty can be resistant to engaging students in this way, as well. Their position is often, "On what basis can students critique faculty performance? They don't know enough." This is the same resistance as with end-of-course evaluations – that such evaluations will be tainted by students' poor performance or other biases. Still, the rewards can be great: "When we are willing to abandon our self-protective professional autonomy and make ourselves as dependent on our students as they are on us, we move closer to the interdependence that the community of truth requires.... [T]eachers and students will meet at new depths of mutuality and meaning, and learning will happen for everyone in surprising and life-giving ways" (Palmer, 1998, p. 140).

Faculty colleagues are the other key ingredient for making teaching public. Strategies for involving colleagues might include such activities as forming teaching circles, developing teaching portfolios, inviting faculty colleagues to conduct peer observations, constructing web-based teaching resources, and the like (Lucal et al, 2003). The definition of colleague here can be extended beyond what we might normally use – a colleague can be within one's department, college, university, discipline, or even beyond. Feedback from knowledgeable observers with varying degrees of familiarity with one's specific area of expertise can be beneficial in providing depth and breadth to the feedback.

While individual and collegial collections of faculty members can undoubtedly enact necessary change, lasting and meaningful change must also happen in the organization itself - the department, division, college, and university. The institution must provide opportunities for the faculty to participate, it must create the conditions under which faculty *can* participate in such a community, and it must reward or at least recognize faculty efforts.

Wright's work (2008) highlights the importance of departmental colleagues in making teaching public. She describes the particular importance of informal systems by which faculty members discuss and share teaching experiences. At the research institution Wright studied, many departments emphasized good teaching in their expectations for faculty. Too often, however, these departments only had poorly defined, ambiguous criteria for evaluating teaching effectiveness. Wright found that in departments that achieved congruence via robust systems for peer review, frequent and widespread conversations about instruction, and detailed and transparent identification of strategies for evaluating the quality of teaching, faculty were more likely to be comfortable about expectations. It was the informal systems that formed the basis of the more formal policies and procedures supporting good teaching.

Since the peer review of teaching can be both formative and summative, perhaps establishing a robust system of formative peer reviews would reduce some of the fear associated with summative peer reviews. Faculty would have a stronger understanding of how their teaching had been reviewed previously, and when it is time for a summative review, there would be less mystery surrounding the criteria and standards employed. Faculty, and especially administrators, must take seriously the fear associated with muddling the relationship between formative and summative evaluations in order to achieve progress in this arena. On some campuses, faculty and administrators work assiduously to create a firewall between the formative peer reviews of teaching carried out by the faculty and the summative reviews executed by chairs, deans, or provosts. Administrators on these campuses recognize the tremendous value of a robust system of collaborative peer review, but they also understand that they can best facilitate it (or get the most impact from it) if they are removed from the process. This requires a leap of faith on the part of administrators and a leap of trust on the part of faculty. Such actions are more difficult for some than others.

The reward structure must change, as well. "The priorities of faculty are a function not simply of their own preferences but also of their institution's concerns and reward structures" (Rhode, 2006). Only when excellence and improvement are rewarded, or at least recognized, will faculty as a group respond. There will always be faculty who strive to improve their teaching, motivated by their own personal and professional goals. However, pervasive and meaningful change will also require recognition and reward. Detailed and transparent criteria for reappointment, merit, tenure, and promotion are necessary as part of the drive to make teaching public. The conversations needed at the department level to articulate what good teaching is and how it is to be evaluated are the same conversations that will lead to clearer expectations about teaching effectiveness for tenure and promotion. Uncertainty about expectations for tenure and promotion is rampant among early career faculty (Collaborative on Academic Careers in Higher

Education, 2008). Improving the organizational expectations, by both clarifying what teaching effectiveness means and by institutionalizing mechanisms to achieve it, will enhance pre-tenure faculty members' lives, make promotion and tenure evaluations easier, and thus less subject to dispute (Higgerson, 1999). This would be good news for all involved.

Department chairs and other academic leaders must also be vocal and visible in their support of making teaching public (Higgerson, 1999; North, 1999). They must be concrete and collaborative in setting goals and expectations for teaching, and proactive in supporting ongoing teaching-related discussions - with individual faculty, collectively with curricular subgroups, and with the faculty as a whole. Rather than general encouragement for faculty to work harder to improve teaching, chairs should offer specific suggestions for improvement (see chapter 13 in this volume). It is also vital to create a culture within which faculty see the value of cooperation and an environment within which differences of opinion are dealt with constructively. Chairs and other academic administrators must provide and support informal and formal ways to recognize the good work people do, and must strive to prioritize the resources necessary to support it.

The scholarly literature suggests a number of organizational factors and practices that contribute to a climate of continuous improvement of teaching. Some changes at the organizational or departmental level may seen tangential or even superfluous, but have been shown to be effective at generating the sense of community argued for here: coffee machines, shared meals, co-located faculty offices, and common gathering spaces (Briggs, 2007; Bolander Laksov et al, 2008). Informal collaboration is an important part of creating the sense of community, shared purpose, and trust necessary to overcome some of the barriers associated with making teaching public. As colleges and universities struggle to fund even the most basic instructional supports, we will face challenges to provide critical community-sustaining resources. But their importance should not be underestimated.

As sociologists, we know that the university is a socially constructed organization, enacted by people in a variety of roles, based in those actors' interpretations, shared assumptions, and relationships. Tierney (2008) reminds us that an organization's solution to a particular problem will necessarily be influenced by its organizational culture. What works in one place will not necessarily work the same way in another. In much the same way (and for the same reasons) that effective teaching must be defined contextually, good solutions to the question of how to make teaching public must be contextualized.

CONCLUSION

Ultimately, the best solutions to the problem of making teaching public will need to originate with faculty. While individual faculty may not recognize that they have much voice in making such changes, faculty as a collective do exercise a considerable degree of influence over the evaluation of teaching effectiveness. There are several routes faculty may follow to enact change related to making teaching public. The best place to start is likely to be the department – the organizational unit where faculty typically exercise the most influence. Alternatively, collaboration with colleagues in another department would be one way to maneuver around a recalcitrant department chair or reluctant departmental colleagues. Also, faculty in the campus teaching and learning center could also be valuable partners in making meaningful change. Finally, chairs, deans, and provosts might also prove to be valuable allies, since they too have a stake in enhancing the effective evaluation of teaching.

The challenges associated with making teaching public are considerable, but manageable. The benefits of making teaching public are equally considerable, and have the potential to transform not only student learning but also faculty careers and institutional effectiveness. The barriers to making teaching public are primarily rooted in institutional practices and structures, and it will not be possible to create learning-centered institutions without attending to the institutional factors that diminish or inhibit the improvement of teaching and learning (Biggs, 2001; Briggs, 2007). We must institutionalize practices that give faculty the freedom to make teaching public. Given the current degree of instability and uncertainty in faculty employment, it is especially incumbent upon academic administrators, in collaboration with faculty, to create the organizational structures and practices that make it possible for faculty to engage in practices that make teaching more public.

REFERENCES

Atkinson, Maxine P. 2000. "The Future of Sociology is Teaching? A Vision of the Possible" *Contemporary Sociology*, Vol. 29, No. 2 (Mar., 2000), pp. 329-332.

____. 2001. "The Scholarship of Teaching and Learning: Reconceptualizing Scholarship and Transforming the Academy" *Social Forces* 79(4):1217-1229.

Beran, Tanya N. and Jennifer L. Rokosh. 2009. "Instructors' perspectives on the utility of student ratings of instruction." *Instructional Science* 37:171-184.

Biggs, John. 2001. The reflective institution: Assuring and enhancing the quality of teaching and learning. *Higher Education* 41: 221-238.

Bolander Laksov, Klara, Sarah Mann, and Lars Owe Dahlgren. 2008. "Developing a Community of Practice Around Teaching: A Case Study" *Higher Education Research and Development* 27(2):121-132.

Briggs, Charlotte L.. 2007. "Curriculum Collaboration: A Key to Continuous Program Renewal" *The Journal of Higher Education* 78(6):676-711.

Cameron, Jeanne, Tina Stavenhaven-Helgren, Philip Walsh, and Barbara Kobritz. 2002. Assessment as Critical Praxis: A Community College Experience" *Teaching Sociology* 30(4): 414-429.

Collaborative on Academic Careers in Higher Education. 2008. *COACHE highlights report 2008.* Cambridge, MA. http://isites.harvard.edu/fs/docs/icb.topic436591.files/COACHE_HighlightsReport2008.pdf

Cox, Rebecca D.. 2009. The College Fear Factor: How Students and Professors Misunderstand One Another. Cambridge: Harvard University Press.

Flexner, Abraham. 1908. The American College: a Criticism. New York: The Century Co..

Higgerson, Mary Lou. 1999. "Building a Climate Conducive to Effective Teaching Evaluation." Pp. 194-212 in Peter Seldin et al., Changing Practices in Evaluating Teaching. Bolton MA: Anker Publishing.

Huber, Mary Taylor. 2001. "Balancing Acts: Designing Careers Around The Scholarship Of Teaching" *Change* 33(4): 21-30.

Huber, Mary Taylor and Pat Hutchings. 2006. "Building the Teaching Commons." *Change* 38(3):25-31

Lindholm, Jennifer A.. 2004. "Pathways to the Professoriate: The Role of Self, Others, and Environment in Shaping Academic Career Aspirations" *The Journal of Higher Education* 75(6): 603-635.

Lucal, Betsy, Cheryl Albers, Jeanne Ballantine, Jodi Burmeister-May, Jeffrey Chin, Sharon Dettmer, and Sharon Larson. 2003 "Assessment of Faculty and the Scholarship of Teaching and Learning: Knowledge Available/Knowledge Needed." *Teaching Sociology* 31(2): 146-61.

Meyer, Luanna H. and Ian M. Evans. 2003. "Motivating the Professoriate: Why Sticks and Carrots are only for Donkeys." *Higher Education Management and Policy* 15(3):151-167.

Morehead, Jere W. and Peter J. Shedd. 1997. "Utilizing Summative Evaluation through External Peer Review of Teaching" *Innovative Higher Education* 22(1): 37-44.

North, Joan DeGuire. 1999. "Administrative Courage to Evaluate the Complexities of Teaching" Pp. 183-193 in Peter Seldin et al., Changing Practices in Evaluating Teaching. Bolton MA: Anker Publishing.

Palmer, Parker J.1993. "Good Talk about Good Teaching: Improving Teaching through Conversation and Community" *Change* 25(6):8-13.

Palmer, Parker J. 1998. The Courage to Teach. San Francisco: Jossey Bass.

Rhode, Deborah L. 2006. In Pursuit of Knowledge: Scholars, Status, and Academic Culture. Stanford: Stanford University Press.

Rice, R. Eugene. 2002. "Beyond *Scholarship Reconsidered*: Toward an Enlarged Vision of the Scholarly Work of Faculty Members" *New Directions for Teaching and Learning* 90: 7-17.

Salmon, Victoria N. 2008. "Preparing Future Teacher-Scholars" Pp 184-192 in Sean P. Murphy, ed., Academic Cultures: Professional Preparation and the Teaching Life. New York: Modern Language Association.

Schiller, Susan A., Marcy M. Taylor, and Pamela S. Gates. 2004. "Teacher Evaluation Within a Community of Truth: Testing the Ideas of Parker Palmer" Innovative Higher Education 28(3):163-186.

Schweizer, Bernard. 2009. "The Dreaded Peer-Teaching Observation." The Chronicle of Higher Education. December 10, 2009. http://chronicle.com/article/The-Dreaded-Peer-Teaching-O/49356/

Shortland, Sue. 2004. "Peer Observation: a tool for staff development or compliance?" *Journal of Further and Higher Education* 28(2):219-228.

Shulman, Lee S. 1993. "Teaching as Community Property: Putting an End to Pedagogical Solitude" *Change* 25(6): 6-7.

Solem, Michael N. and Kenneth E. Foote. 2006. "Concerns, Attitudes, and Abilities of Early-Career Geography Faculty" *Journal of Geography in Higher Education* 30(2):199-234.

Sorcinelli, Mary Deane, Ann E. Austin, Pamela L. Eddy, and Andrea L. Beach. 2006. Creating the Future of Faculty Development. Boston: Anker.

Tierney, William G. 2008. The Impact of Culture on Organizational Decision Making: Theory and Practice in Higher Education. Sterling, VA: Stylus.

Tinto, Vincent. 1997. "Universities as Learning Organizations" *About Campus* Jan/Feb pp. 2-4.

Wright, Mary C.. 2008. Always at Odds? Creating Alignment Between Faculty and Administrative Values. Albany: SUNY Press.

Wright, Mary C., Carla B. Howery, Nandini Assar, Kathleen McKinney, Edward L. Kain, Becky Glass, Laura Kramer, and Maxine Atkinson. 2004. "Greedy Institutions: The Importance of Institutional Context for Teaching in Higher Education." T*eaching Sociology* 32(2): 144-159.

II

MODES OF PEER REVIEW

4

The Teaching Portfolio*

Theodore C. Wagenaar, Miami University

A portfolio is simply a collection of a professional's work, designed to demonstrate the range of one's accomplishments. Professionals such as artists and designers have long used portfolios to document their accomplishments. In higher education, student portfolios – which document students' accomplishments – have become more popular as ways to assess learning (Huba and Freed, 2000). The use of teaching portfolios, however, is relatively new in higher education. Recent assessment concerns have sparked a new level of interest in teaching portfolios (Centra, 2000; Selden, et al., 2010).

Teaching portfolios can be used effectively in almost all disciplines (see Bernstein, et al., [2006] for examples). Like other disciplines, sociology introduces students to alternative ways of thinking about the world–in this case, thinking sociologically– and underscores such other liberal education goals as critical thinking. Effective portfolio use can help document instructors' efforts in these areas and can help enhance a culture of teaching. Teaching portfolios factor prominently in self – evaluation and comprehensive self – evaluation can factor prominently in peer review (Lord, 2009). Both help the self-monitoring process that is necessary for professional advancement and raising the status of the teaching profession in the eyes of the public (Gaff, 2009; Hamilton, 2009). This chapter examines some of the lessons learned from the literature on teaching portfolios.

* *This essay was adapted from an article that appeared in *Teaching Portfolios Within the Discipline*, edited by Daniel Renfrow.

The author acknowledges with appreciation the comments of anonymous *Teaching Sociology* reviewers and Kerry J. Strand

A CULTURE OF TEACHING

Instructors typically close their doors when they teach, both literally and figuratively. This private approach to teaching creates a social structure that inhibits sharing teaching experiences and that stunts the development of a culture of teaching. As a result, a collective responsibility for teaching and learning is slow to emerge. Teaching portfolios can help open those doors by making teaching more public (see Chapter 3 in this volume). Portfolios are documents that can be shared, discussed, and analyzed. Readers of portfolios confront ideas that may work in their own classrooms. Portfolio products can be peer reviewed and can help promote a climate of group inquiry into teaching (Bernstein and Edwards, 2001). In the process, portfolios can help raise teaching closer to the status of research–worthy of review by colleagues and worthy of our best efforts because our work will be displayed publicly. They help nurture a growing "culture of evidence" in teaching akin to the culture of evidence that we have long experienced in research (cf. Halpern, 1994). As a result, teaching portfolios can help generate a public dialogue about topics that include personal teaching experiences, disciplinary content, and other issues. Such analyses can generate ideas for improvement, and they can help construct a dialogue about teaching that puts it center stage, including the role of teaching in the department and in the school. One positive outcome of this sort of dialogue may be that teachers become more comfortable in sharing what they do and in learning from others, so that the social climate of teaching takes on greater collective involvement and representation. A side benefit of the public nature of teaching portfolios is their usefulness in obtaining a job, particularly for newer teachers (Barry and Shannon, 1997, Rose, 2007). Lang (2010), for example, offers specific advice for writing the standard ingredient of a teaching portfolio—the teaching philosophy.

DEFINITION OF SELF

Part of Palmer's (1998) message is that teachers benefit when they address who they are as teachers and what their role is in the learning process. He particularly stresses the need for instructors to know who they are as individuals and to connect that awareness to their teaching. Teaching portfolios can play a role here by helping instructors discover, as well as present, their teaching selves (Anderson-Patton and Bass, 2002). They can help to articulate and clarify our conceptualization of our teaching selves. Formulating a presentation of the teaching self via a teaching portfolio may encourage instructors to crystallize what, in their minds, represents the central ingredients of that self.   In the process, instructors may become more aware of inconsistencies in those ingredients, and may also uncover ideas to improve their teaching that may otherwise be overlooked.   For example, constructing a teaching portfolio may highlight a discrepancy between an instructor's teaching goal of promoting in-class critical thinking with the minimal role given exercises in the grading formula noted on the syllabus. Or, the portfolio may show a greater connection with the school's general education goals than the instructor initially assumed, something that the instructor may now choose to highlight.   Bernstein, et al.   (2006) focus on strengthening the connection between course portfolios and student learning.

Teaching portfolios may also encourage self-reflection and self-appraisal as teachers imagine how they appear to others and respond to these images (Cerbin, 1994). Assembling a portfolio requires instructors to consider carefully what they do in preparing courses, how they teach, what their pedagogical goals are, and who they are as teachers. This sociological exploration and exposition of self may be enhanced through a hermeneutic and interpretive approach to portfolio development and assessment (Tigelaar, Dolmans, Wolfhagen, and van der Vleuten, 2005). The process may also encourage participants to think critically about their teaching as they are forced to articulate reasons for making the pedagogical choices that they did (cf. Shulman, 1988). Thus, the process may encourage teachers to reassess their teaching selves as well as the presentation of their teaching selves. What people define as real often becomes real in its consequences: documenting one's teaching effectiveness may spur further teaching improvement efforts because instructors may now define themselves more clearly as effective teachers.   Of course, a portfolio may also confront a less effective teacher with that reality and produce negative reactions, at least initially. In fact, FitzPatrick and Spiller (2010) used a narrative research methodology to document the complex and often negative emotions that emerge while constructing a portfolio.

APPLICATIONS IN SOCIOLOGY

Many sociological concepts and strategies for teaching them are particularly well suited to portfolio use. Take the sociological imagination, for example, a central concept. Instructors often ask students to apply the sociological imagination to their lives or to a social situation. Student journals could be used to determine how well this is done. Sample entries could be included in a teaching portfolio, perhaps annotated by the instructor to show specifically how entries reflect accomplishment of course goals. Another way to teach this concept might involve asking students to connect what are commonly thought to be private troubles (such as unemployment or divorce) with public issues (such as the economy or changes in the status of women). Students could do this in groups and the results could be included in the portfolio. Yet another approach could be the social class genealogy and poverty lunch projects used by Tynes (2001) to enliven students' understanding of the sociological imagination and to foster collaborative learning.

Community-based learning approaches have also found favor with sociologists because these strategies engage students in the community and require them to apply and integrate their sociological learning (Strand, et al., 2003.). Mooney and Edwards (2001) describe the pedagogical differences and instructional benefits of several types of community-based learning approaches: out-of-class activities, volunteering, service add-ons, internships, service learning, and service learning advocacy. Teaching portfolios can help explicate both the teaching strategies and learner responses in these and other alternative teaching strategies.

Sociologists often have students do brief or extended observational research. For example, Wright (2000) uses short-term exercises in observational research and field trips to promote sociological analytical reflection. Excerpts from students' reports could help describe the course and document what students have learned. Other sociologists use innovative in-class activities. For example, Misra (2000) uses clips from television shows to give sociological concepts more "real" meaning to students and to promote critical thinking and active learning. The written work students complete with such an exercise can be included in a portfolio and content analyzed to show connections with course goals. Moran (1999) uses poetry to teach about inequality and argues that the use of poetry enables students to experience the emotion and feeling of poets' lived experiences. He also provides strategies for using this venue for teaching critical thinking. Again, students' work can be analyzed in a portfolio to document these claims.

PORTFOLIO CONTENTS

Teaching portfolios typically begin with an introductory teaching philosophy statement that summarizes the instructor's approach to teaching and provides an overview of portfolio contents (cf. Lang, 2010). This statement can also introduce any "themes," such as a critical thinking focus. It also typically includes a description of teaching responsibilities and other contextual descriptors, such as teaching load, elective versus required courses, and class size. The core elements follow: syllabi, exams, and assignments. These items should be self-contained, but may need descriptive comments to show how they fit with the statement on teaching presented earlier. For example, an assignment that involves watching a feature-length movie or a television show may need comments linking the assignment to the instructor's approach to teaching. Some instructors explain why they selected particular readings and assignments, and some include responsibilities such as independent studies and advising. Instructors should present course goals and link them to program goals. Teaching strategies should be described, linked to course goals, and assessed.

Many instructors include samples of student exams and written material. Although most display high quality work, less competent work might serve to illustrate the linkage between instructor comments and student improvement. Student evaluation of teaching data are also typically included, often with comments to show how the instructor responded to the results. For example, an instructor described as "unavailable" by some students in student evaluations might explain how she or he increased office hours, established an interactive course web site, or otherwise made it easier for students to make contact. How did the instructor change the readings in a course when they were described as "boring" or "dense" by many students? In other words, how does the instructor use student evaluations in a formative way to improve the teaching and learning experience? Student data could also include student perceptions on how well course goals were attained and, if the course is part of the major, how well the course contributed to program goals. Results from peer reviews of teaching can also be incorporated and perhaps compared and contrasted with student evaluation data (cf. Kumaravadivelu, 1995).

Portfolios are a good venue to display instructional web content and course management software. Web-based assignments and some of the more illustrative examples of student contributions could be included. Instructors could also explain the pedagogical rationale for web-based assignments, and might even solicit external reviews of their course web sites.

Portfolios often conclude with the instructors' reflections about the portfolio, on their teaching, what they have learned from assembling the portfolio, and what they plan to do differently in the future. Instructors often include here their efforts to improve their teaching, perhaps with comments about their contributions to teaching analysis and teacher development on and off campus. In short, portfolios usually contain some combination of descriptive, evaluative, and reflective information (Centra, 1994).

Several analysts offer their own rubrics for organizing portfolios. Murray (1995) suggests these segments: 1) what is taught, 2) who is taught, 3) why courses are taught (program and course goals), 4) documentation of teaching strategies, 5) teaching assessment strategies, and 6) teaching improvement plans. Seldin, Miller, Seldin, and McKeachie (2010) provide detailed examples of effective portfolios and successful implementation strategies in several disciplines. Ross et al. (1995) stress learning and suggest that teachers consider the following questions: 1) What do you want students to learn, and why is this learning important? 2) How do you believe students best learn the course material? 3) What do you do to help students learn? and 4) Why did you select particular teaching strategies--how are they linked to your aims and beliefs about student learning?   I would add to these a fifth, How successful were you in achieving your goals, and how do you know? (See also Urbach's, 1992 list of ingredients.   He includes suggestions about documents and artifacts that might illustrate each topic.) Kulski and Radloff (1998) propose five stages in their framework for portfolio development: 1) collection of materials, 2) compilation in archival format,   3) construction as a compendium for assessing teaching effectiveness against specific criteria, 4) illustrations of linkages with departmental and school goals, and 5) how all this leads to further reflection.

Portfolios are often conceptualized as a "snapshot" – a static picture of the whole of one's work at one point in time. However, portfolios can also be used to establish a benchmark to show changes over time in an instructor's teaching philosophy, teaching methods, assignments, expectations for students, and professional development (Bernstein, et al., 2006). In addition, a review of portfolios in a department over time can provide a portrait of changes in departmental teaching effectiveness and in strategies for improving teaching.

Despite their commonalities, teaching portfolios do vary. Ross et al. (1995) analyzed the portfolios of teaching award winners at the University of Florida and found considerable variability. Such variability makes comparability difficult and can complicate the evaluation of portfolios. They stress the importance of presenting clear and convincing evidence and suggest that instructors should: 1) specify a standard set of contents, 2) include data about the institutional context, 3) include a statement about the instructor's beliefs about teaching and learning, 4) present evidence of instructional improvement efforts, 5) present evidence from multiple sources to support claims of teaching excellence, 6) explain all evidence presented in the portfolio, and 7) critically evaluate the amount of evidence presented (Ross et al. 1995). Finally, Richlin (1995) stresses that teaching portfolios must be seen as part of an overall system for the evaluation of teaching. That is, portfolios are more effective when designed and implemented within the context of a more comprehensive campus-wide program for teaching excellence.

In summary, teaching portfolios can be assembled and presented in many ways. Unfortunately, few empirical studies exist on their use and utility (De Rijdt, Tiquet, Dochy, and Devolder, 2006). Quinlan (2002) encourages campuses to explore various ways of implementing teaching portfolios, consistent with institutional goals. Still, faculty should review several different models before settling on one or more that best address their own personal circumstances and preferences, while adhering to institutional practices. Sung, et al. (2009) describe the use of digital teaching portfolios. Discussions within departments should help identify the collective goals departmental faculty have for teaching portfolios. These discussions help to determine whether one or multiple models should be used in the department, and should take the institution's mission and goals into account.

IMPLEMENTATION

Portfolios may be developed simply for the purpose of seeking employment or even as a means of self-examination. More typically, however, they result from administrative mandates for "multiple sources of data" to evaluate teaching, which in turn may be tied to demands by accreditation agencies or state legislatures for assessment data. Strong institutional and administrative support make the assessment function of teaching portfolios more evident. In fact, in one of the rare studies on portfolios, Liston et al. (1998) found that, absent institutional support, faculty use teaching portfolios almost exclusively for promotion and tenure reasons.

Institutional support is important for other reasons as well (Van Tartwijk, et al., 2007). Departments venturing into portfolios without institutional commitment will usually experience immediate inertia. Effective portfolio implementation is difficult unless portfolios are part of the academic culture on campus. Even division-wide efforts are likely to be constrained and confused without central administrative support.

McColgan and Blackwood (2009) express concern that little attention has been given to the implementation of effective portfolio use. Several elements would help shift the academic culture to support and facilitate teaching portfolio usage. For one, the reward system must recognize teaching portfolios not only as a legitimate measure of teaching effectiveness but also as a valued strategy. Strong statements from high-level administrators that portfolios will be considered seriously in promotion and tenure reviews are important. However, these statements must be corroborated by reports from those on relevant review committees. Consistent messages from chairs that portfolios will be reviewed and used for merit reviews will help, again with evidence that this has actually occurred. Institutional support, such as providing expert assistance, will enable both individuals and departments to implement teaching portfolio usage effectively, so that individual instructors can use them to improve their teaching and departments can use them to strengthen their teaching cultures.

Sufficient resources are even more important than strong statements, because training and implementation cost time and money. Some faculty could attend professional conferences on portfolio usage. Perhaps one faculty member in each department could be granted release time to develop expertise in portfolio usage and serve as the departmental consultant. Expertise could also be developed in the center for teaching and learning on campus. Provisions should be made for the additional clerical work involved. Teaching portfolios involve considerable time and effort if done well. A support structure must be in place such that portfolio implementation does not become one more requirement for already busy faculty to complete, often haphazardly.

However, even campuses with a strong teaching climate and strong administrative support can experience difficulties. Weshah (2010) found that teachers expressed significant concern over the difficulties involved in creating portfolios and notes the centrality of institutional support. Wolverton (1996) detailed the difficulties that accompanied portfolio implementation at Miami-Dade Community College, a school long respected for its strong teaching-centered climate. When portfolios were first implemented, instructors had to produce a 20-page narrative, cross-referenced with extensive documentation, to show how they had met each of 29 attributes of an effective teacher. Not surprisingly, faculty members lost sight of the overall goals while preparing what they considered to be the "perfect portfolio." Moreover, many of the attributes were difficult to support with objective evidence. The procedures were changed subsequently to make the process more manageable. The faculty were asked to describe the teaching/learning process by addressing several questions that covered motivation, interpersonal skills, building a personal knowledge base about teaching and about one's discipline, and application of the knowledge base. The revised, more flexible process, helped mobilize faculty participation while also meeting the goals of addressing teaching and learning, and fostering a collaborative approach to teaching.

Buckridge (2008) expresses concern about using portfolios for both formative and summative purposes and notes that an emphasis on the summative purpose may compromise the goal of the formative purpose. Murray (1995) emphasizes the department's role in making portfolios work. Faculty members identify more closely with their departments and disciplines than with their schools. He suggests several guidelines that promote success at the departmental level: 1) chairs must share control of the evaluation process with faculty members, 2) faculty members must define collectively what constitutes effective teaching in the department, 3) faculty must define the appropriate criteria for reviewing portfolios, 4) chairs must allay faculty resistance, and 5) chairs must promote a collegial climate. Collective responsibility enhances portfolio utility. Others suggest that a sound mentoring program is one way to promote such a departmental climate and to improve the portfolios (Kulski and Radloff, 1998). In such programs, senior faculty serve as mentors for junior faculty. Over time, such a program helps foster communication about various departmental concerns, including teaching.

RELEVANT QUESTIONS

A number of decisions must be made when a department or an institution implements teaching portfolios. *Who will be asked to assemble portfolios–new faculty members only, untenured faculty members only, part-time faculty members, senior faculty members, all faculty members?* It seems prudent to consider carefully the decision to use portfolios for junior faculty members only. Such a decision might underscore status differences, highlight the evaluative aspect of portfolios for promotion and tenure, mitigate the self-assessment and self-improvement aspects of teaching portfolios, and hinder efforts to build a teaching culture in the department. Using portfolios for all faculty is likely to do the most for making teaching a more collective and public enterprise.

How often should portfolios be submitted? Portfolios should be assembled regularly instead of just once; their cumulative nature fosters dialogue about teaching (Anderson, 1993). For probationary faculty members, once a year may be best so that feedback can pinpoint quickly the difficulties new teachers might be experiencing. This timing also helps to develop promotion and tenure dossiers. Assigning a portfolio mentor (or a more general teaching mentor) may also assist new faculty members and fosters a collaborative approach to teaching. For tenured faculty members, every two or three years seems reasonable. Because untenured faculty members need more feedback more promptly than do tenured ones, different expectations seem appropriate. Also, tenured faculty members have more teaching experience and are less likely to change their teaching within a year or two. Moreover, they do not need portfolio review as much for tenure and promotion reasons. This timing also helps alleviate the substantial time investment portfolios require (see Richlin, 1995 for a discussion of time commitments and how to handle them).

Who will see portfolios? The answer to this question depends on the reasons for doing teaching assessment. The formative reasons reflect the more private, self-reflective aspect, while the summative reasons reflect the more public, personnel evaluation aspect (cf. Smith, 1995). Richlin and Manning (1995) note that these assessment purposes are not mutually exclusive, but can be subsumed effectively within a comprehensive evaluation of teaching. However, Centra (2000) argues that portfolios have only limited utility for self-evaluation of teaching because self-ratings do not correlate meaningfully with ratings provided by others.

Formative assessment results should be shared only with whomever the faculty member chooses, whereas summative assessment results must be shared with colleagues and administrators responsible for promotion, merit, and tenure evaluations. Portfolios designed to improve teaching will receive broader faculty support. Programs focusing on evaluation fail more often because they reinforce administrative reasons over faculty improvement reasons. Liston, et al. (1998) found that the private, self-improvement function of portfolios drew more faculty interest than their public, evaluation purpose, suggesting that it might be best to begin with the self-improvement function. Seldin and Miller (2008) offer useful and specific suggestions for using portfolios to do evaluation and provides sample rating scales. Tigelaar, Dolmans, Wolfhagen, and van der Vleuten (2005) suggest that a constructivist approach be used when developing criteria of quality in order to maximize the integrity of the assessment process. Finally, those asked to review portfolios should receive training in how to construct and assess teaching portfolios (Centra 1994).

Smith and Tillema (2007) examined the frameworks used by 35 portfolio assessors in order to improve the standards and practices of portfolio review. If the goal is evaluation, only those in evaluative positions should see the portfolio. In general, portfolios should be shared only with permission. However, portfolios should be shared more widely if the goal is to not only improve teaching but to develop a collaborative teaching culture (Wolf 1991). Peer review could be incorporated in both situations and could include reviews of both classroom teaching and teaching materials.

Should a faculty member have the opportunity to respond to evaluators' comments? The nature and purpose of teaching portfolios suggest that faculty members be given the chance to provide a written response, to be included with the portfolio when it is submitted for personnel actions. This procedure helps reinforce the instructor's ownership of the portfolio and helps present alternative viewpoints in the case of disagreements. It is also underscores the role of portfolios as evolving documents that stimulate dialogue.

How long should portfolios be? This question has no easy answer. Length depends on such factors as the purpose of the review, the number of faculty members in a department, the frequency of submissions, and personal preferences. Discussions among those involved will yield appropriate limits on length (Wolverton, 1996) A guideline of 10-12 pages (plus attachments) seems appropriate. More comprehensive portfolios are appropriate for "one-shot" or for final tenure reviews. For yearly submissions, only modest updates are needed after submission of the initial comprehensive portfolio.

Should student materials be included? Again, this depends on the same kinds of considerations as the length of the document. Student work demonstrates how well students have attained course goals and illustrates the quality and type of feedback given by instructors. Two caveats are in order. First, for obvious reasons, most instructors submit only their students' best work. This is problematic, according to Abrami, d'Apollonia, and Rosenfield (1997), because it is difficult to judge teaching effectiveness using only students' best work. The best samples indicate primarily what is possible and not necessarily what is typical. Abrami, d'Apollonia, and Rosenfield (1997) suggest using a "representative" selection of student work. Second, permission must be sought from the students. This can be accomplished easily by including a permission form with the assignment, making it clear that granting permission is not linked to grades.

Which criteria will be used to assess portfolios? Gibbs (1995) notes the paucity of clear criteria for assessing portfolios. Richlin and Manning (1995) maintain that teaching portfolios should remain private until evaluation criteria are clear. Criteria should be consistent with a school's goals and definition of effective teaching. Criteria should reflect the best thinking on effective teaching, learning, and curricula. For example, *Reports from the Field* (Association of American Colleges, 1990) outlines goals and criteria for assessing study-in-depth in twelve fields. The American Sociological Association (1991) issued a companion report for sociology in *Liberal Learning and the Sociology Major.* Criteria should reflect the collective wisdom of departmental faculty members. These guidelines will help develop clear, fair, and useful criteria for assessing teaching portfolios, which should be achieved before they are used. Van der Schaaf and Stokking (2008) argue that portfolio assessment validity can be enhanced by linking teacher competencies, the criteria for assessing these competencies, the format employed, the completion of the format by teachers, and the scoring by raters.

What format should portfolios take? Teaching portfolios are usually written documents. However, they need not be, at least not exclusively. Video recordings could be used to illustrate both teaching behaviors and students' responses. For example, Wiedmer (1998) describes the use of multimedia, CD-ROM portfolios in the Indiana Electronic Portfolio Project. Other web-based versions of teaching portfolios have also emerged (see electronicportfolios.com and Young, 2001 for examples). Web versions of portfolios can help make teaching more public and can promote dialogue (Guernsey, 1999). They also help facilitate discipline-wide conversations about teaching and provide discipline-specific examples.

A FINAL CONCERN

One issue remains - what are the implications of an increasing use of teaching portfolios? Who will benefit from greater use of teaching portfolios? I have argued that instructors and students will benefit. However, the press for "comparability," for institution-wide assessment practices and standards, and for meeting state and institutional accountability demands may have consequences as well (Gaff, 2009; Hamilton, 2009). For example, widespread use of teaching portfolios may inadvertently lead to some homogenization of teaching styles to conform to "standards." Increased use may alter the balance of power between faculty and administrators. Wholesale, indiscriminate use of teaching portfolios for evaluation and assessment purposes may compromise their useful diagnostic features, much like the subversion of purposes that emerged with widespread use of student evaluation of teaching. In fact, Leggett and Bunker (2006) suggest that voluntary use of teaching portfolios can be very useful, but shifting to mandatory use of a multipurpose teaching portfolio negatively affects the institution's effectiveness by changing the underlying culture to conform more to a market orientation.

Ultimately, the most pressing question is: who benefits? We should do our best to make sure that the answer is "students and faculty," but as sociologists we should also be prepared to respond when this is not the case.

REFERENCES

Abrami, P.C., S. d'Apollonia, and S. Rosenfield. 1997. "The Dimensionality of Student Ratings: What We Know, What We Do Not." Pp. 321-367 in *Effective Teaching in Higher Education: Research and Practice*, edited by R.P. Perry and J.C. Smart. Edison, NJ: Agathon.

American Sociological Association. 1991. *Liberal Learning and the Sociology Major*. Washington, DC: American Sociological Association.

Anderson, E., ed. 1993. *Campus Use of the Teaching Portfolio*. Washington, DC: American Association for Higher Education.

Anderson-Patton, V. and E. Bass. 2002. "Using Narrative Teaching Portfolios for Self-Study." Pp. 101-114 in *Narrative Inquiry in Practice: Advancing the Knowledge of Teaching*. New York: Teachers College Press.

Association of American Colleges. 1990. *Reports From the Field*. Washington, DC: Association of American Colleges.

Barry, N.H. and D.M. Shannon. 1997. "Portfolios in Teacher Education: A Matter of Perspective." *The Educational Forum* 61:320-328.

Bernstein, D., A.N. Burnett, A. Goodburn, and P. Savory. 2006. *Making Teaching and Learning Visible: Course Portfolios and the Peer Review of Teaching*. Bolton, MA: Anker.

Bernstein, D., and R. Edwards. 2001. "We Need Objective, Rigorous Peer Review of Teaching." *Chronicle of Higher Education* January 5:B24.

Buckridge, M. 2008. "Teaching Portfolios: Their Role in Teaching and Learning Policy." *International Journal for Academic Development* 13(2):117-127.

Centra, J.A. 1994. "The Use of the Teaching Portfolio and Student Evaluations for Summative Evaluation." *Journal of Higher Education* 65:555-570.

_____. 2000. "Evaluating the Teaching Portfolio: A Role for Colleagues." Pp. 87-94 in *Evaluating Teaching in Higher Education: A Vision for the Future*, edited by R.E. Ryan. *New Directions for Teaching and Learning*, no. 83. San Francisco: Jossey-Bass.

Cerbin, W. 1994. "The Course Portfolio as a Tool for Continuous Improvement of Teaching and Learning." *Journal on Excellence in College Teaching* 5:95-105.

Costantino, P.M., M.N. De Lorenzo, and C. Tirrell-Corbin. 2008. *Developing a Professional Teaching Portfolio: A Guide for Success* (3rd ed.). Princeton: Allyn & Bacon.

De Rijdt, C., E. Tiquet, F. Dochy, and M. Devolder. 2006. "Teaching Portfolios in Higher Education and Their Effects: An Exploratory Study." *Teaching and Teacher Education* 22:1084-1093.

FitzPatrick, M.A. and D. Spiller. 2010. "The Teaching Portfolio: Institutional Imperative or Teacher's Personal Journey?" *Higher Education Research & Development* 29(2):167-178.

Gaff, J.G. 2009. "Academic Freedom, Peer Review, and Shared Governance in the Face of New Realities." Pp. 19-36 in *The Future of the Professoriate: Academic Freedom, Peer Review, and Shared Governance*, edited by N.W. Hamilton and J.G. Gaff. Washington DC: Association of American Colleges and Universities.

Gibbs, G. 1995. "How can Promoting Excellent Teachers Promote Excellent Teaching? *Innovations in Education and Training International* 32:74-84.

Guernsey, L. 1999. "With Web Skills–and Now Tenure–A Professor Promotes Improved Teaching." *Chronicle of Higher Education* February 26:A24.

Halpern, D.F. 1994. "Rethinking College Instruction for a Changing World." Pp. 1-12 in *Changing College Classrooms*, edited by D.F. Halpern and Associates. San Francisco: Jossey-Bass.

Hamilton, N.W. 2009. "Proactively Justifying the Academic Profession's Social Contract."Pp. 1-18 in *The Future of the Professoriate: Academic Freedom, Peer Review, and Shared Governance*, edited by N.W. Hamilton and J.G. Gaff. Washington DC: Association of American Colleges and Universities.

Huba, M.E., and J.E. Freed. 2000. *Learner-Centered Assessment on College Campuses: Shifting the Focus from Teaching to Learning*. Needham Heights, MA: Allyn and Bacon.

Kulski, M.M. and A. Radloff. 1998. "Adding Value to Teaching: A Framework for Institutional Use of the Teaching Portfolio." *South African Journal of Higher Education* 12:179-185.

Kumaravadivelu, B. 1995. "A Multidimensional Model for Peer Evaluation of Teaching Effectiveness." *Journal on Excellence in College Teaching* 6 (3):95-113.

Lang, J. 2010. "4 Steps to a Memorable Teaching Philosophy." *Chronicle of Higher Education* Aug. 29:online.

Leggett, M. and Bunker, A. 2006. "Teaching Portfolios and University Culture." *Journal of Further and Higher Education* 30:269-282.

Liston, D.D., C.A. Hansman, S.L. Kenney, and C.C. Brewton. 1998. "Teaching Portfolio Use in the Absence of Institutional Support. *Journal on Excellence in College Teaching* 9:121-134.

Lord, T. 2009. "What? Professors Evaluating Themselves? Are You out of Your Mind?: In Defense of Faculty Self – Evaluation." *Journal of College Science Teaching* 38(4):72-74.

McColgan, K. and B. Blackwood. 2009. "A Systematic Review Protocol on the Use of Teaching Portfolios for Educators in Further and Higher Education." *Journal of Advanced Nursing* 65(12):2500-2507.

Misra, J. 2000. "Integrating 'The Real World' Into Introduction to Sociology: Making Sociological Concepts Real." *Teaching Sociology* 28:346-363.

Mooney, L.A., and B. Edwards. "Experiential Learning in Sociology: Service Learning and Other Community-Based Learning Initiatives." *Teaching Sociology* 29:181-194.

Moran, T.P. 1999. "Versifying Your Reading List: Using Poetry to Teach Inequality." *Teaching Sociology* 27:110-125.

Murray, J.P. 1995. "The Teaching Portfolio: A Tool for Department Chairpersons to Create a Climate of Teaching Excellence." *Innovative Higher Education* 19:63-75.

Palmer, P. 1998. *The Courage to Teach: Exploring the Inner Landscape of a Teacher's Life.* San Francisco: Jossey-Bass.

Quinlan, K.M. 2002. "Inside the Peer Review Process: How Academics Review a Colleague's Teaching Portfolio." *Teaching & Teacher* Education 18(8):1035-1050.

Renfrew, D. (ed) 2009 . *Teaching Portfolios Within the Discipline.* Washington, DC: American Sociological Association.

Richlin, L. 1995. "A Different View on Developing Teaching Portfolios: Ensuring Safety While Honoring Practice." *Journal of Excellence in College Teaching* 6:161-178.

_____. and B. Manning. 1995. "Evaluating College and University Teaching: Principles and Decisions for Designing a Workable System." *Journal of Excellence in College Teaching* 6:3-15.

Rose, S. 2007. "Perfecting Your Portfolio: Preparing for Promotion." *FASEB Journal* 21(5):A33-A34.

Ross, D.D., E. Bondy, L. Hartle, L.L. Lamme, and R.B. Webb. 1995. "Guidelines for Portfolio Preparation: Implications from an Analysis of Teaching Portfolios at the University of Florida." *Innovative Higher Education* 20:45-61.

Seldin, P., J.E. Miller, C.A. Seldin, and W. McKeachie. 2010. *The Teaching Portfolio: A Practical Guide to Improved Performance and Promotion/Tenure Decisions* (4th ed.). San Francisco: Jossey Bass.

Seldin, P. and J.E. Miller. 2008. *The Academic Portfolio: A Practical Guide to Documenting Teaching, Research, and Service.* San Francisco: Jossey Bass.

Shulman, L.S. 1988. "A Union of Insufficiencies: Strategies for Teacher Assessment in a Period of Educational Reform." *Educational Leadership* 46 (3):36-41.

Smith, K. and H. Tilema. 2007. "Use of Criteria in Assessing Teaching Portfolios: Judgemental Practices in Summative Evaluation." *Scandinavian Journal of Educational Research* 51(1):103-117.

Smith, R.A. 1995. "Creating a Culture of Teaching Through the Teaching Portfolio." *Journal of Excellence in College Teaching* 6:75-99.

Strand, K., S. Marullo, N. Cutforth, R. Stoecker, and P. Donohue. 2003. *Community – Based Research and Higher Education.* San Francisco: Jossey Bass.

Sung, Y.T., K.E. Chang, W.C. Yu, and T.H. Chang. 2009. "Supporting Teachers' Reflection and Learning through Structured Digital Teaching Portfolios." *Journal of Computer Assisted Learning* 25(4):375-385.

Tigelaar, D.E.H., D.H.J.M. Dolmans, I.H.A. Wolfhagen, and C.P.M. van der Vleuten. 2005. Quality Issues in Judging Portfolios: Implications for Organizing Teaching Portfolio Assessment Procedures." *Studies in Higher Education* 30:595-610.

Tynes, S.R. 2001. "Bringing Social Class Home: The Social Class Genealogy and Poverty Lunch Projects." *Teaching Sociology* 29:286-298.

Urbach, F. 1992. "Developing a Teaching Portfolio." *College Teaching* 40:71-74.

Van der Schaaf, M.F. and K. M. Stokking. 2008. "Developing and Validating a Design for Teacher Portfolio Assessment." *Assessment and Evaluation in Higher* Education 33(3):245-262.

Van Tartwijk, J., E. Driessen, C. van der Vleuten, and K. Stokking. 2007. "Factors Influencing the Successful Introduction of Portfolios." *Quality of Education* 13:69-79.

Weshah, H.A. 2010. "Issues of Developing a Professional Teaching Portfolio in Jordan." *European Journal of Social Science* 15(1):97-114.

Wiedmer, T.L. 1998. "Portfolios: A Means for Documenting Professional Development." *Journal of Staff, Program, and Organization Development* 16:21-37.

Wolf, K. 1991. "The Schoolteacher's Portfolio: Issues in Design, Implementation, and Evaluation. *Phi Delta Kappan* 73:129-136.

Wolverton, M. 1996. "Teaching Portfolios: The Experience at Miami-Dade Community College." *The Journal of General Education* 45:295-305.

Wright, M.C. 2000. "Getting More Out of Less: The Benefits of Short-Term Experiential Learning in Undergraduate Sociology Courses." *Teaching Sociology* 28:116-126.

Young, J.R. 2001. Professors Publish Teaching Portfolios Online." *Chronicle of Higher Education* August 17:A31.

5

The Use of Teaching Circles

Carol Bailey, Virginia Polytechnic Institute
and State University
Thomas L. Van Valey, Western Michigan University

Teaching is an activity that requires constant review and renewal. Changes in instructional technology, class size, student populations, and the scholarship of teaching and learning are only some of the factors that require faculty to periodically rethink their pedagogy. A number of strategies have been developed at both the disciplinary and institutional levels to help faculty keep up to date with current developments in pedagogical techniques (Hutchings, 1995; Quinlan, 1996; Chism, 1999). One of the simpler and more common strategies to date has been the creation of Teaching Circles.

BACKGROUND AND PURPOSE

The term Ateaching circle@ entered the public lexicon of higher education with the publication of Ernest Boyer=s, *Scholarship Reconsidered....@* (Nazareth, 2003) It was elaborated by Hutchings (1995) and Quinlan (1996, 1998), and described as a fundamentally collaborative activity that is flexible enough to meet a variety of needs. These could include individualized objectives, courses with multiple sections, and program review. Hutchings further suggested that three principles would make teaching circles more productive: 1) be clear about the purpose of the group; 2) keep discussion focused on concrete particulars; and 3) think about how to preserve and share the work of the teaching circle.

Loosely defined, a teaching circle is a voluntary group of individuals who meet on a regular basis for the purpose of improving teaching and student learning. Although most teaching circles focus on teaching and learning, the disciplines involved, the composition of the members, the purpose of the circle, the meeting frequency, and the activities of the circle vary widely across institutions. For example, sometimes teaching circles are seen as faculty support groups, and at other times they are seen as faculty study groups B reflecting a different emphasis in group priorities. Those who participate in teaching circles can include a blend of faculty, graduate students who teach, and even students and administrators. The members can be from several disciplines or from the same discipline. Within the context of a single department, teaching circles can consist of those who teach the same course or those who teach across the entire curriculum. Therefore, determining an appropriate mix of members depends upon the purpose of the circle, the needs of those involved, diversity issues, and the blend of personalities that facilitate a supportive environment.

In addition to helping faculty and other teachers keep up to date, the teaching circle is a strategy for developing peer collaboration outside the classroom environment (Cessna and Graf, 2000). Faculty and graduate students can avail themselves of the scholarly literature on teaching and learning, assist others, refine their own teaching, and find a supportive forum for the discussion of teaching as a professional activity (Black and Cessna, 2002, UIOWA). Consequently, teaching circles are unlike most other mentoring-type relationships B no hierarchy is implied among group members. Indeed, teaching circles are places where equal relationships can be formed among those new to the profession and their more experienced colleagues. By working together in teaching circles, faculty and others share a common direction and a sense of collegiality.

Teaching circles also allow the faculty to set informal professional standards for teaching (UTEP). The teaching circle provides a forum that says teaching is scholarly intellectual work, and thus worthy of attention (Hutchings, 1995). This is particularly appropriate in those instances where a teaching circle is incorporated as part of a program review. The discussion that develops often allows the faculty to identify group-level standards for specific practices (e.g., grading, syllabi, academic misconduct). In some instances, it can lead to a more carefully structured curriculum and a better organized academic program

Given the demands on faculty time, the teaching circle can also be an efficient mechanism for keeping faculty informed about the scholarship of teaching and learning. For example, group members can take turns locating, disseminating, and leading discussions on current research (SFASU). Some teaching circles organize pedagogical colloquiums or department brown bags on teaching or other related topics. As ways of enhancing the culture of a department or even an institution, teaching circles have the potential to be an important mechanism for promoting the professional and scholarly nature of teaching.

Teaching circles are also one mechanism for helping a department move from teaching as a private activity to a public activity (Shaw et al, 2002, Mezeske, 2006, Marshall, 2008). They open up conversations about teaching to one's peers (and often others as well), yet do so in a collegial and non-threatening manner. Thus, they legitimate the open, public discussion of teaching related issues, and can even help erode the concerns that some faculty have about the peer review of teaching.

FORMAT AND OPERATIONS

Although there are often broad frameworks established by the institution itself, the format of a teaching circle is typically decided by the members of the group. The emphasis of a particular teaching circle might be to help teachers refine their current skills or to learn new ones. Members of a teaching circle might all work on the same issue - improving class discussion, for example (SPSU, ECU). Alternatively, they might work on individual problems within the group context. Still other circles have created course portfolios, developed teaching philosophies, undertaken classroom visitations, improved course materials, and engaged in collaborative peer reviews (LCC). During the course of a group=s history, the members might work through a series of topics or focus on a single one. Meetings might be highly structured or relatively unstructured. Regardless of the substantive focus, the most effective teaching circles appear to be those that are formative or developmental in nature, and totally removed from the formal (and even informal) summative evaluative process.

Within teaching circles, members typically have a confidential format for companionship, feedback, and support in a nonjudgmental atmosphere. Members are encouraged to be open, risk takers, and focus on positive interactions within the group (Black and Cessna, 2002). Trust among group members is essential. Consequently, members need to agree on group rules and spend time on group dynamics early in the process.

A teaching circle might begin by working on listening skills and giving facilitative comments. Members need to collectively decide who will have access to any minutes generated during meetings or data that the group might collect. The importance of regular attendance and participation by all group members should be stressed, and procedures for ensuring that the same individuals do not dominate the group can be established. A shared understanding of confidentiality issues is extremely important among group members.

Administrative support for teaching circles is useful but not necessary (Mezeske, 2006). A stipend for group members, a place to meet, supplies, and recognition and rewards for participation are all effective incentives, and would be gratefully accepted. However, many teaching circles operate quite well without any formal support. Often, they seem to function on a consensual basis, with one or more individuals taking on the responsibility of finding a meeting place, setting a meeting time, and establishing a particular agenda.

In those institutions that support teaching circles (often through a center for teaching and learning or other faculty development mechanism), it is common for there to be multiple teaching circles in operation at a given time across multiple disciplines (Scharff , 2003, CPP, IUP, LCC, MNSCU). In some instances, they are loosely coordinated; in others, they function independently of one another. Some Sociology departments even have multiple teaching circles. In those instances, they appear to be devoted to specific courses (e.g., the introductory course, social problems, statistics). Periodically, the different teaching circles can share experiences with each other, sometimes during faculty meetings or at other departmental meetings.

A BRIEF EXAMPLE OF A TEACHING CIRCLE

In the Department of Sociology at Western Michigan University, our teaching circle is organized by a doctoral-level graduate student who has been designated for that year by the chair of the department as the Graduate Teaching Mentor. The recipient receives a $1,000 stipend provided from the Dean=s office, and is an advanced student, who has completed the department=s teaching practicum, has substantial experience teaching his/her own courses with outstanding student evaluations, and has a strong interest in pursuing teaching as a high academic priority.

The teaching circle meets about once a month throughout the academic year, and the topics of discussion are usually announced in advance by the Teaching Mentor. As an incentive, lunch (e.g., pizza or sandwiches and drinks) is often provided by the department. The people that attend are mostly graduate students who are teaching or who are going to be teaching, but also a few faculty. There are typically 6-12 people present. Topics covered have included: the design of an introductory course, selection of texts, designing writing assignments, approaches to grading, discipline problems, ethical issues, and research on teaching and learning.

CLOSING COMMENT

It is clear that teaching circles can morph into many different forms, depending on the nature and the interests of the participants. Indeed, it is precisely the reason that teaching circles offer much promise. They can start out small, avoiding the need for departmental consensus. They require little or no resources, and only minimal commitment from the participants. They can include graduate students who are teaching as well as part-time, untenured, and tenured faculty. It is that flexibility and the fact that they are typically defined as sharing and non-threatening that teaching circles can be an extremely useful way of opening the conversation about peer review in a department.

REFERENCES

Black, L. and Cessna, M. A. 2002. "Teaching Circles: Making Inquiry Safe for Faculty." *Teaching Excellence* POD Network, Ft. Collins, CO Vol 14, No 3.

Boyer, E. L. 1990. *Scholarship Reconsidered: New Priorities of the Professoriate*. Stanford, CA. Carnegie Foundation

Cessna, M. A. and Graf, D. 2000. "The Benefits of Teaching Circles." *NEA Higher Education Advocate*. 17(6): 4-8

Chism, N. 1999. *Peer Review of Teaching: A Sourcebook*. Bolton, MA: Anker Publishing.

Hutchings, P. (Ed.) 1995. *From Idea to Prototype: The Peer Review of Teaching*. Washington, DC: American Association for Higher Education.

Hutchings, P. 1996. "The Peer Review of Teaching: Progress, Issues and Prospects." *Innovative Higher Education*. Vol 20, No 4: 221-234.

Marshall, M. J. 2008 "Teaching Circles: Supporting Shared Work and Professional Development." *Pedagogy* Vol 8, No 3: 413-431

Mezeske, B. A. 2006 "Teaching Circles: Low-Cost, High-Impact Faculty Development" *Academic Leader*: 8

Quinlan, K. M. 1996. "Involving Peers in the Evaluation and Improvement of Teaching: A Menu of Strategies." *Innovative Higher Education*. Vol 20, No 4: 299-307.

Quinlan K. M. 1998 "Promoting Faculty Learning about Collaborative Teaching." *College Teaching*. Vol 46, No 2: 43-47.

Scharff, L. F. V. 2003. "Organizing and Maintaining University-wide Teaching Circles. In W. Buskist, V. Hevern, & G. W. Hill, IV, (Eds.). *Essays from E-xcellence in teaching, 2002* (Chap. 8). Retrieved from the Society for the Teaching of Psychology Web site: http://teachpsych.lemoyne.edu/teachpsych/eit/index.html

Shaw D, Belcastro S, Thiessen D. 2002. "A Teaching Discussion Group in your Department – It Can Happen!" *College Teaching*. Vol 50, No 1: 29-33

WEB REFERENCES

CPP, Teaching Circles: Toward a Community of Teacher-Scholars,@ Faculty Center for Professional Development, Cal Poly Pomona. www.csupomona.edu/~faculty_center/special_programs/teachingcirclefly er.pdf

ECU, "Teaching Circles," First-Year Writing, Department of English, East Carolina University. core.ecu.edu/engl/fyw/writing/circles.htm

IUP, The Reflective Practice Project. Center for Teaching Excellence, Indiana University of Pennsylvania. www.iup.edu/page.aspx?id=40531

LCC, "Teaching Circles," Center for Teaching Excellence, Lansing Community College. www.lcc.edu/cte/services_support/teachingcircles/index.html

MNSCU, "Teaching Circles FAQ," Center for Teaching and Learning. Century College, Minnesota State Colleges and Universities. ctlcentury.project.mnscu.edu

Nazareth College, "The Teaching Circle" Center for Teaching Excellence. Nazareth College of Rochester. www.naz.edu/dept/cte/pe/circles/whatisteachingcircle.html

SFASU, "What are Teaching Circles?" Teaching Excellence Center, Stephen F. Austin State University. www2.sfasu.edu/teachingexcellence/Services/TeachingCirclesSFA.htm

SPSU, "The Teaching Circles Program" Center for Teaching Excellence, Southern Polytechnic State University. cte.spsu.edu/newsite/teachingcircles/index.shtml

UIOWA, "Would You Like to Join a Teaching Circle?" Center for Teaching, University of Iowa.
www.uiowa.edu/~centeach/talk/volume3/teaching_circle.html

UTEP, "Teaching Circles," The Center for Effective Teaching and Learning, University of Texas at El Paso.
sunconference.utep.edu/CETaL/resources/portfolios/circles.htm

6

The Use of Student Interviews
in the Review of Teaching

John DeLamater, University of Wisconsin
Thomas L. Van Valey, Western Michigan University

Information from students is an essential part of any comprehensive review of an instructor's teaching. Students are one of the most appropriate sources of information about the learning environment created by the instructor, and certainly about what they have learned as a result of the class. The major issue is how to collect that information from the students in a meaningful and useful way.

STUDENT RATINGS

The most common means of soliciting information about teaching is student ratings of instructors. These tend to be short surveys consisting mostly of closed-end items, usually administered toward the end of the term. The questions or scales on which the instructor is to be rated and the response alternatives are typically specified in advance, and there may also be a few open-ended questions or space provided for comments. While such student ratings of instructors are an efficient means of gathering information, they do have several drawbacks.

First, the survey form is usually standardized. By their nature, they can not allow for dialogue, for the elaboration of details or for the clarification of items that are perceived as ambiguous (Hutchings, 1996, Emery & Tian, 2003). Some or all of the items may be used for all courses in the department, or for all courses in the college, or even the entire campus. Since the survey must cover an enormous variety of courses, the questions therefore are necessarily global and simplistic. While this facilitates comparisons across courses, such general questions may not be applicable to some, perhaps many, specific courses or teaching situations. Moreover, it tends to focus on the degree to which the evaluations can be used in a summative fashion.

Second, it appears that students often appear to answer these surveys in a perfunctory fashion, completing them quickly and skipping over the request for comments (Chen & Hoshower, 2003). Thus, the resulting information may not be particularly helpful to the instructor who wants formative feedback that will help improve his or her classroom instruction (Shevlin et al, 2000). Nevertheless, there is evidence that responses to specific behavioral items can give an instructor information that can result in improvement (McKeachie, 1996).

Third, these surveys are completed by a convenience sample - those students who happen to be in the class on the day they are distributed, usually toward the end of the term. These students are the ones that have remained in the course, and are likely to be those students who have positive attitudes toward the course or the instructor. Thus, it can be argued that they will provide artificially more positive ratings than would be obtained from the entire class or even a carefully drawn representative sample.

STUDENT INTERVIEWS

One alternative to the typical student ratings is to interview students who are taking the course. The interview can be focused on the specific course, and the questions can be tailored to the specific instructor, the instructional situation, and the students taking the course (Buschman, 2001). Interviewing students provides unique information about the nature and consequences of teaching/instruction (Hoban, 2000, Kember, Leung & Kwan, 2002, Steinert, 2004). In addition, the use of this technique signals to students that their opinions are valued. It also demonstrates the instructor's commitment to creating a productive learning environment in the course. The use of student interviews also reflects, and signals to students, a more learning-centered approach to instruction. Moreover, if they are carried out during the term rather than just at the end, student interviews can provide information on how instruction is progressing in the course. Furthermore, it enables students to take an active role in the class, and gives them some responsibility for making contributions to improving the course (Morehead & Shedd, 1996).

Unlike the typical student rating form, there are a number of topics on which student interviews can focus:

- the students' assessment of the required work load.
- the level of effort that students are putting into the course.
- the students' assessment of the value of specific

aspects of instruction, such as lectures, discussions, field experiences, readings, assigned papers, and examinations.

- the classroom climate - students' perceptions of the instructor's openness to their views, support for diverse types of learners.
- the physical environment of the course and the technology that is involved.
- the students' assessment of their progress or accomplishment in learning the material.
- the students= view of the content of the course.
- the students= view of the degree to which norms of behavior were followed (e.g., attendance, tardiness, plagiarism, cheating) and enforced.

GENERAL GUIDELINES

There are some general guidelines that apply to all forms of review of teaching. First, there are no extant universal criteria for the evaluation of teaching (or student learning), nor are such criteria likely to emerge in the near future. The range of teaching situations is so diverse that universal criteria are likely to be too broad to be of practical use. Consequently, reviews must be context-specific. Thus, the criteria to be applied depend upon the discipline, the nature, size and level of the class, as well as the characteristics of both the instructor and the students.

Second, it is essential that the reviewer(s), and the instructor being reviewed, agree in advance about the focus of the review and the criteria to be employed. Since there are many aspects of teaching and learning that can be assessed using student interviews, a narrowing of the focus is essential. The interviews should address the needs of the instructor being reviewed. In particular, the review should focus on, or at least include, those specific aspects of teaching about which the instructor wants feedback. Advance discussion and agreement about the topics to be covered is therefore critical.

Third, it is essential that the reviewer be informed about and open to the instructional approach taken by the instructor. Faculty members have divergent perspectives on how one should teach the content of the discipline. A review of teaching must be respectful of the instructor's perspective. This might suggest that reviewers should be from the same discipline or even sub-discipline, and have the same orientation toward instruction. However, while such similarity may be important in some cases, it does not seem necessary in all cases.

THE TECHNIQUE OF STUDENT INTERVIEWS

Student interviews have been defined as "hour-long sessions wherein a peer meets with a teacher's class or a representative group of the teacher's students" (Morehead & Shedd, 1996, p. 263). These are comparable to focus groups, a qualitative data collection technique that is often used in marketing as well as other social science applications (Atkinson, 1998, Buschman, 2001, Muller, 2006). They can, of course, also be carried out with as few as a single student, and may take a good deal longer than an hour, depending on the circumstances. At the University of Wisconsin, the technique usually involves interviewing small groups of students (5-7 at a time). In any event, the number of students interviewed in a given sitting needs to be relatively small so the reviewer can obtain information from each participant. Typically, the interviews are carried out either near the end of the term or soon after it is over.

Before the interviews, the instructor and the reviewer(s) discuss the instructor's goals for the course, and agree on the specific issues to be addressed. The reviewer(s) then prepare a list of questions to be covered. During the interviews, the reviewer(s) attempt to ensure that all students are heard and all opinions are represented. Also, the reviewer(s) take notes on the tenor as well as the substance of the responses by the students. One option is to record the sessions, although this may raise students' concern about the confidentiality of what they say.

The product of the interviews depends in part on the purpose of the review. If the purpose is **formative** in nature (i.e., to provide feedback to the instructor so he or she can improve their teaching), the reviewer typically meets with the instructor and provides oral feedback summarizing the interviews. The feedback will be most helpful if it is specific - if the reviewer can identify specific aspects of instruction which the students find helpful and specific aspects which the students feel interfere with learning. If the reviewer and instructor agree, the feedback can also be summarized in a written memo, with the memo given only to the instructor. The instructor has the choice of including it as an entry in his/her promotion dossier or teaching portfolio, as additional evidence of student evaluations.

If the purpose of the interviews is **summative** in nature (i.e., to provide evidence of quality of teaching for the evaluation of the instructor by others), a summary memo of the review is written, a copy is provided to the instructor, and the instructor has the opportunity to respond in writing to the review. The summary memo and the instructor=s response together constitute the record of the review, and both should be transmitted to the appropriate party for inclusion in the personnel records.

ISSUES

There are several issues that must be resolved each time this technique is employed. First, there is the question of timing. Interviews for the purpose of formative reviews can be conducted during the course (or even repeated at different times), and the feedback can thus be used as a basis for changes during the remainder of the course or for a subsequent course offering. In contrast, applications of this technique for the purpose of summative reviews normally occur near the end of the course or shortly after the term is completed.

A second issue is the number of students to be interviewed and their selection. In small classes (those with 20 students or less), it is best to interview as many of the students as possible so that every viewpoint is represented. Of course, if interviews include only 5-7 students, this would require interviews with three or four groups of students. In larger classes, the time required to interview every student and compile the results may be prohibitive. In this case, samples of students need to be selected. One could simply ask for volunteers, but the drawback is the potential for bias in the feedback obtained. The most representative sample would be drawn randomly, with each student selected being interviewed. However, this may not always be feasible. Alternatively, one could allow the class as a whole to select representatives to be interviewed. If this alternative is used, it may be best to allow the class to determine how to select their own representatives.

The selection of students does raise an interesting question. If one=s concern about sampling is that the results should be Arepresentative@ and thus more generalizable to the class as a whole, is this an attempt to portray student interviews as somehow better or more scientific than the usual student evaluations? If so, it raises the question of whether the results are indeed more useful and thus justify the additional time and effort involved in collecting and compiling them. If not, then why not simply treat student interviews simply as one more type of information that an instructor (and/or his or her peers) can employ to improve his or her teaching (or that can be used to evaluate it)?

A third issue is the confidentiality of students= remarks. The candor and honesty of student comments almost certainly depends on their sense that what they say is confidential, and that they will not be penalized by the instructor or by others if they provide critical feedback. For this reason, it is clear that student interviews should not be conducted by the instructor. Similarly, the use of graduate assistants assigned to the course is likely to inhibit critical feedback. However, on small campuses or even in buildings that house several departments, the use of other faculty may not alleviate the problem. After all, the students may believe that all faculty protect one another and are likely to share the results informally. As noted above, tape recording the interviews also might arouse students' concern with confidentiality, unless they are assured that only the reviewer (and not the instructor) will have access to the tapes.

What the instructor does (or does not do) as a result of the student interviews can also have substantial repercussions. If the instructor does nothing as a result (or, if the students and colleagues perceive that the instructor does nothing), it may send the signal that student views about instruction are worthless. This can easily result in dramatic declines in the active and credible participation by the students. By the same token, the faculty or graduate student assistants who conduct and compile the interviews may quickly decide it is a waste of their time.

In contrast, when students do perceive that the instructor implements changes in the course as a result of the interviews, it reinforces the importance of their participation. They may develop an increased sense of investment in the course, and an increased sense of the professor's responsiveness. It may even carry over into the effort they put into the course. When they see adjustments in the learning environment that are responsive to them, it reinforces the relationship between them and the instructor. That bodes well for the quality of student learning.

REFERENCES

Atkinson, D. 1998. "Evaluating Teaching/Learning via Groupware Focus Groups" in Black, B. and Stanley, N. (Eds), *Teaching and Learning in Changing Times*. Proceedings of the 7th Annual Teaching Learning Forum, The University of Western Australia, Perth. 22-27.

Buschman, L. 2001.-"Using Student Interviews To Guide Classroom Instruction: An Action Research Project." *Teaching Children Mathematics*, Vol 8, No 4: 222-227.

Chen, Y. and Hoshower, L. B. 2003. "Student Evaluation of Teaching Effectiveness: An Assessment of Student Perception and Motivation" *Assessment & Evaluation in Higher Education*, Vol 28, No 1: 71-88.

Emery, C. R., Kramer, T. R. and Tian,R. G. 2003. "Return to Academic Standards: a Critique of Student Evaluations of Teaching Effectiveness", *Quality Assurance in Education*, Vol 11, No 1: 37-46.

Hoban, G. 2000. "Making Practice Problematic: Listening to Student Interviews as a Catalyst for Teacher Reflection." *Asia-Pacific Journal of Teacher Education*, Vol 28, No 2: 133-147.

Hutchings, P. 1996. *Making Teaching Community Property*. Washington, D.C.: American Association for Higher Education. pp.37-41.

Kember, D., D.Y.P. Leung & K.P. Kwan. 2002. "Does the Use of Student Feedback Questionnaires Improve the Overall quality of Teaching?" Assessment & Evaluation in College Teaching. Vol 27. No. 5: 411-425.

McKeachie, W. J. 1996. "Student Ratings of Teaching." In England, Hutchings, and McKeachie, (Eds) *The Professional Evaluation of Teaching*. New York: American Council of Learned Societies, Occasional Paper No. 33, 1-7.

Morehead, J. W. and Shedd, P. J. 1996. Student interviews: A vital role in the scholarship of teaching. *Innovative Higher Education*, 20: 261-269.

Muller, Robert. 2006. "Focus Groups as a Form of Student Evaluation of Teaching" paper presented at the ATN Evaluation Forum, Perth, Australia.

Sheppard, S. Leifer, L. and Carryer, J. E. 1996. "Commentary on Student Interviews" *Innovative Higher Education* 20: 271-276.

Shevlin, M. Banyard, P. Davies, M. and Griffiths, M. 2000. "The Validity of Student Evaluation of Teaching in Higher Education: Love me, love my lectures?" *Assessment & Evaluation in Higher Education*, Vol 25, No 4: 397-405.

Steinert, Yvonne. 2004. "Student Perceptions of Effective Small Group Teaching" *Medical Education* 38 (3), 286-293.

WEB REFERENCES

Samojlowicz, Gosia, "Structured Focus Groups for Course and Program Assessment" This is from the Excellence in Teaching Program, University of Nevada, Reno
http://teaching.unr.edu/etp/Focus_Groups/focusgroups.html

www.provost.wisc.edu/archives/ccae/MOO/int.proc.form.html. This is from the Peer Review Task Force, University of Wisconsin at Madison. The page also provides links to other pages for those interested in the peer review of teaching.

7

Designing a Peer Observation Instrument

Keith A. Roberts, Hanover College

The peer observation of teaching is an important element in the peer review of teaching. For one thing, reliance solely on student evaluations denigrates the scholarship of teaching and learning, for undergraduates do not know the scholarship that defines the discipline, nor do they comprehend the complex issues and the research underlying choices of teaching methodologies. If we are serious about our professionalism, we must be serious about peer review and peer involvement in our development as teacher scholars. (Arreola, 2000; Roberts and Donahue, 2000; see also Chapters 1 thru 4 in this volume))

A preliminary step in the classroom observation of peers is the determination of whether a focused review or a generalized review is needed. A *focused review* is one in which the classroom visitor is helping to develop one or more *specific* skills. On the other hand, an instructor may want *a general review* of overall teaching skills. If the purpose of peer review of the classroom is formative (i.e., developmental), then it is usually most helpful if the person being reviewed shares with the reviewer those things she wants help in improving. However, in those institutions where peer reviews are summative (i.e., evaluative) these reviews are inevitably *general* reviews. Similarly, the report that is provided in summary of the observation(s) needs to be consistent with the purposes of the review. Traditionally, numeric ranking scales are employed for summative reviews; qualitative summaries are more valuable for formative purposes.

Unfortunately, the research on teaching and learning shows a rather low level of reliability with regard to summative peer observations of teaching (Centra, 1979, Braskamp and Ory, 1994). However, as in any qualitative research, reliability can be substantially improved. Just as in field studies, training in observation techniques can increase skill and improve reliability and validity, training in the observation of a classroom can increase the dependability of those data. One factor that is especially important in increasing the credibility of peer observations is ensuring that the observers look for the same patterns or skills (Braskamp and Ory, 1994; Chism, 1999; Paulsen, 2001; Paulsen, 2002). For this reason a peer observation instrument may be especially valuable. Indeed, departments that are serious about reliability, should look at the research calling for careful training of peer observers and for consideration of the traits that make for especially effective peer observers (Svinicki and Lewis, 2006, UNC Center for Teaching and Learning, 2006, Braskamp and Ory, 1994)

Of course, there is no perfect peer observation instrument, although there can be more and less helpful ones. Faculty ownership of the instrument can be an important asset, however. Designing an instrument that works within the specific academic unit is also critical. In what follows, I suggest a process which may improve the quality of the instrument and may also give the process added credibility within the department.

A PROCESS FOR DEVELOPING AN INSTRUMENT FOR CLASSROOM OBSERVATION

A first step is to develop some level of agreement within the department about the elements of effective teaching that will be considered. A department may want to begin with criteria that have already been established. Several scholars indicate that although there are variations, general consensus exists nationally about the elements of good teaching (Centra, 1979, 1993; Feldman, 1988; Wotruba and Wright, 1975; Johnson and Ryan, 2000; Svinicki and Lewis, 2006; Cashin, 1989). A department could also begin with one or more of the lists of characteristics that have been empirically tested (see Centra, 1993, Feldman, 1988; Svinicki and Lewis, 2006) and establish its own list of eight or ten characteristics which are consistent with the culture of its own institution. Such lists typically include many of the following:
  • Expertise in Subject Matter.
  • Enthusiasm (for the subject and for teaching).
  • Clarity of Communication.
  • Good Organization (daily & during the entire course).
  • Preparation for Class.
  • Rapport with Students (in class and outside of class).
  • Utilization of Diverse Instructional Methodologies.
  • High Expectations.
  • Prompt and Useful Feedback.
  • Student Learning Objectives.
  • Stimulation of Student Interest.

- Ability to Engage Students.
- Students Encouraged to Think for Themselves.
- Fairness of Exams and other Evaluation Strategies.
- Clarity of Course Objectives (tied to the department's/institution's objectives).

A second step is to identify which of the factors identified by the department as indicators of effective teaching can be best assessed by students and which can be best assessed by peers. In some cases only faculty are capable of evaluating a trait. For example, students are not well situated to evaluate scholarly knowledge of the subject matter, the appropriate level of teaching (academic rigor), the scope of the material covered (most often they simply do not know what materials or theoretical perspectives were left out of the course coverage), or whether the course objectives are consistent with departmental or university instructional objectives. Peers are needed to assess these types of information. In other cases—because they see the instructors every day—students may be in the best position to assess other factors. Students are able to assess *acts of commission* (e.g. preparation for class, enthusiasm, promptness of feedback on work, effectiveness as a discussion leader, clarity of communication) but they are very ill prepared to provide feedback on *acts of omission* (e.g., new theoretical developments in the field or teaching strategies which were not used) (Centra, 1976).

Of course, the power relationships in a classroom can cloud student perceptions of instructors or of their decisions, so even when students are capable of assessing a characteristic, corroborating evidence from peers is valuable. If information provided by the instructor is reviewed along with observations by both peers and students, the triangulation of data regarding that aspect of teaching enhances the confidence one can place in the results. This is the case if both student assessments and peer observations concur that a particular aspect of teaching is either especially strong, or is especially in need of improvement. Where student and peer observations differ, further data and/or careful interpretation of the results may be needed. The important point here, however, is that students and colleagues should be asked to assess those characteristics that they are best capable of assessing.

The key, then, is for departments to generate a list of characteristics of effective teaching and then to identify the most reliable and valid evidence for each characteristic. A final list might look something like the following table:

Elements of Effective Teaching:	Most reliable & valid types of evidence:
• Knowledge of the Subject	Self evaluations Peer reviews
• High Expectations	Copies of exams and selected assignments Copies of graded assignments— including comments to students Peer review of materials Grade distributions
• Frequent/Prompt Feedback	Student evaluations
• Students Encouraged to Think for Themselves	Self evaluation Copies of examinations Student evaluations Peer classroom observations
• Participatory (active) learning	Self evaluation Peer classroom observations
• Clarity of Communication (re: class presentations; assignments; feedback)	Student evaluations Syllabi Copies of assignments
• Organization (daily & entire course)	Student evaluations Syllabi Copies of selected student handouts Peer classroom observation
• Enthusiasm (for subject & for teaching)	Student evaluations Peer classroom observation
• Respect for Students (in class & outside of class)	Student evaluations Peer classroom observation
• Fairness of Exams and/or Other Evaluations of Student Work	Student evaluations Review of examinations and a sample of graded papers

A third step is to focus on those items that can be assessed by peers. Some elements of teaching can be assessed by reviewing syllabi and other materials, but other areas may require classroom visits. The instrument used for peer classroom observations should include those factors which peers are well qualified to assess in a limited number of observations of a classroom.

Fourth, the members of the department need to agree on whether they want a written narrative regarding the instructor's skills, or a check-off system that allows an observer simply to mark a number or a point on a continuum ranging from excellent to poor. There are advantages to each approach, and the decision may depend in part on whether the observation instrument will be used for summative reviews, developmental reviews, or both.

Fifth, departments will want to have discussions regarding how the various factors involved in effective classroom teaching are operationalized. For example, an instructor sitting in a circle conducting a class discussion may score either high or low on "enthusiasm" depending on how her passion for learning and for the subject matter comes through. The fact that the instructor is sitting may not necessarily be a sign of low enthusiasm; many students experience enthusiasm through the intensity of the engagement rather than through a "high energy performance." Thus, there may be more than one way some of these factors can be manifested in the classroom, and discussions regarding how they are measured can be fruitful. Familiarizing members of the department with the empirical literature on teaching and learning can also help to make them better peer observers.

Finally, what one does in the classroom is only part of the role of effective teaching. Cashin (1989) makes the case that peer review should examine instructional design issues (e.g., the quality of the syllabus, the effective design of student assignments in or out of the classroom, appropriate and effective exercises for small groups) in addition to content expertise and instructional delivery skills. Instructional design issues are addressed elsewhere, but they can certainly be part of the peer observation process, and a department may want some of those issues included in its peer review process. For example, simply having conversations with the faculty member being observed, both before and after the observation, often elicits useful information about goals for the class, the rationale for a particular approach, or other useful and pertinent information.

It is important for observers to recognize that effective teaching is an art, and sometimes the whole of one's work may be greater than the sum of the parts. No instructor is likely to be "superior" in all of the individual components of teaching. Therefore, it is critical for the peer observer not only to note the positives, but also recognize those areas where improvement could occur. For example, a faculty member may be outstanding at the organization and presentation of material and yet not be particularly good at group process or discussion. In short, it is important to recognize that an instructor may be quite effective, even if he or she is not highly competent in *every* area.

While departments may need to custom design an observation instrument to fit the teaching culture of the unit, two sample observation instruments are provided. Readers should feel free to use them and to improve them. The sample forms appear on the following pages. Still others are available at the websites provided below.

REFERENCES AND RESOURCES

Arreola, R. 2000. *Developing a Comprehensive Faculty Evaluation System: A Handbook for College Faculty and Administrators on Designing and Operating a Comprehensive Faculty Evaluation System.* Bolton, Mass.: Anker.

Braskamp, Larry A, and John C. Ory. 1994: *Assessing Faculty Work: Enhancing Individuals and Institutional Performance.* San Francisco: Jossey-Bass.

Cashin, William E. 1989: "Defining and Evaluating College Teaching" IDEA Paper No. 21. Center for Faculty Evaluation and Development, Kansas State University. http://www.idea.ksu.edu/resources/Papers.html

Centra, John A. 1979: *Determining Faculty Effectiveness.* San Francisco: Jossey-Bass.

Centra, John A. 1993: *Reflective Faculty Evaluation.* San Francisco: Jossey-Bass.

Chickering, Arthur, and Zelda Gamson, editors. 1991: *Applying the Seven Principles for Good Practice in Undergraduate Education.* San Francisco: Jossey-Bass.

Chism, Nancy Van Note and Christine A. Stanley. 1999: *Peer Review of Teaching: A Sourcebook.* Bolton, Mass: Anker

Cohen, P. S. and Wilbert J. McKeachie. 1980: "The Role of Colleagues in the Evaluation of College Teaching" *Improving College and University Teaching* 28: 147-154

Feldman, K. A. 1988: Effective College Teaching From the Students' and Faculty's View: Matched or Mismatched Priorities?" *Research in Higher Education.* 30: 291-344.

Hutchings, Pat. 1996: *Making Teaching Community Property: A Menu for Peer Collaboration and Peer Review.* Washington D.C.: American Association for Higher Education

Johnson, T., and Ryan, K. 2000. "A Comprehensive Approach to the Evaluation of College Teaching." In K. E. Ryan (ed.), *Evaluating Teaching in Higher Education: A Vision for the Future.* New Directions for Teaching and Learning, no. 83. San Francisco: Jossey-Bass,

Keig, Larry. and Michael Waggoner. 1994: *Collaborative Peer Review: The Role of Faculty in Improving College Teaching.* ASHE-ERIC Higher Education—Report 23:2. Washington D.C.: George Washington University School of Education and Human Development

Paulsen, M. B. 2001. "The Relation Between Research and the Scholarship of Teaching." In C. Kreber, (ed.), *Scholarship Revisited: Defining and Implementing the Scholarship of Teaching.* New Directions for Teaching and Learning, no. 86. San Francisco: Jossey-Bass: 19-29.

Paulsen, M. B. 2002. "Evaluating Teaching Performance." New Directions for Institutional Research, no. 114. Wiley Periodicals: 5-18.

Roberts, Keith A. and Karen A. Donahue. 2000. "Professing Professionalism: Bureaucratization and Deprofessionalization in the Academy" *Sociological Focus.* 33: 365-83.

Svinicki, Marilla and Karron Lewis. 2006: *Preparing for Peer Observation: A Guidebook.* Center for Teaching Effectiveness, University of Texas at Austin. http://www.utexas.edu/academic/cte/PeerObserve.html

UNC Center for Teaching and Learning. 2006: *Peer Observation of Classroom Teaching.* Center for Teaching and Learning, University of North Carolina at Chapel Hill. http://ctl.unc.edu/fyc15.html

Wotruba, T. R., and P. L. Wright. 1975: "How to Develop a Teacher Rating Instrument: A Research Approach." *Journal of Higher Education.* 46: 653-663.

WEBSITES WITH INFORMATION ON PEER REVIEW

University of Wisconsin:
http://www.provost.wisc.edu/archives/ccae/MOO/

University of Wisconsin, Department of Psychology peer evaluation form:
http://www.wisc.edu/provost/ccae/MOO/psychology.html

University of North Carolina, Chapel Hill, Center on Teaching and Learning:
http://ctl.unc.edu/fyc15.html

Michigan State University evaluation guidelines and forms for Teaching Assistants: http://tap.msu.edu/PDF/TA_Eval.pdf

National Academy of Sciences: http://www.mathsci.unco.edu/faculty/personal/hauk/med710/EIUTappdxC.pdf

University of Texas Center for Teaching Effectiveness: http://www.utexas.edu/academic/cte/PeerObserve.html

AppendixA: Classroom Observation Form A

(from Richard I. Miller, Department of Higher Education, Ohio University)

Instructor _____   Course _____

Term _____   Academic Year _____

Visitor(s)_____   Title _____

Directions: Rate classroom teaching on each item. Use numbers 12 and 13 for additional questions.

Highest			Middle			Lowest	Don't know or N/A
7	6	5	4	3	2	1	X

_____   1.   Were the major objectives of the course made clear to you in the written materials?

_____   2.   How well was the class presentation planned and organized?

_____   3.   Were important ideas clearly explained?

_____   4.   How would you judge the instructor's mastery of the course content?

_____   5.   Was class time well used?

_____   6.   Did the teacher encourage critical thinking and analysis?

_____   7.   Do you believe the instructor encouraged relevant student involvement in the class?

_____   8.   How did the instructor react to student viewpoints differing from his or her own?

_____   9.   How would you describe the attitude of students in the class toward the teacher?

_____   10. Do you believe that your visitation was at a time when you were able to judge fairly the nature and tenor of the teaching-learning process?

_____   11. Considering the previous 10 items, what is your
                 overall rating of this teacher?

_____   12._____

_____   13._____

_____   Composite rating.

Yes_____   No_____   Did you have a preliminary conference with
the teacher before the visitation?

Yes_____   No_____   Did you have a follow-up conference?

Comments after class visitation: _____
_____
_____
_____
_____
_____

Comments after follow-up conference:_____
_____
_____
_____
_____
_____
_____

(Continue comments on back of the page if necessary.)

Appendix B:Classroom_Observation Form B
(from Keith Roberts, Sociology, Hanover College)

Instructor: _____Date _____

Course: _____

Observer: _____

Clarity of Communication

Organization

Knowledge of Subject Matter

Respect for Students

Student Engagement/Ability of Instructor to Stimulate Interest

Handling of Questions

Stimulation of Higher Order Thinking Skills (application, analysis, synthesis, evaluation)

Appendix C: OVERALL LEARNING ATMOSPHERE

In the following space, the observer is encouraged to comment on any other aspects of the learning experience that might be relevant: quality of syllabus and clarity of course objectives, special circumstances regarding the class observed, use of instructional methodologies which might appeal to various learning styles, effective use of class time, student attitudes or course content which made the teaching unusually difficult, conversations with the instructor about class objectives prior to or following the visitation, and so forth.

Comments:

Effective teaching is an art, and it is certainly the case that when it comes to teaching, the whole of one's work may be greater than the sum of the parts. No instructor is likely to be "superior" in all of the individual components of teaching. The list of characteristics on previous page represents an "ideal type." While each instructor may work toward improvement in those areas in which they are less strong, commendable teaching typically involves a high level of effectiveness in a substantial majority of these aspects of instruction.

8

Video Feedback for Faculty Development: Using Communities of Practice and Role Analysis

Vaneeta-marie D'Andrea, Global Higher Education Consulting
Hans O. Mauksch

INTRODUCTION

For more than four decades, video feedback methods have been employed for professional development in fields as diverse as athletics, counseling, education, engineering, entertainment, and medicine (Garland, 1969, Travers, 1973, Stenson, Smith & Perry, 1983, Braskamp & Ory, 1994, Myers, 1998, Russell & Ng, 2009). Thousands of people have used video feedback for the purposes of education, training and therapy. Most often, video feedback is used to assess job performance and, if necessary, to find ways to improve it. In education, video feedback has been used extensively in pre-service training programs. We contend that possibly the greatest potential for video feedback is for in-service programs; yet it remains underutilized for this purpose. The reasons for this are unclear, especially since the value of the method is understood by many other professions. Most likely, the reasons are related to the fear of the misuse by administrators or the fear of being seen by colleagues in the act of teaching (Mauksch 1985).

The first sociologists to discuss video feedback as a professional development tool were Albert and Hipp (1976). Their paper explained how video feedback was employed in the pre-service training of teaching assistants. However, further reports of the implementation of video feedback by sociologists have not appeared. Yet, video feedback has been an on-going feature of workshops offered through the American Sociological Association's Teaching Resources Center and an important part of some departmental visits made by the ASA's Department Resources Group (DRG).

The purpose of this essay is to summarize the key elements of two models of formative video feedback that have been developed through the ASA's Projects on Teaching (see D'Andrea et al. 1985) and employed in professional development workshops and visits by the DRG. The emphasis will be on the sociological principles underlying the practice and the use of video feedback for professional development purposes. This paper does not consider the use of video feedback to assist with administrative evaluations of teaching for the purpose of summative judgments related to promotion and tenure. It is only concerned with the formative uses of video feedback. Hopefully, as a result, more sociologists will be interested in trying this approach to improving their classroom-based teaching.

OVERVIEW OF VIDEO FEEDBACK

In the simplest terms, video feedback in an educational context involves having a specific teaching /learning experience visually recorded and then reviewed/analyzed. It allows for a concentrated focus on specific aspects of the experience. It also often stimulates recollections of thoughts and feelings which occurred during the activity. Video feedback can provide the instructor with experiences from the perspective of the observer as well as the person being 'observed' (Davis, 2009).

Most important for purposes of improvement, perhaps, the process of video recording a teaching event creates a record that allows the teacher to step back and learn from his or her own practice (Nilson, 2010). In Cooley's sense, video feedback could be described as an electronic looking-glass self, or in Meadian terms a technological process of confronting the social self. For most initial users, it is first and foremost a confrontation with the professional self. Indeed, it is difficult not to be self-conscious when viewing ourselves on videotape in any context. How many times a day do we really get to see ourselves? - usually only when we stand in front of a mirror. Moreover, how much do we see of ourselves when we do look in the mirror? Video observation allows for the total person, in action, to be seen.

In video observations of the teacher/student role set, teachers are doing the thing that is most vital to their self definition - their professional job. Teaching is normally a relatively private activity (at least from the perspective of our colleagues); it can be very disconcerting to see ourselves as others see us. Most of us prefer to think of ourselves as relatively young, reasonably attractive, intelligent, and excellent teachers. Despite the fact that the research suggests that most people find video feedback a relatively pleasant experience, the most common reactions to the initial self-viewing of a videotape are negative. The physical self is forced to be the center of attention, and the focus is on voice characteristics, accent, head shaking, gestures, hand movements, the person's shape, size, degree of hair loss, etc. Responses often range from "I look awful!" to "I use my hands too much!" or "I speak in a monotone!"

Although video feedback is likely to be perceived as less intrusive than having a peer observer present, it is evident that there still are social psychological implications. Thus, it is vital to address these considerations during the process of a video consultation. Faculty being videotaped must be allowed to acknowledge their feelings of self consciousness. At least, they should be able to experience them for a period of time so that they can begin to get over them and focus on themselves in their roles as teachers. In truth, they need to move through such feelings so they can become less subjective and more objective observers of themselves. The two models used by the DRG, and described below, include protocols to address this process.

TWO MODELS OF VIDEO FEEDBACK

The Teaching Clinic: - Microteaching in Communities of Practice.

Micro-teaching is a scaled-down teaching encounter, originally developed at Stanford University, in which faculty are asked to teach brief lessons of 5 to 20 minutes to small groups of 'students' (Fortune et al, 1967). The sequence is a teach/analyze/re-teach process which focuses on a specific teaching skill (Bergquist & Phillips, 1975, Myers, 1998). It uses simulation techniques to break down the teaching process into smaller, more easily understood units. "Microteaching allows the instructor to work on one teaching skill at a time, provides a safe environment in which to experiment and practice, gives rapid feedback, and ... breaks down the 'art' of teaching into identifiable skills." (Jimerson & D'Andrea, 1984: 3-4).

Central to the idea of microteaching is the belief that teaching consists of a number of discrete, identifiable activities that can be isolated and taught. Allen & Ryan (1986) identify seven skill areas relevant to college teaching: 1) stimulus variation, 2) set induction, 3) closure, 4) silence and nonverbal cues, 5) reinforcement of student participation, 6) questioning, and 7) use of examples (Bergquist & Phillips, 1975: 106). Such a set of skills does not imply that there is an ideal or prescribed model of the good teacher. Instead, microteaching aims at refining and increasing the range of skills available to teachers in different situations. Thus, this approach to video feedback combines a conceptual system for identifying precisely-specified teaching skills with the use of video to facilitate growth in these same teaching skills (Travers, 1973: 951).

After using this approach, Klingstedt reported that the majority of the student teachers felt that videotaped microteaching: gave them a more positive self-image; promoted mutual understanding; gave them a feeling of competence as a teacher, while at the same time pointed out areas where they could make improvement; was time well spent; aided self-evaluation; and should be offered early in a teacher education program (1976: 20). Similarly, Mangan (1992) reported that the videotaping of a mini-lecture she delivered was the most helpful part of an orientation program she attended. After her fellow TA's viewed her tape and offered constructive criticisms, she delivered another lecture, which was also videotaped. "It's the biggest confidence boost you could have", she said (1992: 18).

In 1985, Mauksch created a process which uses micro-teaching principles as the corner stone of professional development for university teachers. Coming from the field of medical sociology, he saw this process in terms of his sub-discipline and called them *Teaching Clinics.* These 'Clinics' offered faculty the opportunity to participate in a micro-teaching exercise with peers who were teaching sociologists. The key advantage of engaging in a micro-teaching experience of this type is that those taking the part of 'students' have special knowledge of the subject and previous experience with the challenges of making sociological concepts understandable to undergraduate students. Mauksch's view was that *Teaching Clinics* were most useful if they were part of a professional workshop outside of the departmental boundaries, for example, as part of a regional or national conference session on teaching. In such contexts, the usual power relations would be minimized, while at the same time special knowledge of teaching in sociology would be maximized. Following from the work of Leve and Wenger (1991), these would now be called "communities of practice."

In the community of practice setting, individual faculty members should be assured in advance that they will have the opportunity to comment on the video recording first, followed by comments from group members. Once this is completed, then, and only then, would the consultant/facilitator be called upon to make any comments. In this way, each faculty member feels she/he has more control in the process. For the most useful outcomes, it is important that this three part process is followed carefully. The participants should be given the opportunity to prepare their 'teaching' in advance, are aware of the rules of engagement, and everyone in the group has a turn at micro-teaching. Most importantly the group needs to be aware of the reasons each member wants feedback, and on what issue(s) they specifically want feedback. The pre-video form (see Appendix A) is a useful tool to communicate this information to the group. For a group of 4-6 people, this process takes about 3 hours.

The Teaching/Learning Consultation: Role Analysis for Professional Development.

Different from the *Teaching Clinic*, the *Teaching/Learning Consultation* involves an individual faculty member outside of their peer group as a consultant. It is often part of an institution-wide faculty development program which employs educational consultants. Most often it involves the recording of an <u>actual</u> classroom experience. This model is different from microteaching, because the teacher is videotaped in her/his natural environment, no single skill is singled out for emphasis, and the feedback is usually not quite as fast (Jimerson & D'Andrea, 1984: 4). D'Andrea (1985) has further suggested that this process is most useful when it focuses the individual's attention on his or her overall role as teacher, rather than on teaching skills per se.

The role of the consultant in this model is two-fold: 1) to help provide focus for the video analysis, and 2) to facilitate its review by helping the teachers see themselves in the role of a teacher. With respect to the former, the faculty member can be encouraged to review his/her goals for the video observation by reflecting on its purpose and completing the pre-video form. This should help stimulate the faculty member's thinking about the reason and goal for having a video observation. For the latter, the consultant needs to help steer the teacher away from focusing on individual idiosyncrasies and towards reviewing the video recording within the parameters of role analysis. Guided questions from the consultant about how the teacher being viewed fits the social expectations of a teacher can shift the emphasis away from personal features and traits to a social role analysis (see Appendix B). Psychologically, there is less resistance to change if the change is about the enactment of the role rather than the personal traits of the individual being reviewed. Thus, positive change is more likely to occur.

The emphasis of the one-on-one consultation can help faculty understand that their perceived problems are not always obvious to students and can be improved (Garland, 1969: 621). Indeed, a good consultant can make the difference between a fair or even poor video feedback experience and an excellent one. "... explicitly crowding a person into a corner may in many instances be not only unwarranted but also counterproductive" (Pascale 1978:156). Here, as above, it is important that the consultant emphasizes the person's autonomy by providing him/her the first response to the viewing. In addition, however, the consultant can also help to refocus any initial negative response to the video observation by identifying positive aspects of the teaching role and suggesting ways to build on what is working well for the student experience (Cooperrider & Whitney, 2005) (see Appendix C).

The usual approach to this type of professional development has been to focus on teaching skills (Boehrer, n.d, Strasser, n.d). By placing the emphasis instead on the teaching role and the teacher-student role set, the process allows for greater distance away from a direct confrontation with the self and allows for greater objectivity in each individual analysis. It is also helpful for the faculty member watching the videotape to think of themselves in the role of a student in the class. By either becoming aware of themselves in the role of the teacher or thinking of themselves as a student in the class, they are more likely to analyze the video observation rather than simply watch it and react to it (see Appendix D).

With regard to the technical aspects of the video feedback process, we have found that no more than a half hour of recorded data should be considered in any one consultation session. This amount will take from one to two hours to review completely. However, it should be remembered that the faculty member will expect to have the entire class recorded. This is positive, but we suggest that the consultant take the opportunity to choose the beginning, middle, or end of the class session for specific analysis. Indeed, determining the part of the tape to be reviewed should be connected to the purpose and goals that the faculty member has established in advance. It is more efficient for the consultant to point out a few specific areas to focus on, and replay small segments to emphasize or clarify certain points, rather than go through the entire tape minute by minute (Fortune et al., 1967: 388). It is also more helpful to the change process to limit the changes to two or three at any one time.

DISCUSSION

There are important features of video feedback that are part of both the clinic and the consultation models. Video recording is especially useful when faculty look at their teaching in a systematic manner since it provides data that can be analyzed. Video feedback provides a mirror to faculty. It is the only way that they can see themselves teaching or get the view from the students' perspective. Video feedback also arouses a multitude of sensory responses -- more than just hearing or seeing a person teach. Therefore, it has the potential for greater impact on the faculty member. Once faculty begin to get involved in the video review process, it stimulates their thinking about what constitutes good teaching, and they begin to view their own teaching in a new light. In short, the experience of being videotaped heightens concern for teaching.

In addition to simply creating a greater level of awareness of the importance of teaching interactions, pedagogical skill development can be accomplished via video feedback. For teachers who have been in the classroom for a while, it is important for them to identify what they know and what they don't know about teaching. Video feedback can verify what is going well in addition to what needs improvement. Moreover, video recordings provide the only opportunity for immediate review of an actual classroom situation. The replay facility of a video recording lends itself to repeated analysis. Specific areas can be reviewed repeatedly for personal reflection or for consultant comment. Since it provides a more accurate and 'objective' observation of the teaching/learning process, it can even be used as supporting data to refute or confirm student evaluations.

Not unlike other forms of behavior change, pedagogical change is dependent on the readiness of the instructor to change. Often, the instructor is responding to negative student evaluations, or in some cases, is required by an administrator to seek help from a faculty development consultant. The person's job may even be on the line. In such cases, anxiety is likely to be extremely high. Therefore, it is particularly important for the consultant to be the instructor's advocate for improvement. Generally speaking, the pattern of change tends to follow a common sequence. In the first semester that a video consultation takes place; several areas of change are identified. This is usually followed by a period of working on these areas outside the classroom, sometimes in a microteaching setting. In the next step, which may need to take place during the next semester of consultation, the instructor implements the changes in the classroom, gets student feedback, and records an additional session for further review. In successive semesters, additional adjustments can be made, and changes in student evaluations tend to be significant enough to be evident.

Nearly everyone whose teaching is videotaped experiences some stressful reactions. These are especially acute the first time it is done. The intense focus on the self can create stress and may produce anxiety at a level that can be disorganizing. It is important to take measures to minimize anxiety as much as possible. This can be done by providing the faculty member to be taped with as much choice in the process as possible and a guarantee that he/she will control the actual recording once completed and can do whatever they wish to do with it (save it for future reference, destroy it etc). Anxiety will also decrease when practice is provided and when constructive criticism principles are used - reinforce the best, and the worst will change. In any case, video feedback can be a powerful tool for positive change in higher education.

Note: The authors wish to acknowledge the work of the following colleagues who contributed to the development of this paper: Sheila Cordray, Dean Dorn, Reed Geerstsen, Ed Kain, Ted Wagenaar, and Tom Van Valey.

REFERENCES

Albert, R and R. Hipp. 1976. "Videotape Recording in the Preparation of College Sociology Teachers," *Teaching Sociology*, 3: 327-338

Allen, D. and K. Ryan. 1969. *Microteaching*. Reading, MA: Addison-Wesley.

Bergquist, W. and S. Phillips. 1975. *A Handbook for Faculty Development*. Washington, D.C.: Council for the Advancement of Small Colleges.

Boehrer, J. n.d. *Suggestions for Watching Tapes with TA's*. Boston: Harvard-Danforth Teaching Lab.

Braskamp, L. A. and J. C. Ory. 1994. *Assessing Faculty Work: Enhancing Individual and Institutional Performance*. San Francisco, Jossey-Bass

Cooperrider, D. and D. Whitney. 2005. *Appreciative Inquiry*. San Francisco: Barrett-Koehler Publishers

D'Andrea, V. 1985. *Teaching Advisory Service Consultant Handbook*. Storrs, CT: University of Connecticut, Center for Educational Innovation

D'Andrea, V., S. Cordray, D. Dorn, R. Geertsen and E. Kain. 1985. *Summary Transcript: Topical Development Group A-6 -- The Teaching Clinic: Skills,*

Style, and Structure, Wingspread Conference on Postsecondary Instructional Improvement, Racine, Wisconsin.

D'Andrea, V. and D. Gosling. 2005. *Improving Teaching and Learning: a whole institution approach*, Buckinghamshire: Open University/SRHE Press

Davis, B. G. 2009. Tools for Teaching, 2nd Edition. San Francisco: Jossey-Bass.
Fortune, J.C., J.M. Cooper and D.W. Allen. 1967. "The Stanford Summer Micro-teaching Clinic, 1965," *Journal of Teacher Education*, 18: 389-393.

Garland, J.K.. 1969. "Training for Teaching Assistants: Trial Classes and IV Taping," *Journal of Chemical Education*, 46: 621.

Jimerson, J and V. D'Andrea. 1984. "Techniques of Training with Video-Feedback." Paper presented at the Annual Meeting of the Association for Educational Communications and Technology, Dallas, Texas.

Klingstedt, J.L.. 1976. "Video Taped Microteaching: Students Rate It Great," *Improving College and University Teaching*, 24: 20-21.

Leve, J and E. Wenger. 1991. .Situated Learning: Legitimate Peripheral Participation. Cambridge: Cambridge University Press

Mangan, K.. 1992. "Colleges Expand Efforts to Help Teaching Assistants Learn to Teach," *The Chronicle Of Higher Education*, (March 4): A17-A18.

Mauksch, H.O. 1985. Memorandum to Topical Development Group A-6, "The Teaching Clinic: Skills, Style, and Structure," Wingspread Conference on Postsecondary Instructional Improvement, Racine, Wisconsin.

Myers, J. 1998. "Videotaping: A Tool for Teachers" GSAS Bulletin 27:6 January. Derek Bok Center for Teaching and Learning, Harvard University.

Nilson, L. B. 2010. Teaching at its Best: a Research-Based Resource for College Instructors, 3rd Edition. San Francisco: Jossey-Bass.

Pascale, R.T. 1978. "Zen and the Art of Management," *Harvard Business Review*, March-April: 153-162.

Russell, G, and A. Ng. 2009. "Observation and Learning in Family Practice" Can Fam Physician Vol. 55, No. 9: 948 - 950

Stenson, N., J. Smith and W. Perry. 1983. "Facilitating Teacher Growth: An Approach to Training and Evaluation." *The MinneTESOL Journal*, 3:42-55.

Strasser, G. F. n.d. *Videotape Resources and Techniques for TA Feedback and Training.* State College: Pennsylvania State University.

Travers, R.M.W. (ed) 1973. *Second Handbook or Research on Teaching.* Chicago: Rand McNally and Company.

Wright, G. 2008. "The Use of Digital Video to Increase Teacher Reflection for Action Aptitude and Ability." In J. Luca & E. Weippl (Eds.), *Proceedings of World Conference on Educational Multimedia, Hypermedia and Telecommunications 2008* (pp. 3341-3347). Chesapeake, VA: AACE.

Appendix A: Pre-Video Reflection Form

Name: _____Institution: _____
Date of Video Recording: _____

Please take a few minutes to answer the questions which apply to your interests in having your teaching visually recorded.

1. What do you wish to gain from being visually recorded?

2. What do you want to learn about yourself in your role as a teacher?

3. What do you want to learn about your students' learning?

4. What do you want to learn about your teaching style or methods?

5. Describe briefly your plans for the teaching session which will be recorded.

6. Is there anything else you feel would be useful for the camera person or consultant to know?

Please complete at least one week in advance of the scheduled recording session.

Revised version of: V. D'Andrea, "Pre-videotaping Information" form, Center for Educational Innovation, University of Connecticut, 1982.

Appendix B: Video Feedback Consultant's Guide

Begin by asking a few questions about the professional
development process generally, and then move to the video
feedback process more specifically.

Q1. Realistically, where does improving your teaching fit into your
professional priorities?

Q2. What do you want to learn about yourself as a teacher from the
video recording?[Reviewing the Pre-video Information Form here
is often useful]

Next, play a short segment of the video recording (no more than
three to five minutes). Focus the review of the recording around
the questions listed below. Begin by focusing on the teaching role,
and avoid discussing any personal idiosyncrasies. If this is not
done, the review may become misdirected to areas of change which
will have the least affect on the students' learning experience.
Questions to pose at this point would be along the following lines:

1. Describe what the teacher is doing?

2. Is this what you would expect to see a teacher do?

3. What one thing would you suggest that this teacher do again and
why?

4. What one thing would you suggest this teacher avoid doing
again and why?

Next, in collaboration with the faculty member, select a few areas
where he/she can actually make changes to get positive
reinforcement for having made the change. Do not make a long list
of areas for change. Changes can only be made incrementally.

Make a record of the actions identified and ensure that they align
with the learning outcomes for the course and/or the session
observed. Agree on a timeline for implementation.

Appendix C: Characteristics of Constructive Feedback

It is *descriptive* rather than evaluative. By describing one's own reactions, it leaves the individual free to use it or not to use it as she/he sees fit. By avoiding evaluative language, it reduces the need for the individual to respond defensively.

It is *specific* rather than general. To be told that one is "dominating" will probably not be as useful as to be told that "in the conversation that just took place, you did not appear to be listening to what others were saying, and I felt forced to accept your arguments."

It is focused on *behavior* rather than on the person. It is important that we refer to what a person does rather than to what we think or imagine he is. Thus, we might say that a person "talked more than anyone else in this meeting" rather than that he is a "loud-mouth." The former allows for the possibility of change; the latter implies a fixed personality trait.

It takes into account the *needs of both the receiver and the giver of feedback.* Feedback can be destructive when it serves only our own needs and fails to consider the needs of the person on the receiving end. It should be given to help, not to hurt. We too often give feedback because it makes us feel better or gives us a psychological advantage.

It is directed toward *behavior which the receiver can do something about.* Frustration is only increased when a person is reminded of some shortcoming over which he has no control.

It is *solicited* rather than imposed. Feedback is most useful when the receiver himself has formulated the kind of question which those observing him can answer or when he actively seeks feedback.

It is *well-timed.* In general, feedback is most useful at the earliest opportunity after the given behavior (depending, of course, on the person's readiness to hear it and support available from others). The reception and use of feedback involves many possible emotional reactions. Excellent feedback presented at an inappropriate time may do more harm than good.

It involves *sharing of information,* rather than giving advice. By sharing information, we leave a person free to decide for himself, in accordance with his/her own goals and needs. When we give advice we tell a person what to do, and to some degree take away his/her freedom to make an independent decision.

It involves the *amount of information the receiver can use* rather than the amount we would like to give. To overload a person with feedback is to reduce the possibility that he may be able to use what he receives effectively.

It concerns *what is said and done,* or how, not why. The *"why"* takes us from the observable to the inferred and involves assumptions regarding motive or intent. Telling a person what his/her motivations or intentions are more often than not tends to alienate the person and contributes to a climate of resentment, suspicion, and distrust; it does not contribute to learning or development. If we are uncertain of one's motives or intent, this uncertainty itself is feedback, however, and should be revealed.

It is *checked to insure clear communication.* One way of doing this is to have the receiver try to rephrase the feedback to see if it corresponds to what the sender had in mind. No matter what the intent, feedback is often threatening and thus subject to considerable distortion or misinterpretation.

It is *checked to determine degree of agreement from others.* When feedback is given in the presence of other people, both giver and receiver have an opportunity to check with others in the group about the accuracy of the feedback. Is this one person's impression or an impression shared by others. Such "consensual validation" is of value to both sender and receiver.

It is followed by *attention to the consequences of the feedback.* The person who is giving feedback may greatly improve his helping skills by becoming acutely aware of the effects of his feedback. He can also be of continuing help to the recipient of the feedback.

It is an important step toward *authenticity.* Constructive feedback opens the way to a relationship which is built on trust, honesty, and genuine concern. Through such a relationship, we will have achieved one of the most rewarding experiences that a person can achieve and will have opened a very important door to personal learning and growth.

Source: W. Bergquist and S. Phillips, *A Handbook for Faculty Development*. Washington DC: Council for the Advancement of Small Colleges, 1975:. 224-225.

Appendix D: Guide for Self-viewing

WARNING !!! Get used to seeing yourself. You may be delighted to see how pleasing you look, or you may be dismayed. Spend a few minutes taking in your image. Having thus confronted yourself, begin to assess your teaching role by using the suggestions outlined below.

Before turning on the recording, take a few minutes to list some specific teaching activities you expect to see or would like to see. Use the following as an initial checklist for viewing your recording. You might like to focus on:

1. The Teacher's Style - is she/he:
>   reading from notes?
>   moving or standing still?
>   talking to the ceiling, the power point projector, the
>   wall, or the students?
>   speaking too fast, too slow, just right?
>   aware of any special tone in the voice? Do you like it?
>   using any repetitive gestures or words?

>   **Turn off the sound**!
>   Check the Teacher's eye contact and gestures

2. The Teacher's Classroom Skills - did she/he:
>   give the class an outline of what was planned to be
>   covered?
>   did she/he stick to it?
>   were the goals of the session clearly communicated?
>   were the classroom materials clear and legible?
>   was the material organized and presented logically?
>   do you think the students found note-taking easy?
>   were the students involved?

>   Watch any ten-minute segment and note how often
>   the Teacher:
>   defined/elaborated new ideas or concepts
>   provided illustrative examples of major concepts
>   challenged the students with new ideas
>   asked questions
>   repeated/rephrased/clarified questions that were
>   asked

Revised version of: V. D'Andrea, "Self-Viewing Guide," University of Connecticut, Center for Educational Innovation, 1982.

III

PREPARING, IDENTIFYING, AND USING PEERS

9

Preparing Graduate Students for Teaching as Peers

Brent Bruton, Iowa State University
Thomas L. Van Valey, Western Michigan University

This essay simply offers some advice to departments of sociology that train graduate students. It is based on our combined experience at training graduate students to teach and ultimately to become peers. We feel that such preparation is the first step in helping these potential new faculty understand, accept, and even embrace the peer review of teaching.

In our view, there are three general principles involved in the preparation of graduate students for teaching as future peers. First, and without question most important, we believe that faculty must model the behavior we desire in our students. We cannot simply tell them what to do -- we must <u>show</u> them. Second, while they are still graduate students, we should encourage our students to participate in collaborative activities of all kinds - research and teaching in particular. This could even be extended to service activities, both in the institution and in the community. Third, we believe that departments as well as faculty need to reward students who work collaboratively. For most, efforts expended without recognition of some kind will, in time, no longer be offered.

WE MUST BE WHAT WE EXPECT
OUR GRADUATE STUDENTS TO BECOME

In their preparation for academic roles, it is critical for graduate students to routinely observe their faculty participating in collaborative teaching activities. Faculty already model the kinds of research-related behaviors we expect graduate students to exhibit - research, writing, presentations at professional meetings, publications, all often in collaboration with other faculty. In order for the students to believe that teaching is important, and that collaborative approaches to teaching are acceptable, they must see that it is being done in their own departments.

Many faculty, however, do not approach teaching in a collaborative manner. They tend to treat teaching as a private activity (see Chapter 3 in this volume). If we and our faculty colleagues are to expect graduate students to approach teaching collaboratively, the graduate students must see how we do it. They need role models to emulate. Those of us who believe teaching is an important professional activity, one that deserves to be public, cannot simply exhort our colleagues to join in the effort, we must serve as change agents and lead our departments from the front; we must lead by example.

WE MUST ENCOURAGE COLLABORATIVE ACTIVITIES

For a few faculty to exhibit collaborative efforts is not enough by itself, however. Graduate students must also be encouraged to engage in them. There are a range of collaborative activities that can easily be put in place as encouragement for graduate students. Indeed, many will be easier to implement with graduate students than they will with faculty. For example, in departments where a number of students all serve as teaching assistants for the same course, Teaching Circles can be established (see Chapter 5 in this volume). This can be done informally at first, but over time could be included as part of the regular responsibilities of an assistantship. Once Teaching Circles are operating for the graduate students, it also should become easier to include faculty who teach the same course to participate. They can then be expanded to other courses or topics.

Colloquia on teaching issues are also relatively easy to implement. Faculty, as well as graduate students, are frequently interested in presentations/discussions on the use of technology in teaching, alternative approaches to evaluating student performance, models of active learning, the skills involved in critical thinking, internships and other forms of service learning, as well as other topics. Again, these can begin informally, but they do need to be nurtured. The normal time pressures associated with being a graduate student (or a faculty member, for that matter) tend to work against participation in such activities unless they are recognized as beneficial. The support of the chair is at least helpful, probably critical, in establishing such norms (see Chapter 13 in this volume). For those departments with an established speaker series, it is a simple matter to occasionally invite someone in to make a presentation on a teaching topic instead of a research topic. For those departments that do not have such resources, they can recommend speakers to their institutions, since they often sponsor such series on a campus-wide basis.

One approach that would be particularly useful in preparing graduate students for collaborative teaching is to ask those that teach to prepare a Teaching Portfolio (see Chapter 4 in this volume). Portfolios have been receiving much attention of late within national associations of higher education as simple devices that help instructors (both graduate students and faculty) treat their teaching in the same way they treat their research - as a matter for public scrutiny and peer review. Portfolios allow instructors to include all the materials they believe are relevant to the design and development of their courses and the assessment of their teaching. Sometimes it is easier to begin with a single course (i.e., to prepare a Course Portfolio), especially for graduate students who often have not taught many different courses. In those departments that have classes on the preparation for teaching, the construction of such a document can even be required as a component. The portfolio may also be useful to those students who are entering the job market, because it may give them an edge over other students who have less experience or who have not approached teaching with as much clarity of purpose.

One clear way of sending a message to graduate students about the importance of teaching is to ask any candidates invited to the institution for a job interview to make two presentations. One can be the usual presentation related to the candidate's area of research. The other, however, could be a Pedagogical Colloquium (see Chapter 14 in this volume), in which the candidate makes a presentation on a teaching topic, or even teaches a session of a real class. At minimum, a department can simply request that the candidate's teaching portfolio be included in the job application packet. Departmental actions of this kind powerfully communicate the importance of teaching to graduate students. Moreover, they also allow a department to more accurately assess the full range of qualifications of their job candidates. This is especially important as the quality of teaching and learning becomes a more important element in the accountability of a department and its program.

Of course, those departments that already offer classes preparing graduate students to teach are ahead of the game. They already have a vehicle in place that is the basis for many of these innovations. Many of these courses require the students to observe faculty or one another (or both), to work together on designing courses and preparing course syllabi, to discuss teaching techniques and to critically examine new teaching approaches. Increasingly, however, institutions that train PhDs are also implementing workshops, colloquia, and other programs in an effort to improve the quality of instruction by graduate students.

Departments that do not have internal resources to carry out some of these activities may find resources readily available at the college or university level.

WE MUST REWARD STUDENTS WHO TEACH COLLABORATIVELY

It is not enough to just encourage students, even by promoting teaching activities. Students and faculty as well should receive a tangible message that teaching is important and that teaching collaboratively is an excellent strategy for achieving teaching excellence. Quite simply, people who take teaching seriously, and who are good at it, should be rewarded. It must be demonstrated that teaching counts in decisions that matter - for tenure and promotion, as well as for periodic merit salary increases. For graduate students, departments can usually manage at least some forms of reward. These might include small monetary awards, letters of recommendation for jobs, certificates or other public recognition of teaching achievements, support for travel to professional meetings, or access to staff and other teaching resources. It might even include preferential treatment for work/teaching assignments.

For faculty, the situation is quite different. Even today at many institutions that train PhD students, the traditional reward structure is heavily biased in favor of research and other traditionally defined scholarly activities. Rewards for teaching and service have typically been relegated to secondary status, if they exist at all. Nevertheless, small financial and other rewards are often possible, and they may have substantial symbolic impact for individual faculty. To alter the basic nature of the institutional award structure is, of course, beyond the means of departments since it is likely to require fundamental changes across the entire institution. Still, departments can make it clear that they would like to see such changes.

Although social change proceeds slowly (perhaps especially in higher education), it can occur if departments share common purposes and common means of achieving those purposes. It is now beginning to appear that the changes taking place in higher education may forge a set of common purposes around the basic goal of accountability. Moreover, it is possible that making teaching a professional activity as public as research - the principle that underlies collaborative approaches - will serve as the means to achieving those goals.

10

The Peer Review of Teaching in Post-Tenure Review

Maxine Atkinson and Andrea N. Hunt,
North Carolina State University

We work in a time of unrest, challenge, redefinition, excitement, and hope. Many of the issues and opportunities we face center on definitions of scholarship, including the scholarship of teaching and learning. What it means to be a teacher-scholar and the importance of teaching excellence are at the core of many conversations about the academy today. Post-tenure review and the peer review of teaching are practices central to the current challenges and exciting expectations we all encounter but with which we have not yet made peace. In this chapter, we discuss the peer review of teaching within the context of post-tenure review.

Our reluctance, resistance, or even hostility to the peer review of teaching and post-tenure review is likely to be at least partially motivated by similar factors. Autonomy is an important component of academic life. "The ability to do w*hat* I want, *when* I want and *how* I want" is one of the best descriptions of how many of us see faculty autonomy (Rushing, Chapter 4 in this volume [originally quoted in Lindholm, 2004:611, italics in original]). Indeed, faculty work can be described as the closest you can get to being self-employed without taking the financial risks of a small business owner, and autonomy is one of the most appealing aspects of being a faculty member. But, if our teaching is to be publicly reviewed, and post-tenure review puts us under regular scrutiny, will we continue to be able to do what we want, when we want and how we want?

The peer review of teaching takes us out of our safe, private place where we are queens or kings of our own realms, and thrusts us into a position of being evaluated by others. While teaching was once a private affair, the peer review of teaching makes it more public. Post-tenure review puts us in a similar and perhaps even more defensive position (or creates similar opportunities, depending on one's perspective). Tenure is an attractive structure because it suggests that once you have passed this high bar, your job will be stable and your autonomy assured. Post-tenure review challenges the strength of the tenure system.

Post-tenure review, like the peer review of teaching, disrupts our security with the possibility that we can be evaluated in ways that most of us did not foresee when we were awarded tenure. This change of expectations in higher education creates a cultural shift that can be uncomfortable, and often leaves faculty feeling uneasy. While we expect to have our research reviewed by our peers, those reviews are anonymous and impersonal, and if our research is rejected, we can "revise and resubmit" or turn our attention to other projects. Peer reviews of teaching and post-tenure review are both much more personal, and may be perceived as overly risky to the previously taken-for-granted privilege of being a tenured faculty member. The peer review of teaching and post-tenure review, therefore, can easily be seen as a threat to the professoriate by both individuals and academic organizations. The American Association of University Professors (1998) clearly takes such a position, arguing that post-tenure review is a direct threat to academic freedom.

The origins of post-tenure review and the peer review of teaching may be responsible for some of our unease. Colleges and universities created post-tenure review in the 1980's as a response to public concerns over tenure and the perceived lack of faculty accountability. Some argue that post-tenure review originated to protect tenure, by providing the assurance that faculty are indeed evaluated in a more comprehensive manner than simple annual reviews and, perhaps, promotion (Bataille and Brown, 2006). Supporters of post-tenure review believe that it might actually help save the tenure system, ensure accountability, and encourage faculty development (Edwards, 1997; Licata and Morreale, 2006; Montell, 2002; Neal, 2008).

The peer review of teaching evolved for some of the same reasons as post-tenure review. However, while some of the pressure to more carefully evaluate teaching certainly came from academic insiders, as Boyer's (1990) classic *Scholarship of Teaching* attests, external forces have been central to the demands for more accountability in our teaching (Seldin, 1997). Moreover, our critics have not always been gentle. For example, Sykes' (1988) *Profscam* argues that higher education is a sham, teaching is a lucrative racket, and professors are selfish and corrupt. More recently we are charged with offering no "value added" to education (Kors, 2008). That is, if our students simply gained another 4-6 years of experience, they would be just as well off as they are when they graduate from our colleges and universities. Faculty are too often seen as lazy parasites, feasting at the public trough, small clans of warring factions fighting political battles whose fates are best decided by other players. Or, on a more positive note, they are seen as irrelevant societal actors who spend their time playing with esoteric ideas (Atkinson, 2000).

Our critics have not only been limited to those without expertise. Recently, Bok (2006) joined the chorus of critics with his book, *Our Underachieving Colleges: A Candid Look at How Much Students Learn and Why They Should Be Learning More*. The title alone tells us that this former Harvard president is not impressed with what we are doing for our students in higher education. While Bok's critique has its sting, the commonly referred to "Spellings Commission report" was perhaps even more damning in its findings and recommendations. The commission stated, "We are disturbed by evidence that the quality of student learning at U.S. colleges and universities is inadequate and, in some cases, declining" (U.S. Department of Education, 2006: 3). The report also uses the dreaded "accountability argument." Thus, while the peer review of teaching and post-tenure review are intended to help us address our critics and improve the academy, we are not always comfortable with either.

TYPES OF POST-TENURE REVIEW

There are two primary types of post-tenure reviews. The most common type of post-tenure review is a periodic, comprehensive review, which is regularly scheduled. Five to seven years seems to be a common interval for periodic, comprehensive reviews. For example, North Carolina State University (2009), the university system of Georgia (2010), the University of Missouri system (2007), and the University of Colorado (2006) all require regular five-year reviews of all tenured faculty. Their previous annual reviews are examined, in addition to peer reviews of their teaching, their curriculum vitae, and their performance plans. Other institutions may opt for a shorter time interval such as the University of Oregon (1999) which conducts post-tenure reviews every three years to encourage, reward, and support continuous development. Some institutions, for example, the College of William and Mary (1999) and the Texas A & M University system (2008), provide individual departments with more flexibility as to when the post-tenure review is to be conducted.

The second type of review is the triggered review. Triggered post-tenure reviews are episodic and result from concerns about faculty performance, usually demonstrated on the annual review (Licata and Morreale, 1999). Virginia Tech (2004) uses a triggered model. There, faculty undergo a post-tenure review if they receive two consecutive annual reviews with unsatisfactory performance levels. Similarly, Kansas State University's (2006) triggered reviews occur if faculty receive unsatisfactory annual reviews. They too have the goal of improved performance in the areas needing it as indicated by the annual review. The University of Nebraska-Lincoln's (1998) triggered review is based on a more comprehensive peer review if the annual review is unsatisfactory.

Formative and Summative Post-Tenure Review

The purpose and the results of post-tenure peer review are contested territory. In 1983, the AAUP issued the statement, "The Association believes that periodic formal institutional evaluation of each post probationary faculty member would bring scant benefit, would incur unacceptable costs, not only in money and time but also in dampening of creativity and of collegial relationships, and would threaten academic freedom" (AAUP, 1998: 61). In 1998, the AAUP reaffirmed their stance on post-tenure review. However, they did recognize that post-tenure review is becoming mandatory at many institutions and provided some guidelines for facilitating the process. The AAUP insisted that, above all, post-tenure review should be about faculty development rather than accountability. The AAUP (1998) further recommended that faculty should be central in the process, by developing and carrying out post-tenure review. Post-tenure review should not be a reevaluation of tenure and must be conducted in a manner that protects academic freedom. However, Aper's (2003) findings suggest faculty and administrators differ in their perceived purpose of post-tenure review. While faculty tend to prefer post tenure review to be a form of faculty development, many perceive it as a way for administrators to use it in personnel decisions. At the same time, while many administrators may view it as a way to get faculty development, they also may make personnel decisions using the information it provides.

While post-tenure review originated to assure accountability, the AAUP insists that post-tenure review should be a formative rather than a summative process. Formative evaluations emphasize professional development and rarely have the types of consequences associated with summative evaluations (Licata, 2004). Of the post-tenure review policies of which we are aware, Hanover College's emphasizes a formative process more than any other. Hanover College gives faculty the option to choose either a summative or formative review. If faculty choose the formative review, they must complete two reviews in a seven-year period. Moreover, faculty have a number of options for ways to enhance their professional development (e.g., peer mentoring groups, individual mentoring, or completing a series of formative workshops). The policy also provides guidelines for the options under the formative review.

The Peer Review of Teaching in Post-Tenure Review

The literature on the peer review of teaching provides us with important lessons about post-tenure review. The peer review literature provides support for the argument that post tenure review would be more effective if it were formative. Wagenaar (see Chapter 1 in this volume) argues that it is best to focus peer reviews of teaching on diagnosis and feedback because it reduces anxiety and helps institutionalize the process. If post-tenure review were more diagnostic and less threatening, faculty would be less likely to resist it. Few faculty are likely to fully embrace an assessment process that is summative and evaluative.

Faculty tend to see the post-tenure review process as more meaningful when it is based on peer review (Licata and Morreale, 1999). Tierney (1997) suggests that peer review facilitates the development of a community of scholars which in turn helps develop the community members' individual performance. If one accepts this premise, then post-tenure review becomes more developmental in nature. In addition, the peer review of teaching in post-tenure review provides faculty with more control of the materials and process of assessment, and even though it is a way to hold faculty accountable, encourages better teaching and learning, and facilitates faculty and course renewal (Mignon and Langsam, 1999). Above all, the peer review of teaching can provide additional evidence of continuing growth as teacher-scholars for the post-tenure review.

Morreale (1999) identifies some necessary components for evaluating teaching within post-tenure review: 1) settings the standards in teaching performance - including effective classroom instruction, faculty availability, and knowledge of the discipline; 2) constructing a development plan that addresses faculty goals for teaching and the resources needed to improve teaching; 3) determining the purpose of teaching; 4) generating evidence for teaching and providing the necessary feedback to faculty; 5) interpretation of the evidence of teaching by peers and chairs; 6) evaluation of the collective contribution of faculty so that an individual's teaching is not seen in isolation but within the context of the entire department; 7) rewards and recognitions for quality teaching; 8) the need to provide resources for the continued development of teaching; and 9) consequences for unsatisfactory performance on the post-tenure review. If our post-tenure review processes were indeed this robust, perhaps fewer of us would be resistant.

CONCLUSION

Post-tenure review goes beyond the traditional review practices of tenure and promotion, and is much more comprehensive than annual reviews. While some state systems have conducted post-tenure reviews for quite some time (e.g., California and Oregon), it is still a relatively new practice for most institutions of higher learning. There is not yet a consensus on post-tenure review practices, and some universities have policies with direct consequences for faculty while others do not. Policies that have "no teeth" (and that includes those with "teeth" but no rewards) are frustrating for faculty. At best, they are a waste of time. On the other hand, when policies are ill-designed, faculty are fortunate if it is only our time that is wasted.

Ironically, the peer review of teaching may actually be strengthened by post-tenure review. For those of us in institutions that stress research, without post-tenure review, the peer review of teaching would be less likely to exist. It may only be in the creation of policies that are comprehensive, such as post-tenure review that teaching comes to the forefront. While tenure decisions certainly include reviews of teaching, the highest bar is set for research. This may still be the case for post-tenure review, but in the absence of such a policy, teaching might be ignored all together. For schools with a stronger teaching mission, teaching is much less likely to be ignored.

We agree with the AAUP that two characteristics of post-tenure review are most likely to be useful and productive. First, post-tenure review policies should require significant faculty input. The post-tenure review process should be conducted by peers. Any comprehensive evaluation system that is not firmly in the hands of the faculty threatens academic freedom and challenges the basis for membership on a faculty. Evaluating academic expertise and performance should never be relegated solely to administrators. If faculty misconduct is the issue, procedures other that post-tenure review can be used. Second, post-tenure review is more useful to both the individuals and the institutions if the review is formative rather than summative. Post-tenure review (and the peer review of teaching) has the potential to be a source of self-reflection and revitalization, and is more likely to accomplish those goals if faculty development is the major focus.

Proponents of post-tenure review argue that annual reviews are not always the most effective tool for identifying faculty needs, whereas post-tenure review is designed for this purpose and can redirect institutional resources to provide assistance where and when it is most needed.   Furthermore, academic freedom is not compromised when post-tenure review is carried out primarily by peers.   It may even encourage a greater sense of collective purpose and the development of a stronger learning community (AAUP, 1998).   Opponents of post-tenure review suggest that it erodes the tenure process and encourages faculty to focus on the quantity rather than the quality of scholarship (Montell, 2002).   Moreover, since evaluative measures are already in place in the form of annual reviews, it is highly unlikely that a more structured and focused system will benefit faculty (AAUP, 1998).   Opponents also insist that post-tenure review diminishes faculty authority and creates more managerial accountability and administrative intrusion (AAUP, 1998; Montell, 2002).

We argue that post-tenure review and the peer review of teaching both challenge our sense of autonomy, both originate from similar influences, and both have the potential to be positive forces in the academy.   However, both post-tenure review and the peer review of teaching must be firmly in the hands of faculty and both must include formative evaluations.   If those two conditions are met, post-tenure review may serve the academy well and encourage us to serve our students better.

REFERENCES

American Association of University Professors. 1998. "Post-Tenure Review: An AAUP Response. *Academe* 84(5): 61-67.

Aper, Jeffery P. and Judith E. Fry. 2003. "Post-Tenure Review at Graduate Institutions in the United States: Recommendations and Reality." *The Journal of Higher Education* 74(3): 241-260.

Atkinson, Maxine P. 2000. "The Scholarship of Teaching: Conceptualizations and Implications for Sociologists." Presidential Address, Southern Sociological Society. New Orleans, LA. April.

Bataille, Gretchen M. and Betsy E. Brown. 2006. *Faculty Career Paths: Multiple Routes to Academic Success and Satisfaction.* American Council on Education. Westport: CT: Praeger Publishers.

Bok, Derek. 2006. *Our Underachieving Colleges: A Candid Look at How Much Students Learn and Why They Should Be Learning More.* Princeton, NJ: Princeton University Press.

Boyer, Ernest L. 1990. *Scholarship Reconsidered: Priorities of the Professorate.* Princeton, NJ: Carnegie Foundation for the Advancement of Teaching.

College of William & Mary. 1996, 1998-1999. "Section III. B.2.a. Policy on Post-Tenure Review." *Faculty Handbook.* Williamsburg, VA: College of William & Mary. Retrieved April 30, 2010 (http://web.wm.edu/sacs/accdoc/3/7/2/documents/FacultyHandbook,Chapter3,SectionB.2.pdf?svr=www).

Edwards, Richard. 1997. "Can Post-Tenure Review Help Us Save the Tenure System?" *Academe* 83(3): 26-31.

Hanover College. n.d. *Post-Tenure Review Policy.* Personal Correspondence with Dr. Keith Roberts, Professor of Sociology, Hanover College. April 21, 2010.

Hutchings, Pat. 1996. *Making Teaching Community Property: A Menu for Peer Collaboration and Peer Review.* Washington, DC: American Association for Higher Education.

Kansas State University. 2006. "Sections 31.5 to 31.8." *University Handbook.* Manhattan, KS: Kansas State University. Retrieved April 30, 2010 (http://www.k-state.edu/provost/aahe/overview_post_tenure.html).

Kors, Alan Charles. 2008. "On The Sadness of Higher Education." *The Wall Street Journal.* Retrieved May 3, 2010 (http://online.wsj.com/article/SB121184146283621055.html).

Licata, Christine M. 2004. "Post-Tenure Faculty Review Practices: Context and Framework." Pp. 6-11 in *Post-Tenure Faculty Review and Renewal II: Reporting Results and Shaping Policy,* edited by Christine M. Licata and Betsy Brown. Bolton, MA: Anker Publishing Company, Inc.

Licata, Christine M. and Joseph C. Morrele. 1999. "Post-tenure Review: National Trends,Questions and Concerns." *Innovative Higher Education* 24(1): 5-15.

------. 2006. *Post-Tenure Faculty Review and Renewal III: Outcomes and Impact.* Bolton, MA: Anker Publishing Company, Inc.

Lindholm, Jennifer A. 2004. "Pathways to the Professoriate: The Role of Self, Others, and Environment in Shaping Academic Career Aspirations" *The Journal of Higher Education* 75(6): 603-635.

Middlebury College. 2009. "Rules of Appointment and Tenure for Academic Faculty." Faculty Handbook. Middlebury, VT: Middlebury College. Retrieved April 30, 2010 (http://www.middlebury.edu/about/handbook/faculty/Faculty_Rules).

Mignon, Charles and Deborah Langsam. 1999. "Peer Review and Post-Tenure Review." *Innovative Higher Education* 24(1): 49-59.

Montell, Gabriela. 2002. "The Fallout from Post-Tenure Review." *Chronicle of Higher Education*. Retrieved March 10, 2010 (http://chronicle.com/article/The-Fallout-From-Post-Tenure/46063/).

Morreale, Joseph C. 1999. "Post-Tenure Review: Evaluating Teaching." Pp. 116 – 138 In *Changing Practices in Evaluating Teaching: A Practical Guide to Improved Faculty Performance and Promotion/Tenure Decision*, edited by Peter Seldin and Associates. Bolton, MA: Anker Publishing, Inc.

North Carolina State University. 1998, 2009. "Post Tenure Review of Faculty REG 05.20.4." *Policies, Regulations, and Rules*. Raleigh, NC: North Carolina State University. Retrieved April 30, 2010 (http://www.ncsu.edu/policies/employment/epa/REG05.20.4.php).

Neal, Anne D. 2008. "Reviewing Post-Tenure Review." *Academe Online* 94 (5). Retrieved March 10, 2010 (AAUP.org).

Seldin, Peter. 1997. *The Teaching Portfolio: A Practical guide to Improved Performance and Promotion/Tenure Decisions* (Second Edition). Bolton, MA: Anker Publishing, Inc.

Sullivan, Teresa A. 1995. "Teaching Evaluation by Peers." *Teaching Sociology* 23(1): 61-63.

Sykes, Charles J. 1998. *Profscam: Professors and the Demise of Higher Education*. Washington, DC: Regnery Gateway.

Texas A & M University System. 1995, 1997, 2008. *12.06 Post-Tenure Review of Faculty and Teaching Effectiveness*. College Station, TX: The System Office of Academic Affairs. Retrieved April 30, 2010 (http://www.tamus.edu/offices/policy/policies/pdf/12-06.pdf).

Tierney, William G. 1997. "Academic Community and Post-Tenure Review." *Academe* 83(5): 23-25.

University of Colorado. 2006. "Administrative Policy Statement: Post-Tenure Review (IV-89)." *Principles & Policies Related to Appointment, Reappointment, Promotion and Tenure*. Denver, CO: University of Colorado. Retrieved April 30, 2010 (https://www.cu.edu/content/principles-and-policies-related-appointment-reappointment-promotion-and-tenure).

University System of Georgia. 2010. "4.6 Post-Tenure Review." *Academic Affairs Handbook*. Atlanta, GA: University System of Georgia. Retrieved April 30, 2010 (http://www.usg.edu/academic_affairs_handbook/section4/handbook/4.6_post-tenure_review/).

University of Minnesota. 1998. "Rules and Procedures for Annual and Special Post-Tenure Review." *Faculty Senate Tenure Documents*. Minneapolis, MN: University of Minnesota. Retrieved April 30, 2010 (http://www1.umn.edu/usenate/fsen/guidelines.html).

University of Missouri System. 2007. "310.015 Procedures for Review of Faculty Performance." *Collected Rules and Regulations: Faculty Bylaws and Tenure Regulations*. Colombia, MO: University of Missouri System. Retrieved April 30, 2010 (http://www.umsystem.edu/ums/departments/gc/rules/bylaws/310/015.shtml).

University of Nebraska-Lincoln. 1998. "Faculty Resources: Post-Tenure Reviews." *Office of the Senior Vice Chancellor for Academic Affairs*. Lincoln, NE: University of Nebraska-Lincoln. Retrieved April 30, 2010 (http://www.unl.edu/svcaa/policies/posttenure_review.shtml).

University of Oregon. 1999. "02.01.17 Post Tenure Review." *University of Oregon Policy Library*. Eugene, OR: University of Oregon. Retrieved April 30, 2010 (http://policies.uoregon.edu/policy/by/1/03000-human-resources/post-tenure-review).

University of South Carolina. 2009, 2010. "Post-Tenure Review." *Tenure and Promotion*. Colombia, SC: University of South Carolina. Retrieved April 30, 2010 (http://www.sc.edu/tenure/post-tenurereview.shtml).

U.S. Department of Education. 2006. *A Test of Leadership: Charting the Future of Higher Education*. Washington, DC: U.S. Department of Education. Retrieved May 3, 2010 (http://www2.ed.gov/about/bdscomm/list/hiedfuture/reports/final-report.pdf).

Virginia Tech. 2004, 2009. "2.10.4 Post-Tenure Review." *Faculty Handbook*. Blacksburg, VA: Virginia Tech. Retrieved April 30, 2010 (http://www.provost.vt.edu/documents/FHB_Section_2.pdf).

Appendix A. Examples of Post-Tenure Review Policies

College of William and Mary has three types of post-tenure review: scheduled reviews, unscheduled reviews, and follow-up reviews. The purpose of the scheduled reviews is to enhance faculty development and ensure quality of faculty teaching, scholarship, and service. They are not to exceed every 6 years. Unscheduled reviews occur when faculty receive two consecutive unsatisfactory annual merit evaluations. Follow-up reviews occur after unsatisfactory scheduled or unscheduled reviews. Disciplinary actions are taken for continued unsatisfactory performances. (http://web.wm.edu/sacs/accdoc/3/7/2/documents/FacultyHandbook,C hapter3,SectionB.2.pdf?svr=www)

Hanover College conducts post-tenure reviews every seven years. The purpose of the post-tenure review is two-fold: to provide professional development in teaching, scholarship, and service; and may serve as a summative evaluation conducted by a peer review committee. If faculty chooses to have a formative review, they complete two such reviews in the seven-year period. Faculty have options under the formative review process for ways to enhance their professional development (e.g., peer mentoring groups, individual mentoring, or completing a series of formative workshops). The policy provides guidelines for the options under the formative review.

Kansas State University has triggered post-tenure reviews that occur if faculty receives unsatisfactory annual reviews. The goal is to improve performance in the areas needing it as indicated by the annual review. The post-tenure review often results in the development of an action plan. If faculty have two consecutive evaluations or a total of three in any five-year period that are unsatisfactory then can for dismissal can be considered. (http://www.k-state.edu/provost/aahe/overview post tenure.html

North Carolina State University conducts post-tenure reviews every five years. The goal is to protect academic freedom and ensure quality education. The post-tenure review is an evaluation of cumulative performance over time. Faculty submit a current curriculum vitae, a Statement of Mutual Expectations, an annual activity report since the last review, peer teaching evaluations since the last review, and an optional two-page candidate statement. (http://www.ncsu.edu/policies/employment/epa/REG05.20.4.php)

Middlebury College uses post-tenure review as a way to promote associate professors to full professors. Associate professors are first reviewed by the Promotions Committee sometime between the fifth and eighth year after tenure for possible promotion to professor. The review focuses on professional achievements and continued excellence in teaching, scholarship, and service. Criteria are provided for each of these areas including peer review of teaching. If the faculty member is not promoted to full professor then post-tenure review will be conducted between three and five years following the unsuccessful review until the faculty member has been promoted to professor or has departed from the faculty. Full professors are required to complete a ten-year review by the Reappointments Committee to assess professional achievements since promotion to full professor (or since the last ten-year review) and to aid

continued professional development.
(http://www.middlebury.edu/about/handbook/faculty/Faculty_rules)
Texas A & M University System conducts post-tenure reviews every one to
six years after tenure. The focus is on teaching effectiveness, research,
student advising, and university and community service. The policy
outlines criteria for teaching effectiveness including peer review.
(http://tamus.edu/offices/policy/policies/pdf/12-06.pdf)

University of Colorado normally uses scheduled post-tenure reviews every
five years. However, if annual evaluations are below expectations then a
triggered post-tenure review occurs. An extensive review occurs with two
below expectations ratings on annual reviews or when faculty has a
performance improvement agreement that was unsatisfactory.
(https://www.cu.edu/content/principles-and-policies-related-
appointment-reappointment-promotion-and-tenure)

University system of Georgia conducts post-tenure reviews every five years
after the most recent promotion and continues at five-year intervals. The
review is linked to rewards and professional development. If faculty with
unsatisfactory post-tenure review does not improve after three years then
there is cause for dismissal.
http://www.usg.edu/academic_affairs_handbook/section4/handbook/4.6
_post-tenure_review/)

University of Minnesota combines their annual review and post-tenure
review in the same process. The department elects a peer-review
committee who evaluates faculty performance. A special review occurs
when faculty demonstrate substandard performance.
(http://www1.umn.edu/usenate/fsen/guidelines.html)

University of Missouri conducts post-tenure reviews every five years.
Faculty has to develop and publish minimum standards for overall
satisfactory performance. They must also demonstrate their research,
teaching, and service activities. The department chair evaluates faculty
performance and if it is unsatisfactory then faculty peers do another
evaluation. The review is complete if the peer committee gives a
satisfactory rating. If the chair and peer committee both judge the faculty
as unsatisfactory then it is sent to the dean. The consequences for an
unsatisfactory post-tenure review include a development plan and
assessment of progress. If there is no improvement over time then it is
cause for dismissal.
(http://www.umsystem.edu/ums/departments/gc/rules/bylaws/310/01
5.shtml)

University of Nebraska-Lincoln uses a triggered post-tenure review based
upon peer review if the annual review is unsatisfactory. In addition, any
faculty who has had continuous employment for three or more years may
elect or be required to do a post-tenure review no more than one every

four years.
(http://www.unl.edu/svcaa/policies/posttenure_review.shtml)

University of Oregon conducts post-tenure reviews every three years to encourage, reward, and support continuous development. There are two types of reviews: substantive review and major review. A substantive review occurs at the three-year point after a prior major review or after promotion. Other reviews (e.g., merit reviews) cannot substitute for the three-year review. A major review occurs every six years after a prior major review or after being promoted or receiving tenure. Both types of review are based upon peer review and focus on high-quality teaching, continued professional growth, and leadership and service.
(http??policies.uoregon.edu/policy/by/1/03000-human-resources/post-tenure-review)

University of South Carolina conducts post-tenure reviews every six years. Each department sets their own criteria for post-tenure review. In Sociology, a peer review committee evaluates teaching (using peer evaluations, student evaluations, and other documentation), scholarship, service, annual evaluations, and sabbatical reports. If faculty receive an unsatisfactory rating in teaching, research, or service then they have to develop a plan for improvement.
(http://www.sc.edu/tenure/post-tenurereview.shtml)

Virginia Tech uses a triggered review when faculty has two consecutive unsatisfactory annual evaluations. The departmental promotion and tenure committee carries out the review. The purpose is to provide the perspective of faculty peers of the faculty member's professional competence, performance, and contributions to the department, college, and university. The peer review committee evaluates the performance and makes a recommendation to the Chair who then makes the final decision. If a severe sanction is recommended then the case is referred to the college-level promotion and review committee.(see 2.10
http://www.provost.vt.edu/documents/FHB_section_2.pdf)

11

Some Ethical Issues
in the Peer Review of Teaching

Thomas L. Van Valey, Western Michigan University

The following essay is intended to raise some of the fundamental
ethical considerations that are involved in the peer review of
teaching. Before focusing on peer review, though, it is reasonable
to ask how academics can be guided in decisions about
professional behavior in general. One place to look for guidance is
in the codes of ethics of the professional societies. For example, the
Preamble to the code of the American Sociological Association
states:

> This Code of Ethics articulates a common set of values
> upon which sociologists build their professional and
> scientific work. The Code is intended to provide both the
> general principles and the rules to cover professional
> situations encountered by sociologists. It has as its
> primary goal the welfare and protection of the individuals
> and groups with whom sociologists work ... The
> development of a dynamic set of ethical standards for a
> sociologist's work-related conduct requires a personal
> commitment to a lifelong effort to act ethically; to
> encourage ethical behavior by students, supervisors,
> supervisees, employers, employees, and colleagues ...
> (ASA, p. 3)

While the five general principles and the twenty ethical standards
that constitute the bulk of the ASA Code of Ethics are said to apply
to the full range of professional behavior, many of its elements do
not apply particularly well to the teaching enterprise. This is also
the case for ethical codes of many of the other professional
associations. Instead they often appear to be aimed primarily at
the other components of a professional's life - research and
publication (and clinical practice for some associations), along with
the interpersonal relationships that are implicit in an academic or
applied setting - employment decisions, conflicts of interest,

informed consent, authorship credit, and the publication process itself (Van Valey and Hillsman, 2007).

In contrast, our colleagues in Canada at the Society for Teaching and Learning in Higher Education have produced a set of nine "Ethical Principles for College and University Teaching." The preamble to this set of guidelines is quite clear:

> The purpose of this document is to provide a set of basic ethical principles that define the professional responsibilities of university professors in their role as teachers. Ethical principles are conceptualized here as general guidelines, ideals or expectations that need to be taken into account, along with other relevant conditions and circumstances, in the design and analysis of university teaching. (Murray, et al, 1996, p.3)

These principles were carefully articulated to focus on the variety of issues that are directly related to the teaching enterprise:

1. Content Competence,
2. Pedagogical Competence,
3. Dealing with Sensitive Topics,
4. Student Development,
5. Dual Relationships with Students,
6. Confidentiality,
7. Respect for Colleagues,
8. Valid Assessment of Students,
9. Respect for Institution.

While some of these issues are self evident (e.g., Competence, Confidentiality, Assessment of Students, Respect for Colleagues and Institution), a few are not. For example, under Dealing with Sensitive Topics, faculty are encouraged to deal with a given topic in an open, honest, and positive way. This means that the instructor must acknowledge, from the beginning, that a given topic is sensitive or controversial, and explain its relevance to the course. She/he should also provide (or allow others to provide) multiple perspectives on the topic. Given actions by Horowitz (2004, 2005) and other proponents of the "Academic Bill of Rights," this kind of clarification is critical.

This is paralleled in the section on Student Development. Faculty are advised to avoid exploiting and discriminating actions which would disturb the focus on the intellectual development of the student. Similarly, with respect to Dual Relationships with Students, faculty are admonished not to form close, personal relationships with students (especially those that are sexual in nature) that have the potential of harming the impartiality that faculty must maintain or detracting from the intellectual development of the student. Such relationships, of course, create a conflict of interest, or the perception of a conflict of interest, that can seriously undermine the faculty member's credibility and effectiveness.

Of course, neither the ASA nor the STLHE codes were created with peer review in mind, although the STLHE code is specifically aimed at teaching. Nevertheless, both codes do offer principles and guidelines for faculty to use in guiding their own behavior. This, of course, also provides colleagues with principles and guidelines to guide them as they move through the process of peer review.

Another source of ethical guidance, this one specific to the peer review of teaching, is in "From Idea to Prototype: The Peer Review of Teaching - a Project Workbook," by Hutchins and Edgerton (1995). They identified four issues for analysis and action that certainly have ethical dimensions:

1. What shall be peer reviewed? ... the major issue being who decides?
2. Who shall conduct peer reviews? ... and on whom?
3. How should teaching be reviewed by one's peers? ... again, who decides?.
4. In which contexts is the peer review of teaching most likely to bring about improvement of teaching? ... assuming that the goal of peer review is the improvement of teaching and not something else.

These issues provide many opportunities for faculty to determine the areas of consensus and concern, and to lay the groundwork for an ethical approach to peer review.

THE PURPOSE OF PEER REVIEW

From these several sources, it is apparent that there are some common themes that may be applied in the discussion of ethical issues. One of the key considerations is the purpose of peer review. Is it intended to assist the instructor in improving his/her teaching (and, presumably - or maybe even demonstrably, the improvement of student learning)? Or, is it intended as a means of assuring institutional or programmatic accountability - to evaluate the effectiveness of teaching -with a wide range of possible consequences, depending on the outcome? If it is clearly a summative or outcome approach, without significant components of a formative or process approach, then faculty and students may be wary about peer review for good reason. As a rule, purely summative evaluations tend to objectify the subjects of the evaluations (i.e., they are done to faculty), thereby demeaning faculty by removing any vestiges of control over their professional destinies. Formative approaches, in contrast, include faculty as actors in the process, thereby tending to increase faculty ownership and commitment to the process and any outcomes that may result. (See Chapters 1 and 3 in this volume for additional discussions of formative and summative evaluations.)

By the same token, mixing both formative and summative approaches to the peer review of teaching requires a good deal of trust on the part of the faculty, and may well fail as an administrative strategy unless it is carefully implemented (Irby, 1983, Lomas and Nicholls, 2005). Formative reviews frequently call for risk-taking activities on the part of faculty - trying new teaching techniques, employing new technology, incorporating new subject matters. The goal, of course, is to improve teaching and student learning.   However, when the same people (i.e., administrators) who call for formative reviews also make summative decisions – about merit, tenure, and promotion - faculty often may not see any incentive in risk-taking (Cavanaugh, 1996. Keig, 2000, Helms et al, 2001). Indeed, they may come to the quite reasonable conclusion, given the nature of the reward structure at most institutions, that significant investments in teaching take away from their likelihood of success in research and publication. Thus, any risk-taking is likely to be invested in research and publication, which, they have learned, will be most likely to advance their careers.

A parallel consideration has to do with the source of the pressure for peer review. Has it been initiated by the faculty as a whole, or in individual departments, or by the institution's administration or governing body, or has it come from a state legislature or an accrediting body? The answer to this question, of course, is specific to the state and the institution. Some states have moved aggressively in the direction of assessing teaching and student learning with the clear goal of improvement (Hutchins, 1996).   Others have clearly targeted the assessment of faculty effectiveness and productivity, especially certain senior faculty - the so-called "deadwood"(Tierney, 2000). In the latter instance, faculty often confuse peer review with post tenure review (perhaps rightfully so in some cases – see Chapter 1 in this volume).

Regardless of the source of peer review, some departments have taken the position that, in order to minimize the chance of negative impact and also to retain a maximum of faculty control, they and their institutions need to be proactive with respect to peer review. Thus, they believe it is wise for them to design/implement their own system of peer review (perhaps even deliberately including some form of post tenure review) that anticipates the goals of their various stakeholders and constituencies, yet does not disrupt their operations any more than necessary.

There are many models of peer review. Some target all institutions in a state, others focus on some or all programs in a single institution. Some involve all faculty and all courses, while others may only identify selected faculty or selected courses. Whatever the model, an important ethical consideration is the degree of inequity and divisiveness that may result from the process. In particular, this concerns the identification of individuals or programs as "deficient" (usually with a concomitant loss of resources). Fortunately, most (though certainly not all) institutions seem to be taking the approach that minimizing such divisiveness can be accomplished more effectively with a formative approach to peer review (Purdue, 2003). Indeed, some have found that additional faculty development resources may actually be an outcome of peer review.

THE PROCESS OF PEER REVIEW

The process of peer review itself often raises important ethical issues. Because many faculty still see teaching as an essentially private activity, peer review is frequently perceived as unduly intrusive. Indeed, such faculty often see the peer review process itself as a potential infringement on their academic freedom. What they do in their own classrooms, from their point of view, should be up to them and only them. They, after all, are professionals. Here, there is often confusion among the notions of peer review, academic freedom, and censorship (Keig, 2000). Others may in fact be concerned with the specific practice of classroom observation by peers (which may or may not be an element in a peer review process), and how it is carried out.

The peer review process can raise some thorny issues. As the saying goes, "the devil is in the details." For example, once peer review is put in place, who actually does the reviewing? Is it to be done by peers from within the department, by other colleagues from elsewhere in the institution, or even by individuals from outside the institution? In each of these instances, faculty see the potential for bias and abuse (e.g., reviewers selected specifically to "stack the deck" either in favor or opposition to the individuals under review). This is especially the case when the people being subjected to a largely summative peer review are in a vulnerable position (e.g., part-time, or untenured, or being considered for tenure or promotion).

One of the issues routinely raised by departments concerning peer review is the time required to carry out the process. This includes the time for the faculty member being reviewed to prepare the necessary materials (e.g., dossiers and/or teaching portfolios) and to meet with the reviewers, as well as the time required for the reviewers to carry out the actual reviews and write them up. As teaching loads are increased and new pressures are added (e.g., technology, distance learning, service learning), many faculty already feel overburdened. They see the peer review of their teaching as interfering in their "real" responsibilities - research, teaching, and service, especially the former. Moreover, they often feel that asking them to carry out what they see as an essentially administrative procedure is particularly inappropriate. The question in their minds, of course, is why they should potentially jeopardize the success of their own careers to carry out a task that they see as irrelevant to their "real" work.

Along with the issue of the time involved is the question of who is being reviewed. Is it the faculty who are being reviewed, is it the courses they teach, or is it the performance (or learning) of the students in those courses? Or is it perhaps all of them? All are legitimate objects of review, depending on the goals that are set for the process. Part of the concern is over who makes these kinds of decisions, and whether or not there is faculty participation in the decision-making process. This, like many other issues, relates back to the issue of the nature of the review and whether it is primarily formative or summative.

The question of what materials are to be reviewed also raises a number of considerations that have clear ethical components. Assuming that it is faculty who are to be reviewed (rather than courses or student performance), are there clear guidelines as to what will be included? Is there consensus on those guidelines, or the criteria to be employed, or the standards to be used? Are all faculty to be reviewed using the same criteria, or will they differ for those engaged primarily in research versus those who primarily teach, or those who teach primarily at the graduate level versus those who teach undergraduates? Here again, the issues of equity and divisiveness become prominent.

While similar considerations apply if it is courses that are being reviewed, questions of comparability can also be raised. Should multiple sections of the same course be treated differently than different courses? What about large versus small classes, undergraduate versus graduate classes, or those with a special focus (e.g., statistics, writing intensive, distance learning, or honors)? By the same token, if it is student performance that is to be reviewed, to what extent will the process separate out issues of student satisfaction with in-classroom teaching, the central element of most student evaluations of teaching? Similarly, questions of short term versus long term performance become salient.

One of the most important ethical questions revolves around the way people to be reviewed are identified. Some institutions have selected specific programs or departments for review on a rotating basis, with all persons within those programs being reviewed at the same time. Others have used a more or less random process, deciding that a given proportion of all faculty will be reviewed each year (thus building in a cycle of reviews). Still others have adopted what some have called the "worst first" approach, where faculty with previously reported "weaknesses" (of one kind or another) are singled out to be reviewed first. Even setting aside the self-fulfilling prophecy and its potential consequences, a major concern with this latter approach, of course, is the possibility that the individuals who will be targeted for review and potential negative consequences are those who have been controversial within the institution or the communities they serve. It is this latter kind of approach that often helps to confound peer review with academic freedom, censorship and post tenure review. Nevertheless, the fact that there is confusion underscores the importance of the selection process.

When it comes to the actual materials that are to be reviewed, the peer review of teaching appears to be more complicated than the peer review of research. In reviewing research, the review normally focuses only on the end product of the research process - the proposal, paper, monograph, or book. All the intermediate steps (including many possible false starts, errors, previous versions, etc.) are typically invisible to the reviewer. In contrast, with the peer review of teaching, it is the entire teaching process that is put under scrutiny. For example, teaching portfolios routinely include information from multiple offerings of the same course over time, pointing out weaknesses in early versions that have been confronted and, hopefully, addressed. They also typically contain student-based and self-evaluative materials which often contain negative as well as positive components. In addition, while the criteria for the peer review of research have been reasonably well developed, the criteria for the peer review of teaching are still in a developmental stage.

Perhaps in part because the teaching process has been a relatively private activity (see Chapter 4 in this volume), faculty have been largely free to "try out" new approaches, technologies, content, and techniques to see how they work in a given classroom situation. Indeed, there are a number of pedagogical journals (like *Teaching Sociology*) that offer their readers a wide range of such innovations. There is concern among some faculty that the peer review of teaching could have a chilling effect on faculty creativity and innovation, and that certain approaches will become defined as "standard." As the reasoning goes, if the peer review of teaching becomes linked to the reward structure of an institution, the range of approaches to teaching that are <u>acceptable</u> may be constricted.

This same reasoning can be extended to subject matters. At some institutions, the subject matter of certain courses may be controversial (e.g., sexuality, human rights, race and ethnic relations). Because of the controversy that can be associated with such courses, the faculty who dare to teach them must be especially careful not only about the content of the course but also their teaching methods. The safe approach is to do what has been done before (regardless of whether it appears to have been an effective pedagogical approach). To try things that are innovative in such courses may be tantamount to the faculty member setting him/herself up for a negative review, or, what can be even worse from the point of view of the institution, bad publicity. Again, some of the recent conservative attacks, especially in the social sciences, have underscored this concern. (Horowitz, 2004)

Finally, there is widespread concern among faculty that the typical materials to be peer reviewed simply do not express the full range of measures for the quality of teaching (Keig, 2000, Lomas and Nicholls, 2005). Some protest that it is student outcomes that should be used in determining the effectiveness of teaching, and that they already do that by assigning grades. Yet, even they often argue among each other over such issues as recency effects (e.g., how long and how frequently after the completion of a skill or objective should a student's competence be evaluated). Others argue that the typical materials reviewed (e.g., syllabi, student evaluations, classroom observations, teaching or course portfolios, examples of student work) are just not representative of the entire teaching process and are thus weak measures. They often note that student advising, both formal and informal, mentoring, collaboration, and providing research opportunities to students, are components of quality teaching that are seldom included in the peer review process, yet are important components. These faculty sometimes come very close to saying that unlike research, teaching is an art, and thus cannot be properly evaluated in any meaningful way.

CONCLUSION

Some of the other ethical issues that are related to teaching, and that are often explicit in the professional associations' codes of ethics (e.g., the exploitation of students, sexual harassment, respect for people's rights and dignity, confidentiality, overall professional competence and integrity), may be less directly related to the forms of peer review of teaching that exist today, but should certainly not be ignored. A number of exposés of academic life have been written in response to abuses that have occurred, and they have sold well, and not just to academics (e.g., *Profscam, The Lecherous Professor, Moo*). There have also been a number of other critiques of higher education (e.g., *Publish and Perish, Straight Man, The Last Intellectuals*), one, *Poisoning the Ivy*, by a sociologist. It is in the context of these kinds of publicity that higher education must exist, especially today when many states appear to be systematically reducing their support of public higher education.

It is increasingly apparent that teaching in institutions of higher education in the United States is being subjected to ever closer scrutiny (Boyer, 1990 and others would include professional service as well). Not to do so opens the academy up to the kinds of comments and criticisms that some would say are in part responsible for the recent retrenchments in higher education. Therefore, since teaching is typically viewed by the general public as the primary mission of all institutions of higher education, it is critical that these and any other ethical concerns about the peer review of teaching be addressed.

REFERENCES

American Sociological Association. 1997. *ASA Code of Ethics*, Washington, D.C., Also at www.asanet.org/about/ethics.cfm

Boyer, E. 1990. *Scholarship Reconsidered: Priorities of the Professoriate.* Lawrenceville, NJ: Princeton University Press.

Cavanaugh, R. R., 1996. "Formative and Summative Evaluation in the Faculty Peer Review of Teaching." *Innovative Higher Education* Vol 20, No 4: 235-240.

Dziech, B. W, and L. Weiner, 1990. *The Lecherous Professor: Sexual Harassment on Campus, 2nd Edition.* University of Illinois Press, Urbana and Chicago, IL

Helms, M. M., Williams, A. B., Nixon, J. C. 2001. "TQM Principles and their Relevance to Higher Education: the Question of Tenure and Post-tenure Review", *International Journal of Educational Management*, Vol 15, No 7: 322-331.

Horowitz, D. 2004. "In Defense of Intellectual Diversity." *The Chronicle of Higher Education.* February, 13, Retrieved 12/10/2004. (http://chronicle.com/).

Horowitz, D. 2005. "Academic Bill of Rights." Students for Academic Freedom . Retrieved 1/2/2005. (http://www.studentsforacademicfreedom.org).

Hutchings. P. (ed). 1995. *From Idea to Prototype: The Peer Review of Teaching A Project Workbook,* Washington, D.C., American Association for Higher Education

Hutchins, P. 1996. "The Peer Review of Teaching: Progress, Issues and Prospects." Innovative Higher Education. Vol 20, No 4: 221-234

Hynes, J. 1997. *Publish and Perish: Three Tales of Tenure and Terror.* New York: St. Martin's Press

Irby, D M. 1983. "Peer Review of Teaching in Medicine." *Journal of Medical Education.* Vol 58 No 6: 457-461.

Jacoby, R. 1987. *The Last Intellectuals: American Culture in the Age of Academe.* New York: Basic Books

Keig, L. 2000. "Formative Peer Review of Teaching: Attitudes of Faculty at Liberal Arts Colleges Toward Colleague Assessment." *Journal of Personnel Evaluation in Education.* Vol 14, No 1: 67-87.

Lewis, M. 1997. *Poisoning the Ivy: The Seven Deadly Sins and Other Vices of Higher Education in America.* Armonk, NY: M. E. Sharpe, Inc

Lomas, L. and Nicholls, G. 2005. "Enhancing Teaching Quality Through Peer Review of Teaching" *Quality in Higher Education,* Vol 11, No 2: 137–149.

Murray, H. E. Gillese, M. Lennon, P. Mercer, and M. Robinson. 1996. *Ethical Principles for College and University Teaching,* Society for Teaching and Learning in Higher Education, York University: Reprinted in *AAHE Bulletin* Volume 49, Number 4, (December, 1996): 3-6.

Purdue University. 2003. "Building a Foundation for Career Long Faculty Development at Purdue University"
http://www.purdue.edu/faculty/documents/faculty.pdf

Russo, R. 1998. *Straight Man*. New York: Vintage Books

Smiley, J. 1995. *Moo*. New York: Ivy Books

Sykes, C. J. 1988. *ProfScam: Professors and the Demise of Higher Education*. Washington, DC: Regency Gateway

Tierney, William G. 2000. "Dealing with Deadwood." *The Department Chair*, Vol 10, No 3: 1-3.

Van Valey, T. L. and Hillsman, S. 2007. "The Code of Ethics of the American Sociological Association" *Bulletin of the Swiss Society of Sociology*, 132: 11-15

IV

IMPLEMENTATION STRATEGIES

12

Ways to Start the Peer Review Conversation within a Department

Edward L. Kain, Southwestern University

How the peer review of teaching is introduced into the departmental discourse can be important in determining the path those discussions take as they evolve. If, for example, there is an institution-wide mandate for a particular type of peer review—post-tenure review implementing classroom visits, for example—the ways in which the department embraces or resists peer review of teaching will be decidedly different than if the topic emerges from a department discussion of ways to improve student learning outcomes measured by papers and presentations produced in a required senior capstone course. This chapter is designed to help departments and programs think through some productive ways in which they might start conversations about the peer review of teaching. It is divided into two sections. The first presents three important key issues that need to be addressed near the beginning in any discussion of the peer review of teaching: 1) defining what we mean by peer review of teaching, 2) formative versus summative evaluations, and 3) how we structure the timing of peer review of teaching within a program. The second section suggests several ways in which the conversation about peer review of teaching can continue beyond these introductory issues. In particular, it is fruitful to link discussions to structures, activities and groups that are already part of the fabric of the department and the institution.

KEY ISSUES

A complete examination of the peer review of teaching will involve a variety of nuanced discussions about all of the central questions - what, why, how, who, when, and where. Other chapters in this volume address a number of these topics. Beginning the departmental conversation fruitfully, however, requires attention to at least three questions—What do we mean by peer review?;

Why should we do it (in essence, what do we gain from it and how is it going to be used)?; and When do we find ways to integrate the peer review of teaching into our sociology department/program? Examining aspects of these three questions can lead to much broader discussions of ways in which the peer review of teaching can improve the teaching and learning of sociology within a department or program.

Defining the Peer Review of Teaching

Chism defines the peer review of teaching as "informed colleague judgment about faculty teaching for either fostering improvement or making personnel decisions." (2007:3) This definition provides an excellent starting point. First, by insisting upon "informed colleague judgment" it helps to place the evaluation of teaching on a par with the evaluation of research within an academic career. Second, inclusion of the word "informed" makes it clear that the peer review of teaching requires some type of training or systematic evaluation techniques. Third, it opens the door for discussing the range of activities and evidence that might be used to make that informed judgment. Both implicitly and explicitly, this argues for movement beyond the exclusive use of student evaluations of instruction as a way of evaluating teaching. (This issue was central to two early reflections upon peer review and the evaluation of teaching in sociology by Sullivan, 1995 and Wagenaar, 1995). Finally, it builds the distinction between formative and summative evaluation (discussed below) directly into the definition.

One promising way to get people thinking about definitional issues is to ask department members to say the first thing that comes to their minds when they hear the phrase "peer review of teaching." To avoid early responses influencing later ones, have each person write a few sentences, shuffle the sheets of paper, pass them out, and have colleagues read the responses aloud. My suspicion is that the patterning of responses may be somewhat linked to experience. Faculty members who are in their first decade of teaching are more likely to have been trained in a program where they discussed (and may have been required to develop) teaching portfolios. In contrast, faculty who are in their second or third decades of teaching are more likely to have been involved in discussions of post-tenure review.

An important goal of early departmental discussions of the topic is to make people aware of the range of types of activities and information that can be used in the process of the peer review of teaching. Chapters 4 through 8 in this volume can help introduce colleagues to (or expand their understanding of) teaching circles, teaching portfolios, peer observation and other techniques for the peer review of teaching. (Several other excellent sources are Chism, 2007; Hutchings, 1995; and Quinlan, 1996.)

Formative versus Summative Evaluation
Throughout the literature on the evaluation of teaching, a critical distinction is made between formative evaluations, which are focused upon improving the quality of pedagogy, and summative evaluations, which are used for personnel decisions. (Arreola, 2007; Centra, 1993; Chism, 2006). This distinction is a key part of any department discussion of peer review. It is important that both types of peer evaluation are built into a system—peer review for faculty development, and peer review for faculty rewards. Indeed, some of the most productive early discussions about the peer review of teaching may be those which focus upon why and how both types of peer review can strengthen the teaching and learning of sociology. Framing formative peer review as a set of opportunities for faculty development can transform the ways colleagues think and talk about this topic. Again, a key aspect of variation will likely be the career stages of the faculty members. In departments with a significant number of senior faculty, for example, discussion of peer coaching as one type of professional development might be useful (Huston and Weaver, 2008).

Ultimately, discussions of formative and summative evaluation will need to address which colleagues will serve as peer reviewers. While this is a complex topic, one suggestion emerging from the national project on peer review spearheaded by the AAHE is to use reviewers from the same campus for formative evaluations, while external reviewers from other campuses are used for summative evaluations (Morehead and Shedd, 1997). Whatever decisions are made about this issue, the broader the range of reviewers, the more productive the system of peer review of teaching is likely to be.

Exploring the many reasons *why* a department might want to implement peer review of teaching clearly goes far beyond the distinction between formative and summative evaluation. Indeed, the opening chapters of this collection point to some important dimensions of the context of peer review, including assessment, the rewards that are linked to teaching, and moving pedagogical discourse and practice out from behind closed doors into the regular public and professional discourse of sociology departments. In the early (and even the later) stages of talking about the peer review of teaching in a department, it is important to remember that there will likely also be discussions of why *not* to do peer review. Some colleagues will resist. Chism (2007) provides a nice discussion of objections to the peer review of teaching, and argues "a good system for the evaluation of teaching that incorporates peer review must address the objections that are raised to the satisfaction of the faculty community." (2007:25).

The Timing of Peer Review in an Academic Career

A third key issue that may generate productive conversations about the peer review of teaching involves when it occurs within an academic career. The central argument here is that we should move away from thinking about the peer review of teaching as something that occurs only at key points in a career, and move toward thinking about it as a continuous process for improving the quality of teaching and learning. As we expand the repertoire of activities that we include as part of the process (e.g., the development of teaching portfolios, teaching circles, peer coaching, and peer observation), the peer review of teaching becomes a regular part of the academic life course, just as it is a regular part of the research done by academic sociologists.

A starting point for this conversation might be to delineate when the department/program currently uses some type of peer review of teaching. In some departments, the answer to this may be that it is seldom, if ever, used. Upon reflection, however, colleagues may note a number of places where it already exists - when a new faculty member is hired into the department, when junior faculty members move through the pre-tenure years and are reviewed for promotion and tenure, when a colleague is considered for promotion to full professor, or when a faculty member is nominated for a teaching award, either on campus or externally (note also that most of these are more likely to involve summative evaluations). Similarly, if the department has a graduate program, peer review of teaching may also occur within the context of any training of graduate students to teach. In all of these situations, the discussion can then turn to how the peer review of teaching can be integrated into the department and move from discrete points in time toward a more continuous part of academic life.

These three key issues - the definition of peer review of teaching, formative vs. summative evaluation, and when peer review of teaching fits into an academic career - are all critical aspects of beginning discussions about the peer review of teaching in a sociology department or program. The next section suggests several strategies for where these conversations might take place within the structure of the department.

STRATEGIES FOR CONTINUING THE CONVERSATION

Demands on faculty time are a major challenge in the academy. Recent data from the UCLA Higher Education Research Institute indicate that only about a third of college and university faculty feel that the balance between their professional and personal lives is healthy. Nearly three quarters feel that a lack of personal time is a stressor in their lives (HERI, 2009). Given this context, it is critical that peer review of teaching is built into structures and processes that already exist within a department. Rather than creating new and separate tasks and activities, the peer review of teaching needs to be incorporated as one of the ways in which we rethink our current work and build a better environment for the teaching and learning of sociology. This section suggests four places where these conversations might fit within existing department activities: 1) during the training of graduate students, 2) when new faculty members are hired, 3) during the regular cycle of external program review, and 4) as part of the annual assessment of student learning outcomes.

Training Graduate Students to Teach

The most logical place to start any pedagogical conversation is at the beginning of an academic career. Thus, examination of the issues related to the peer review of teaching should be built into courses on pedagogy that are offered in graduate programs in sociology (see Chapter 9 in this volume). Many such courses have students develop a range of teaching credentials, often including a teaching portfolio (see Chapter 4 in this volume). There is some evidence, however, that few job listings in sociology request teaching credentials. Analyzing listings in the 1999 ASA Employment Bulletin, Mahaffy and Caffrey (2003) found that while the majority of job advertisements in sociology listed teaching experience, very few requested teaching evaluations, syllabi, or statements of teaching philosophy, and virtually none requested a teaching portfolio. Not surprisingly, data from their analysis indicates that research institutions are much less likely to request these other types of teaching credentials than are colleges and universities with more of a focus upon teaching. Even in those settings, however, less than 20 percent of the listings in their study requested these additional pieces of evidence about the quality of teaching (Mahaffy and Caffrey, 2003: 209).

This situation may well have changed during the past decade. Other analyses of sociology job advertisements indicate clear changes over time in the relative emphasis upon teaching and research (Rau and Baker, 1989; Kain, 2006). In addition, it may be that more evidence of teaching effectiveness may be requested at a later stage in the hiring process, particularly from final candidates. This leads to the next area in which departments might have very productive conversations about the peer review of teaching - during the hiring process itself.

Enriching the Hiring Process

An important and obvious place to have expanded conversations about the peer review of teaching is when a sociology program is making the decision to hire new faculty. In addition to determining what is requested in job listings, planning and carrying out a search is a perfect time for department faculty to talk about how teaching is evaluated. At teaching institutions, it is relatively standard for job candidates to teach a class (or at least present their research as if it were being taught to a group of undergraduates) while they do their on-campus interview (Piker-King *et al.*, 2006). This is less often the case at institutions with a greater focus upon research. Chapter 14 in this volume expands upon this idea of developing a pedagogical colloquium for hiring new faculty.

While many search committee members may have a good sense of how they will evaluate the research productivity/potential of job applicants, they may have thought less about how to evaluate teaching credentials. Indeed, a thorough conversation about how to evaluate the teaching credentials and potential of job applicants can provide the foundation for later conversations about the peer review of teaching of all faculty members in the department.

A productive exercise is to have colleagues work on the development of a rubric for evaluating the teaching credentials found in job candidates' application materials. Appendix A includes a portion of a larger rubric developed by colleagues in my department for a tenure-track search to evaluate all of the parts of applicants' folders, including graduate training, grant support, cover letter, teaching, publications and writing samples, etc. The part reproduced in Appendix A focuses only upon the teaching aspects of the applicants' credentials. Moreover, the types of things included directly reflect items that were enumerated in the job listing. The general rubric has been used for multiple searches, and each time it is modified to reflect the current search. Indeed, it has evolved over time. There is also a distinction between what is peer-reviewed in the original application folders, in comparison to additional materials that are peer-reviewed for finalists who come to campus for an interview. Finally, I would note that this rubric was clearly the result of collaboration among faculty in the department, along with students and external members of various search committees. It is not intended as the end point, rather it is an illustration to help faculty members think about some of the types of things they might want to evaluate as they are peer reviewing the teaching materials provided by job candidates.

External Program Reviews

Most institutions have a regular cycle during which departments and programs are evaluated by an external reviewer. If that external reviewer is a member of the ASA's Department Resources Group, then the evaluation of the undergraduate program is typically organized around a set of national guidelines found in *Liberal Learning and the Sociology Major: Meeting the Challenge of Teaching Sociology in the Twenty-First Century* (McKinney *et al.*, 2004). An external review is typically preceded by an extended period of time during which a department does a careful self-study, usually following specified guidelines prescribed by the home institution.

A number of the recommendations in *Liberal Learning* can lead to discussions about the peer review of teaching, particularly in the context of a formative review. For example, the extent to which course syllabi and activities reflect national recommendations about the sociology major can provide a relevant set of criteria for the peer review of teaching in a sociology department. Some departments have also found it productive to have a periodic retreat, during which all of the faculty review the year and evaluate the strengths and weaknesses in the program. Choosing several of the recommendations in *Liberal Learning* as the focus of the retreat can be a way to build a stronger program over time. Colleagues can share teaching materials and activities related to those recommendations in a way that resembles a type of teaching circle (see Chapter 5 in this volume), and it can provide a forum for the formative peer review of teaching that focuses upon one or two specific curricular issues.

Assessment of Student Learning Outcomes

One of the recommendations in *Liberal Learning* is "Departments should assess the sociology program on a regular basis using multiple sources of data, including data on student learning" (McKinney *et al.*, 2004: iii). This is a reflection of a growing interest in assessment and accountability at all levels of the academic enterprise. On an annual basis, a department can focus upon a few of the specific student learning outcomes that are included in their assessment plan. (For guidance on developing an assessment plan in sociology, see Lowry *et al.*, 2005). This is yet another place where departments can have fruitful discussions about how both the formative and summative peer review of teaching can improve the teaching and learning of sociology.

SUMMARY COMMENTS

Increased attention upon the peer review of teaching is but one aspect of the many changes in higher education that have occurred over the past three decades. The goal of this chapter has been to provide some guidance for ways to begin conversations about the peer review of teaching is sociology departments and programs. As outlined in the first half of the chapter, three issues are central to those discussions—defining peer review, formative versus summative evaluation, and the timing of peer review. Several key processes in which these conversations may be fruitfully developed are during the training of graduate students, when new faculty members are hired in sociology, when the sociology program has an external review, and as part of the yearly assessment of student learning outcomes in sociology

REFERENCES

Arreola, Raoul A. 2006. *Developing a Comprehensive Faculty Evaluation System: A Guide to Designing, Building, and Operating Large-Scale Faculty Evaluation Systems.* (3rd ed.), Bolton, MA: Anker.

Centra, John A. 1993. *Reflective Faculty Evaluation: Enhancing Teaching and Determining Faculty Effectiveness.* San Francisco, CA: Jossey-Bass.

Chism, Nancy Van Note. 2007. *Peer Review of Teaching: A Sourcebook*, Second Edition. Anker Publishing.

Higher Education Research Institute at UCLA. 2009. "The American College Teacher: National Norms for 2007-2008." *HERI Research Brief.* Los Angeles, CA: HERI. Downloaded 26 February, 2010. (http://www.heri.ucla.edu/publications-brp.php)

Huston, Therese, and Carol L. Weaver. 2008. "Peer Coaching: Professional Development for Experienced Faculty." *Innovative Higher Education* 33:5-20.

Hutchings, Pat, (ed.). 1995. *From Idea to Prototype: The Peer Review of Teaching: A Project Workbook.* Sterling, VA: Stylus.

Kain, Edward L. 2006. "Bridging the Gap between Cultures of Teaching and Cultures of Research." *Teaching Sociology* 34(4):325-340.

Lowry, Janet Huber, et al. 2005. *Creating an Effective Assessment Plan for the Sociology Major.* Washington, DC: American Sociological Association.

Mahaffy, Kimberly A., and Elizabeth M. Caffrey. 2003. "Are Requests for Teaching Credentials Customary? A Content Analysis of the 1999 *Employment Bulletin.*" *Teaching Sociology* 31(2):203-211.

McKinney, Kathleen, Carla B. Howery, Kerry J. Strand, Edward L. Kain, and Catherine White Berheide. 2004. *Liberal Learning and the Sociology Major Updated: Meeting the Challenge of Teaching Sociology in the Twenty-First Century.* Washington, DC: American Sociological Association.

Morehead, Jere W., and Peter J. Shedd. 1997. "Utilizing Summative Evaluation Through External Peer Review of Teaching." *Innovative Higher Education* Vol. 22, No. 1, Fall 1997: 37-44.

Piker-King, Kathleen, Edward L. Kain, Keith A. Roberts, and Gregory L. Weiss. 2006. *Applying for a Faculty Position in a Teaching-Oriented Institution* (2nd Edition). Washington, DC: ASA Teaching Resources Center.

Quinlan, Kathleen M. 1996. "Involving Peers in the Evaluation and Improvement of Teaching: A Menu of Strategies." *Innovative Higher Education*, 20(4):299-307.

Rau, William, and Paul J. Baker. 1989. "The Organized Contradictions of Academe: Barriers Facing the Next Academic Revolution." *Teaching Sociology* 17:161-75.

Sullivan, Teresa A. 1995. "Teaching Evaluation by Peers." *Teaching Sociology* 23(1):61-63.

Wagenaar, Theodore C. 1995. "Student Evaluation of Teaching: Some Cautions and Suggestions." *Teaching Sociology* 23(10:64-68.

Appendix A: Sample rubric for evaluating the teaching credentials and potential of job applicants*

Exceptional teacher and mentor, and Demonstrated excellence, creativity in undergraduate teaching	Range of Experience	Multiple	One	Only TA'd	
	Statement of Teaching Philosophy	Impressive	Good	Weak	
	Creative Imaginative Teaching	Has done, evidence	Talks about wanting to do	No mention	
	Mentors well	Has done, well	Talks about wanting to do	No mention	
	Teaching Award	Has Won multiple	Has won one	none	
	Teaches Reflexively	Has done	Talks about doing	No mention	
Intro	Introductory course	Has taught (well)	Statement says could teach well	No mention weak version	
Methods	Ethnographic Methods	Has Taught (well)	Statement says could teach well	No mention Weak version	
Senior	Senior Research Capstone	Has taught?	Talks about smartly in teaching statement or letter	No mention Weak version	
Upper level electives	Expands our course offerings	With 2-3 courses	With 1 course	No mention	List courses
Experiential	Experiential (research/Study)	Has done (well)	Writes well about doing	No mention	
Activist	Activist/Service Learning/ Social Justice	Has done (well)	Writes well about doing	No mention	
Interdisc.	Interdisciplinary Programs	Has worked in/with-list:	Mentions in teaching statement/letter	No mention	List programs
In a liberal arts context	Understands Liberal Arts	Went to or Taught At	Writes Smartly About	Does not mention	
	Enthusiastic about being at a liberal arts school	Writes exuberantly about	Interested	Does not mention	
	Specifically interested in our campus	Writes smartly about	Somewhat notes	Does not mention	
	To Be Assessed For Finalists				
	Writing Sample	Impressive	Good	Weak	Comments
	Letters Consider both quality of letter, and letter writer	Impressive	Good	Weak	
	Course Descriptions	Impressive	Good	Weak	
	Course Syllabi	Impressive	Good	Weak	
	Teaching Evaluations	Impressive	Good	Weak	
Language Proficiency		Impressive	Good	Weak	

*This is drawn from a more complete rubric that has evolved in the Department of Sociology and Anthropology at Southwestern University. It is updated and revised to reflect the current job listing. This most recent version reflects input from current faculty members: Reginald A. Byron, Melissa Johnson, Maria R. Lowe, and Sandi Kawecka Nenga.

13

Peer Review: The Role of the Department Chair

J. Michael Brooks, South University

INTRODUCTION

As one looks back to the not-so-distant past, being a department chair may seem to have been much easier than it now is. Whether one looks to issues of curriculum development and planning, faculty recruitment and promotion, the role of graduate and undergraduate students in the department, the generation of resources, equity and human rights issues, or the processes of building a collegial environment, we live and work in an era characterized by accountability, assessment, a fear of the litigious, threats to tenure, and the rapid growth of online education. Sorcinelli (2007) found that survey respondents typically worried most commonly about the issues of changes in the nature of the professoriate, the changing nature of the student body, and changes in the nature of teaching, learning, and scholarship. For some, these seem to interact in ways that threaten those virtues that drew them to the academy in the first place. Indeed, Chairs find themselves fending off budget cuts, legislators who would micro-manage, accreditation agencies requiring ever-increasing levels of assessment, and students who are becoming sophisticated consumers and "system-workers", shopping for what they perceive to be the "best deal" in higher education.

All of these issues make being a department chair difficult and challenging at best. While most colleges and universities have gone to chair systems, many still use a headship system. In theory, the difference is significant, with the chair usually serving an elected and/or fixed term at the pleasure of his/her colleagues, while the head serves at the pleasure of the dean for as long as either wants the person in the headship to continue. Reality suggests, however, that chairs who ignore the wishes of the dean and higher administration, or heads who dismiss the views of their departmental colleagues, do so at significant risk to their careers or to their departments.

An additional consideration, however, is that the role of the chair is itself fuzzy. Being a department chair (the term chair in this chapter will be used to include department heads) is a difficult and challenging role, arguably the hardest job in the academy. It requires the person to negotiate often conflicting realities that lie between two very differently constructed social arenas, that of the faculty and that of the administration. Whether the issue is the evaluation of colleagues or any of the other issues mentioned above, the chair must be organizationally savvy and interpersonally adept to survive in the world of higher education as presently constructed.

The purpose of this chapter is to examine the role of the chair in developing, implementing, and interpreting peer review programs. Stated more broadly, this chapter will seek to identify ways that department chairs can lead their faculty colleagues in developing innovative ways of collaborating in their cooperative endeavors (including the evaluation of each other in both formative and summative ways), while also helping the department accommodate to the demands being made on it by the administration and those to whom that administration is accountable. Issues surrounding the peer review of teaching will form the basis of this discussion, which will hopefully provide insights that may be generalized to other issues of departmental governance as well. This discussion will first look briefly at some of the major changes in higher education to provide a context for a discussion of peer review and the chair's role in it. Next will be a more focused look at peer review and the role of the chair in facilitating this process. Finally, a discussion of some specific actions a chair might pursue in the interest of developing a peer review program will be presented.

CHANGES IN HIGHER EDUCATION

In 1995, Barr and Tagg boldly announced a new paradigm for undergraduate education. They argued that the paradigm which has governed higher education has been what they call an "instructional paradigm," with the main mission of providing instruction. What they saw emerging in higher education was a paradigm that stresses students learning "by whatever means work best" (Barr and Tagg, 1995: 13). They continued in some detail spelling out the assumptions of the new "learning paradigm" and contrasting it to dominant "instructional paradigm."

One of the missions associated with the learning paradigm is improving the quality of the student learning that occurs. Thus, learning is emphasized within environments that stress cross-disciplinary and inter-departmental collaboration. (Hamilton & Gaff, 2009) In turn, this changes the roles and relationships within the academy. Notably, faculty move away from the role of the sole provider of a unit of instruction (e.g., a certain number of lectures over a certain period of time to a large number of students) to the role of collaborator. However, this can only occur in an environment that stresses teamwork and collaboration, working with peers and with students to find those methods that produce learning. All of this occurs in a collegial and cooperative environment that is minimally hierarchical, stressing open-ended procedures and asynchronous learning rather than the dominant bureaucratized model that serves only to turn faculty into private entrepreneurs alienated from each other and from students.

If student learning is the most obvious casualty under the traditional paradigm, we can also argue that collegiality becomes a serious problem as well. Many department chairs will agree that creating an atmosphere of true collegiality is difficult at best. While we all hear of such places, we also know that they are few and far between. Massy, Wilger, and Colbeck (1994) coined the term "hollowed collegiality" to describe the fragmented and isolated qualities of life in most academic departments. They attribute this inability to collaborate on teaching to three key features of academic life:
1. Fragmented communication patterns, which isolate individual faculty members and prevent them from interacting around issues of undergraduate education;
2. Tight resources, which limit opportunities and strain faculty relationships;
3. The prevailing methods of evaluation and reward, which undermine attempts to create an environment more conducive to faculty interaction. (Massy, et. Al, 1994: 11)

In a similar vein, Schulman (1993) suggested that teaching will never be seen as a scholarly act equal to that of research and publication until such time as it becomes what he called "community property" (Schulman, 1993: 6-7). He went on to say "...we celebrate those aspects of our lives and work that can become... community property" (Schulman, 1993: 6-7). To raise the status of teaching, we must reconnect it to the disciplines rather than ceding its improvement to outside centers. We must also make the artifacts of teaching visible and then judge them. If teaching is community property and is to be valued, there must be a visible, tangible product that is evaluated.

For Schulman, this meant the peer review of teaching (Schulman, 1993: 6-7). Peer review, in turn, means a change in the culture of teaching, locating teaching in the academic enterprise where it can be valued, and where positive outcomes can be rewarded for all who participate in the learning environment. Indeed, peer review goes to the heart of the social contract that guides many professions in the performance of their duties (Hamilton, 2007). In the case of higher education, peer review refers to the practice whereby faculty members and the college or university administration assume the responsibility of reviewing the qualifications and the performance of their fellow faculty members, whether it is in the areas of research and professional development, service, or teaching.

One important benefit from this practice is academic freedom, which is cherished as a way to protect academics and teachers in the extreme from arbitrary and ideologically based dismissal (Hamilton & Gaff, 2009: 28). However, as student learning and the assessment of learning rubrics begin to take precedence, and the teaching and learning process becomes more interdisciplinary, the importance of the individual teacher and the assessment of teaching as an act may diminish while the assessment of products produced in the name of learning may increase (Reder, 2007: 9, Hamilton & Gaff, 2009: 29).

DEVELOPING PEER REVIEW

It seems clear that peer review offers us an opportunity to address some of the issues that plague the academic department, not to mention the life of the chair. As Weimer (1990) has pointed out, "Faculty, like other people, look to their leaders for all sorts of abstract qualities and characteristics. They look for role models... (and) given this fact, academic leaders must not underestimate the power of their own example to motivate faculty to pursue instructional excellence" (Weimer, 1990: 143). Perhaps the first rule for any department chair, then, is to pursue peer review only after being sure that the approach is one that s/he already practices and can support.

It may not be as difficult as it sounds to begin moving toward peer review. Hutchings (1995) offers us a number of insights into beginning the process, the first being that under the right circumstances, faculty actually want to talk to colleagues about teaching. She points out that even faculty whose primary identity is that of researchers eagerly discuss teaching when it involves talking about their own fields and their own students (Hutchings, 1995). In such discussions, teaching becomes less technique and more the transformation of ideas (Hutchings, 1995), a scholarly act, to use Boyer's (1990) concept.

More recent research does seem to indicate that the peer review of teaching is generally supported by faculty in many settings, and that it can have positive outcomes (Kohut, et al, 2007; Switkes, 1999; Douglas and Douglas, 2006). Peer review can range from the deceptively simple act of getting faculty to talk to one another about their teaching, to sharing their scholarly approaches and successes as well as their problems (see Chapter 3 in this volume). In addition, peer review includes the documentation of teaching - the production of artifacts that allow others from within the department or discipline (as well as those from other departments or other campuses), to assess the quality of what is occurring in the name of teaching and learning. In other words, it can be used for both formative and summative purposes, with its most basic agenda being the sharing of ideas and practices that encourage and support the improvement of faculty teaching and student learning.

If others are to reflect on these artifacts, the faculty member being reviewed should also be given the opportunity to reflect on what they are doing. Many faculty across many types of colleges and universities are now commonly required to produce what amounts to a teaching portfolio (see Chapter 4 in this volume) as a part of their promotion or tenure packet. These usually include a statement by the candidate of their philosophy of teaching as well as their reflections on their actual teaching, including examples of student work and student evaluations. Indeed, the process of reflection, as a part of the peer review process, is a significant and valuable component in the development and improvement of the quality of teaching.

Change is clearly in the wind. If we believe the reports published in the *Chronicle of Higher Education* and other works cited in this volume, faculty value teaching and want to elevate it. Many likely embrace the new "paradigm of learning" as the focal point. Why, then, should we include peer review in the changes that are on the horizon? Edgerton, et. al: (1995) offers us five reasons:

1. Learning to teach involves learning from experience; and to learn from experience requires the assistance of colleagues.
2. In reaching sophisticated judgments about the quality of teaching, "peer perspectives" are essential.

3. Faculty value, more than anything else, the regard of their scholarly peers. Thus, teaching will not be considered a scholarly endeavor until it is evaluated and reviewed by peers.
4. Public concern for the cost and quality of higher education is leading to policies designed to make higher education more accountable. The best antidote to bureaucratic accountability is for higher education to strengthen its own mechanisms of professional accountability. Peer review is one of these.
5. Peer review is a professional responsibility; we owe it to ourselves and to our students to ensure the quality of what we do as teachers (Edgerton, et al, 1995: 1–5).

The question of what to include in a peer review program can only be answered over time, and in close discussions with one's faculty colleagues. Approaches to peer review vary greatly and include virtually any activity that a collection of faculty might consider relevant. Most commonly, activities include at least some of the following, although this list is by no means exhaustive:

1. Portfolios: Course, Teaching, and Student Learning
2. Mentoring systems for:
   a. Graduate teaching assistants
   b. Part-time faculty
   c. New faculty/untenured faculty
   d. All teaching faculty
3. Group Collaboration
   a. Pairing up for mutual assistance
   b. Teaching Circles for individuals, multi-sectioned courses, general education courses
   c. As part of program reviews (e.g., for accreditation)
4. Classroom Observations/Videotaping
5. Development of an in-house teaching-oriented listserv
6. Development of teaching libraries
   a. General references on teaching and learning
   b. Collections of portfolios from the department
   c. Collections of online references and sites to which faculty can turn for support and information
7. Pedagogical Colloquia
8. Graduate courses on pedagogy in the field
9. Faculty Retreats
10. Rewards/Recognition for teaching excellence
11. Active involvement of students in peer review beyond the standard end-of-term ratings sheets

12. Regular use of peer review information in the assessment of programs

The menu of possibilities above likely only scratches the surface of the possibilities available to any department chair under the general rubric of peer review. Programs are in place at many colleges and universities including such highly regarded institutions as the University of California at Berkeley. But how does one move from an imposing list of possibilities to a plan in place? The role of the chair might include at least the following activities.

1. Disseminate information regarding skillful instructional practices in the discipline, and encourage frequent discussions of effective teaching and learning practices among one's colleagues.
2. Create and support significant departmentally-based training programs for all graduate teaching assistants (and part-time faculty) that models and promotes exemplary teaching and learning.
3. Focus on teaching excellence as well as scholarly productivity in hiring new faculty. Never take teaching skills as a given based only on degrees achieved and schools attended.
4. Create and support formal, though voluntary, mentoring programs for new or untenured faculty that pay significant attention to enhancing the quality of teaching and learning.
5. Visibly recognize and reward teaching excellence in the department.
6. Create activities that require faculty collaboration within the department to address important instructional issues and concerns.
7. Model ways faculty can use technological or other innovative approaches to teaching and learning, and support the efforts of others to do so.
8. Encourage all faculty (and graduate students entering the job market) to create teaching and/or course portfolios.
9. Recognize that even the most seasoned faculty member may have questions about how to improve teaching or reach students with their ideas and objectives. (Huston and Weaver, 2008: 5).
10. Design and pursue a professional development plan to become a more skillful and effective chair.

CONCLUSIONS

In moving forward with any peer review process, one must certainly avoid two huge pitfalls. First, one must not attempt to do too much too soon, and certainly not more than can be handled by one's colleagues or accepted by the administration. On the other hand, doing nothing in the face of pressures for accountability, assessment, and the need to improve teaching and learning is simply no longer an option. The other major pitfall is to develop a plan that has the support of the dean or others up the ladder, but lacks the blessings of the faculty who will be most affected by it. As one of my faculty colleagues stated in a departmental meeting, "Teaching circles are fine as long as they are voluntary". The organizationally savvy chair will recognize the wisdom inherent in that comment. If faculty do not feel a sense of investment and ownership, the best laid plans will founder on the rocks of resistance by the very people you sought to benefit.

Creamer and Creamer (1990) have developed a plan for the implementation of change that takes into account significant organizational and interpersonal dimensions. They refer to it as the Probability of Acceptance (PAC) model. A number of key variables are involved, each of which a wise chair will consider in developing a peer review plan. These include the circumstances driving the proposed change and the compatibility of the change with existing values that define the organizational culture. The comprehensibility of the idea , its perceived practicality, and the degree of top-level support that may exist (or be developed) are also important. Also important for success are the leadership to focus the issues and to coordinate the strategies that might be used to implement the idea, along with the need for someone to champion the idea. Lastly, perceptions regarding whether anything is to be gained and by whom are important (Creamer and Creamer, 1990). All of these dimensions help focus the activities of the chair who likely will become the champion of the peer review system, the one who may provide the focus from which the final plan emerges, and the liaison between the department to the rest of the college and university.

Resistance will come and criticisms can and will be raised, not only of particular components of any plan that emerges, but also of the entire concept of peer review. Singer (1989) and Lamont (2009), for example, discusses critiques of the process of peer review for grants and refereed journals that point out the difficulties of doing a proper review, and the fact that originality and significance are often buried under layers of bureaucratic or other criteria that may or may not have anything to do with quality.

What he is pointing out, however, is that structure has been allowed to subdue process. In the interest of getting the evaluation done, we have allowed criteria to overwhelm the real mission of recognizing when knowledge is truly being encouraged or developed.

Peer review, properly done, is an on-going process, not just a structure or a menu of items applied to whatever set of credentials happens to be in front of us. Perhaps the chair's single greatest challenge, then, is to assure that once the commitment is made to embark on a program of peer review, the dialogue of development and discovery continues, thus maintaining and enhancing the process. To do otherwise is to allow structure to overwhelm process, to the detriment of the innovations we all seek.

REFERENCES

Barr, R. B. and Tagg, J. 1995. "From Teaching to Learning: A New Paradigm for Undergraduate Education". *Change* (November/December: 13–25.

Boyer, E. 1990. *Scholarship Reconsidered: Priorities of the Professoriate.* Lawrenceville, NJ: Princeton University Press.

Creamer, D. G. and Creamer, E. G. 1990. "Use of a Planned Change Model to Modify Student Affairs Programs" in D. Creamer, (Ed.), *College Student Development: Theory and Practice for the 1990s* Alexandria, VA: American College Personnel Assoc. 181-192.

Douglas, J. and Douglas, A. 2006. *Evaluating Teaching Quality* (April) 12 (1): 3–13.

Edgerton, R., Hutchings, P., Quinlan, P. & Schulman, L.. 1995. "From Idea to Prototype: The Peer Review of Teaching – Starting the Conversation. *From Idea to Prototype: The Peer Review of Teaching* by Pat Hutchings. Washington, DC: AAHE.

Hamilton, N. W. 2007. "Faculty Autonomy and Obligation". *Academe* 93(1): 36–43.

Hamilton, N. W. and Gaff, J. G.. 2009. *The Future of the Professoriate: Academic Freedom, Peer Review, and Shared Governance.* Washington, DC: Association of American Colleges and Universities.

Huston, T. and Weaver, C. L.. 2008. "Peer Coaching: Professional Development for Experienced Faculty". *Innovative Higher Education* 33: 5–20.

Hutchings, P. 1995. *From Idea to Prototype: The Peer Review of Teaching, A Project Workbook.* Washington, DC: AAHE.

Lamont, M. 2009. *How Professors Think: Inside the Curious World of Academic Judgment.* Cambridge: Harvard University Press

Kohut, G. F., Burnap, C. and Yon, M. G. 2007. "Peer Observation of Teaching: Perceptions of the Observer and the Observed". *College Teaching* 55 (1): 19–25.

Massy, W. F., Wilger, A. K., and Colbeck, C. 1994. "Overcoming 'Hollowed' Collegiality". *Change* (July/August): 11–19.

Reder, M. 2007. "Does Your College *Really* Support Teaching and Learning?". *Peer Review* 9: 9–13.

Schulman, L. 1993. "Teaching as Community Property: Putting an End to Pedagogical Solitude". *Change* (November/December): 6–7.

Singer, B. D. 1989. "The Criterial Crisis of the Academic World". *Sociological Inquiry* 59 (May): 127–141.

Sorcinelli, M. D. 2007. "Faculty Development: The Challenge Going Forward". *Peer Review* 9: 4–8.

Switkes, E.1999. "University of California Peer Review System and Post-tenure Evaluation". *Innovative Higher Education* 24 (1): 39–48.

Weimer, M. E. 1990. *Improving College Teaching.* San Francisco: Jossey-Bass.

14

The Pedagogical Colloquium*

Carla Howery

It can reasonably be argued that the two most important decisions in a department are hiring and tenure. While departments have invested considerable time and effort (as well as considerable rancor) in determining the procedures and standards for awarding tenure, it is often not the case for hiring new tenure-track (or other) faculty. How odd that we hire faculty to teach and often do not advertise for the specific teaching skills for which they are hired. In addition, rarely do we ask for any documentation of class preparation, an evaluation of teaching talents, or a demonstration of ability in the classroom. Instead we focus on their research experience, skills, and potential for future publications.

In recent years, that situation has been changing. A Harvard task force (2006) was charged with exploring the use of a number of promising opportunities to improve teaching. "What if applicants for professorships presented not only their research but a 'pedagogical colloquium' in which they dissected a syllabus, explained how to help students master an especially difficult concept, or detailed a teaching innovation?" (p. 63) Similarly, at the University of Wisconsin, their web-based information on peer review makes it clear - "Important things get talked about. To help instructors ... raise the profile of teaching, we must, therefore, create opportunities that encourage instructors to take time to talk about teaching and learning on a regular basis." (Wisconsin)

Others (Theall 1999, Braxton 2008, Chism 2006) have argued that pedagogical colloquia are among the basic characteristics of peer exchange and review that are central to the development of campus cultures that motivate faculty to teach. Moreover, the utility of the device clearly crosses disciplinary boundaries. Scholars from disparate fields such as mathematics (Bruff 2007), occupational therapy (Nolinske 1997), religious studies (Stanford 1997), and political science (McClellan 2007) argue that pedagogical colloquia have clear benefits for the hiring process.

In Atlanta some years ago, at an American Association for Higher Education conference on "Faculty Roles and Rewards," a panel presented models of effective "pedagogical colloquia" to address the weakness of teaching credentials in the hiring process. The idea of the pedagogical colloquium was initially suggested by Shulman (1995) in part as a response to the concern from faculty at liberal arts and other teaching-oriented institutions to identify candidates who were clearly capable of teaching. He saw it as a means for departments to evaluate both the teaching and the research potential of a candidate, since both were going to be important to the future career of the candidate and to the future of the department.

In general, the pedagogical colloquium is modeled after the standard research colloquium, a session of an hour or two where candidates for a faculty position lay out their interests and accomplishments, and then field questions. In this case the agenda is teaching. One desired outcome of asking all candidates to do both a research and a pedagogical colloquium (or a single session combining both elements) is the message it sends about the importance of effective teaching in the department and the commitment to collegial discussion about teaching. As Hutchings (1996) points out, in addition to the additional information for evaluation it provides of the candidate, it also serves the improvement of teaching by opening up the conversation about departmental expectations regarding teaching. Hutchings goes on to say, "Indeed, this seemingly secondary consequence of the pedagogical colloquium may be as important as its primary purpose." (1996:PAGE)

Some departments ask a candidate to actually teach a class. This approach is valuable, primarily because it allows faculty to see the candidate interact with students, manage subject matter, and communicate orally. The candidate benefits by meeting some of the students at the institution and gains some understanding about their pedagogical challenges. However, having a candidate teach a class could disrupt the flow of a course, and it is often difficult to coordinate the timing of the candidate visit, the candidate's expertise, and the appropriate unit in a course. The pedagogical colloquium not only gets around those logistic problems but also has other advantages: a forum to showcase not only the candidate's pedagogical and communication skills, but the *intellectual underpinnings* and scholarly engagement she or he brings to teaching.

SOME SUCCESS STORIES

Panelists at the Atlanta conference who reported on pedagogical colloquia in their departments included a historian at Stanford University and a mathematician at the University of Georgia. They reported that their faculty learned a great deal more about a candidate by having multiple sources of evidence about scholarly performance. In some cases, a candidate who was strong in one colloquium was weak in the other, and the faculty wrestled with these inconsistencies. They also felt they made better hires as a result, because the conversations about teaching gave each party a better sense of the degree to which the candidate and the department "fit." The discussion which resulted from the pedagogical colloquia provided considerable information about the candidate, and about the department as well. After all, an interview flows both ways, and it is important for a candidate to see how the faculty interact, how their questions and discussion reveals their commitments, and the nature of the department's teaching mission.

In addition, graduate students attending the colloquia commented on its usefulness, and asked for faculty help in preparing a presentation on teaching for their own job interviews. Finally, most departments began to scrutinize other aspects of their hiring process as well as their instructional mission. Employment ads spoke more precisely about the types of teaching skills sought (e.g., experience with large classes, or educational technology, or with simulations). No longer acceptable were the reference letters saying, "although I have never seen him teach, I am sure he is excellent."

Questions could be asked about candidates who had been fully funded for their graduate work, or who for other reasons had had no teaching experience. Some faculty have suggested they would simply not invite such a candidate for an interview. This seems particularly appropriate for a teaching oriented institution. Wright et al (2004) and Howery (1998) underscore this position when they discuss the need to take institutional context into account. Others felt there might be ways in which a candidate could prepare, nonetheless. The candidate could speak about his/her own intellectual history, the qualities of those faculty who were particularly effective (and – unnamed - perhaps ineffective) as teachers, the teaching implications of her/his research, and the core ideas in the field which would be important to include in an introductory course. Candidates could even prepare hypothetical syllabi and course activities.

Shulman (1995) has called for the academy "to make

teaching community property." Teaching needs to be part of public scholarly discourse. The pedagogical colloquium allows departments to evaluate a candidate in a new and important way, to have triangulation of multiple sources of information about different forms of scholarship, and to take seriously the link between demonstrable qualifications and the job for which someone is hired. This innovation is an idea whose time has come.

* This essay was adapted in part from an article that appeared in *Footnotes*, February, 1996, p. 4

REFERENCES

----------. 2006. "Taking Teaching Seriously." *Harvard Magazine.* November/December: 60-65

Braxton, J. M. 2008. "Toward a Theory of Faculty Professional Choices in Teaching that Foster College Student Success." Pp. 181-208 in J. C. Smart (ed). *Higher Education: Handbook of Theory and Research*, Springer

Bruff, D. 2007. "Valuing and Evaluating Teaching in the Mathematics Hiring Process." Notices of the American Mathematical Society. 54 (120): 1308-1315.

Chism, N. V. N. 2006. "Examples of Peer Exchange and Review." Peer-to-Peer Protocols: Faculty Peer Evaluation of Teaching, winter Teaching and Learning Conference, Temple University, January: 1-3.

England, J. 1996. "How Evaluations of Teaching are Used in Personnel decisions." In England, J, Hutchings, P. and McKeachie, W. *The Professional Evaluation of Teaching*, Occasional Paper 33, American Council of Learned Societies.
http://archives.acls.org/op/33 Professional Evaluation of Teaching.htm

Howery, C. 1998 "Making Teaching and Small College Faculty More Cosmopolitan." In Godfrey, E. (ed), *Teaching Sociology in Small Institutions*, American Sociological Association, 1998.:253-266

McMclellan, E. F. 2007. "One Size Does not Fit All: Incorporating Peer Review of Teaching in Departmental Assessment Programs." Presented at the American Political Science Association Teaching and Learning Conference, Charlotte, NC,: 1-13.

Nolinkse, T. 1997. "Preparing and Developing faculty Through Faculty Development Initiatives." *The American Journal of Occupational Therapy.* 53(1): 9-13

Shulman, L. 1988 "Teaching as Community Property." *Change*. 20:6-7

Shulman, L. 1995. "Faculty Hiring: The Pedagogical Colloquium: Three Models." AAHE Bulletin. 47(9): 6-9

----------. "Promoting a Culture of Teaching: The Pedagogical Colloquium." *Speaking of Teaching*. Stanford University Newsletter on Teaching, Spring, 1997: 1-4

Theall, M. 1999. "Motivation from Within: Approaches for Encouraging Faculty and Students to Excel." *New Directions for Teaching and Learning*. Jossey-Bass.

----------. 2010. "How can I help raise the profile of teaching in my department?" University of Wisconsin Teaching Academy. http://teachingacademy.wisc.edu/archive/assistance/MOO/profile.htm

Wright, et al. 2004. "Greedy Institutions: The Importance of Institutional context for Teaching in Higher Education" *Teaching Sociology*. 32 (2): 144-159

V

RESOURCES

15

Bibliography on the Peer Review of Teaching

Carla Howery

This material was compiled over a period of years by Carla, with the assistance of ASA staff from the Academic and Professional Affairs Program. I updated it from the references provided in the preceding chapters. However, it also includes a large number of relevant materials that do not appear in any of the chapters. Similarly, the individual chapters often contain web-based references that are not included in this bibliography.

American Association for Higher Education. 1985. *Integrity in the College Curriculum: A Report to the Academic Community.* Washington DC: American Association for Higher Education.

----------. 1994. "Peer Review of Teaching Initiative." *AAHE Bulletin.* 46(10):16+

----------. 1995. *From Idea to Prototype: The Peer Review of Teaching (A Project Workbook).* Washington, DC: American Association for Higher Education.

----------. 1998. 'About AAHE's Peer Review of Teaching Project', *AAHE Bulletin.* Feb: 12.

American Association of University Professors. 1998. "Post-Tenure Review: An AAUP Response. *Academe* 84(5): 61-67.

American Historical Association. 1993. "Redefining Historical Scholarship." Report of the American Historical Association Ad Hoc Committee on Redefining Scholarly Work. December.

American Mathematical Society. 1994. "Recognition and Rewards in the Mathematical Sciences." Report of the Joint Policy Board for Mathematics Committee on Professional Recognition and Rewards May.

American Sociological Association. 1991. *Liberal Learning and the Sociology Major*. Washington, DC: American Sociological Association.

Abrami, P.C. 1985. "Dimensions of Effective College Instruction." *Review of Higher Education*. 8: 211-28.

Abrami, P.C., S. d'Apollonia, and S. Rosenfield. 1997. "The Dimensionality of Student Ratings: What We Know, What We Do Not." Pp. 321-367 in *Effective Teaching in Higher Education: Research and Practice*, edited by R.P. Perry and J.C. Smart. Edison, NJ: Agathon.

Alagna, Sheryle Whitcher. 1982. "Sex Role Identity, Peer Evaluation of Competition, and the Responses of Women and Men in a Competitive Situation." *Journal of Personality and Social Psychology* 43 (3):546-554.

Albert, R and R. Hipp. 1976. "Videotape Recording in the Preparation of College Sociology Teachers," *Teaching Sociology*, 3: 327-338

Aleamoni, L.M. and M. Yimer. 1973. "An Investigation of the Relationship Between Colleague Rating, Student Rating, Research Productivity, and Academic Rank in Rating Instructional Effectiveness." *Journal of Educational Psychology* 64 (3): 274-77.

Allen, D. and K. Ryan. 1969. *Microteaching*. Reading, MA: Addison-Wesley.

Anderson, Erin, ed. 1993. *Campus Use of the Teaching Portfolio: 25 Profiles*. Washington, DC: American Association for Higher Education.

Anderson-Patton, V. and E. Bass. 2002. "Using Narrative Teaching Portfolios for Self-Study." Pp. 101-114 in *Narrative Inquiry in Practice: Advancing the Knowledge of Teaching*. New York: Teachers College Press.

Angelo, Thomas A. 1989. "Faculty Development for Learning: The Promise of Classroom Research" *To Improve the Academy: Resources for Student, Faculty and Institutional Development.* 35-60.

Angelo, Thomas A. and K. Patricia Cross. 1993. *Classroom Assessment Techniques: A Handbook for College Teachers.* San Francisco: Jossey-Bass Publishers.

Angelo, Thomas A., ed., *Classroom Research: Early Lessons From Success.* New Directions for Teaching and Learning, no.46. San Francisco: Jossey-Bass.

Aper, Jeffery P. and Judith E. Fry. 2003. "Post-Tenure Review at Graduate Institutions in the United States: Recommendations and Reality." *The Journal of Higher Education* 74(3): 241-260.

Arden, E. Summer. 1989. "Who Should Judge the Faculty?" *The College Board Review*: 37-39. Armstrong, Paul B. 1994. "Deprivatizing the Classroom." *ADE Bulletin* (107):13-19.

Arreola, R.A. 1984. "Evaluation of Faculty Performance: Key Issues." *Changing Practices in Faculty Evaluation*, by P. Seldin. San Francisco: Jossey-Bass.

Arreola, R. (1995). *Developing a Comprehensive Faculty Evaluation System: A Handbook for College Faculty and Administrators on Designing and Operating a Comprehensive Faculty Evaluation System.* Bolton, MA: Anker

Arreola, R. 2000. *Developing a Comprehensive Faculty Evaluation System: A Handbook for College Faculty and Administrators on Designing and Operating a Comprehensive Faculty Evaluation System.* Bolton, Mass.: Anker.

Arreola, Raoul A. 2006. *Developing a Comprehensive Faculty Evaluation System: A Guide to Designing, Building, and Operating Large-Scale Faculty Evaluation Systems.* (3rd ed.), Bolton, MA: Anker.

Ashford, S.J. and L.L. Cummings. 1983. "Feedback as an Individual Resource: Personal Strategies of Creating Information." *Organizational Behavior and Human Performance* 32: 370-98.

Association of American Colleges. 1985. *Integrity in the College Curriculum: A Report to the Academic Community*. Washington, DC: Association of American Colleges.

---------. 1990. *Reports From the Field.* Washington, DC: Association of American Colleges.

Astin, Alexander. 1985. *Achieving Educational Excellence*. San Francisco: Jossey-Bass.

Astin, Alexander. 1996. "Involvement in Learning Revisited: Lessons We Have Learned". *Journal of College Student Development* 37 (March/April): 123–134.

Astin, A.W., and C.B.T. Lee. 1996. "Current Practices in the Evaluation and Training of College Teachers." *Educational Record* 47: 361-75.

Atkinson, D. 1998. "Evaluating Teaching/Learning via Groupware Focus Groups" in Black, B. and Stanley, N. (Eds), *Teaching and Learning in Changing Times*. Proceedings of the 7th Annual Teaching Learning Forum, The University of Western Australia, Perth. 22-27.

Atkinson, Maxine P. 2000. "The Future of Sociology is Teaching? A Vision of the Possible" *Contemporary Sociology*, Vol. 29, No. 2 (Mar., 2000), pp. 329-332.

____. 2001. "The Scholarship of Teaching and Learning: Reconceptualizing Scholarship and Transforming the Academy" *Social Forces* 79(4):1217-1229.

Aubrecht, J.D. 1984. "Better Faculty Evaluation Systems." *Changing Practices in Faculty Evaluation*, by P. Seldin. San Francisco: Jossey-Bass.

Austin, A.E. 1990a. "Supporting the Professor as Teacher: An Evaluation Study of the Lilly Teaching Fellows Program." Paper presented at the 15th annual meeting of the American Association for the Study of Higher Education, Portland, OR., ED 232 554. 38 pp. MF-01; PC-02.

----------. 1990b. *To Leave an Indelible Mark: Encouraging Good Teaching in Research Universities Through Faculty Development: A Study of the Lilly Endowment's Teaching Fellows Program, 1974-1988.* Nashville: Peabody College, Vanderbilt.

----------. 1992a. "Supporting Junior Faculty Through a Teaching Fellows Program." *Developing New and Junior Faculty.* edited by M.D. Sorcinelli and A.E. Austin. New Directions for Teaching and Learning No. 50. San Francisco: Jossey-Bass.

----------. 1992b. "Supporting the Professor as Teacher: The Lilly Teaching Fellows Program." *Review of Higher Education* 16:85-106.

Austin, A.E. and R.G. Baldwin. 1991. *Faculty Collaboration: Enhancing the Quality of Scholarship and Teaching.* ASHE-ERIC Higher Education Report No.7. Washington: Association for the Study of Higher Education. ED 346 805. 138 pp.MF-01; PC-06.

Austin, Ann E., and Roger G. Baldwin. 1991. *Faculty Collaboration: Enhancing the Quality of Scholarship and Teaching.* ASHE-ERIC Higher Education Report, no.7 Washington: The George Washington University School of Education and Human Development.

Aylett, Robert and Kenneth Gregory. 1996. *Evaluating Teacher Quality in Higher Education.* Routledge.

Bachrach, Samuel and Bryan Mundell. 1995. *Images of Schools: Structures and Roles in Organizational Behavior.* Corwin Press.

Baeher, M. 2003. "Overview of Assessment." In S. Beyerlein and D. Apple, *Faculty Guidebook: A Comprehensive Tool for Improving Faculty Performance,* Hampton Beach, NH: Pacific Crest.

Baker, Paul J. 1986. "The Helter-Skelter Relationship Between Teaching and Research." *Teaching Sociology,* 14:50-66.

Baldwin, R.G. and R.T. Blackburn. November/December 1981. "The Academic Career as a Developmental Process." *Journal of Higher Education* 52:598-614.

Baldwin, R.G. March/April 1990. "Faculty Vitality Beyond the Research University." *Journal of Higher Education* 61:160-80.

Ballad, M.J., J. Reardon, and L. Nelson. 1976. "Student and Peer Ratings of Faculty." *Teaching of Psychology* 3:88-91.

Banta, Trudy, Jon P. Lund, Karen E. Black, and Frances W. Oblander. *Assessment in Practice: Putting Principles to Work on College Campuses.* San Francisco: Jossey-Bass, 1996.

Barnes, L.B., C.R. Christiansen, and A.J. Hansen. 1994. *Teaching the Case Method.* Boston, MA: Harvard Business School Press.

Barr, Robert B. and John Tagg. 1995, November/December. "From Teaching to Learning: A New Paradigm for Undergraduate Education." *Change* 13-25.

Barry, N.H. and D.M. Shannon. 1997. "Portfolios in Teacher Education: A Matter of Perspective." *The Educational Forum* 61:320-328.

Barton, J. and A. Collins. 1993. "Portfolios in Teacher Education." *Journal of Teacher Education* 44:200-210.

Bataille, Gretchen M. and Betsy E. Brown. 2006. *Faculty Career Paths: Multiple Routes to Academic Success and Satisfaction.* American Council on Education. Westport: CT: Praeger Publishers.

Batista, E.E. 1976. "The Place of Colleague Evaluation in the Appraisal of College Teaching: A Review of the Literature." *Research in Higher Education* 4:257-71.

Bell, M.E., E.C. Dobson, and J.M. Gram. Fall 1977. "Peer Evaluation As a Method of Faculty Development." *Journal of the College and University Personnel Administration* 28:15-17.

Bennett, W.E. 1987. "Small Group Instructional Diagnosis: A Dialogic Approach to Instructional Improvement for Tenured Faculty." *The Journal of Staff, Program, and Organizational Development* 5(3):100-04.

Bennett, S. and J. Santy. 2009. "A Window on Our Teaching Practice: Enhancing Individual Online Teaching Quality Through Online Peer Observation and Support. A UK Case Study." *Nurse Education in Practice* 9(6):403-406.

Beran, Tanya N. and Jennifer L. Rokosh. 2009. "Instructors' perspectives on the utility of student ratings of instruction." *Instructional Science* 37:171-184.

Bergman, J. 1979. "The Effectiveness of Peer Ratings at the University Level." *Journal of Teaching and Learning* 4(3):34-37.

----------. 1980. "Peer Evaluation of University Faculty." *College Student Journal* (monograph ed.) 14(3, Pt. II):1-21.

Berk, R.A., P.L. Naumann, and S.E. Appling. 2004. "Beyond Student Ratings: Peer Observation of Classroom and Clinical Teaching." *International Journal of Nursing Education Scholarship* 1(1):article 10.

Berkenkotter, Carol. 1995. "The Power and Perils of Peer Review." *Rhetoric Review* 13 (2):245-48. Abraham, M.R. and D.H. Ost. 1978. "Improving Teaching Through Formative Evaluation." *Journal of College Science Teaching* 7: 227-29.

Bernstein, Daniel J. 1996. "A Departmental System for Balancing the Development and Evaluation of College Teaching: A Commentary on Cavanagh." *Innovative Higher Education* 20(4):241-248.

Bernstein, D. et al. 2001. "We Need Objective, Rigorous Peer Review of Teaching." *The Chronicle of Higher Education* 47(17): B24.

Bernstein, D., A.N. Burnett, A. Goodburn, and P. Savory. 2006. *Making Teaching and Learning Visible: Course Portfolios and the Peer Review of Teaching.* Bolton, MA: Anker.

Bernstein, D.J. 2008. "Peer Review and Evaluation of the Intellectual Work of Teaching." *Change: The Magazine of Higher Learning* 40(2):48-51.

Bernstein, D.; Jonson, J.; and Smith, K. 2000. *An Examination of the Implementation of Peer Review of Teaching.* New Directions for Teaching & Learning, no. 83: 73-86.

Berquist, W. 1979. "The Liberal Arts College." *Designing Teaching Improvement Programs*, edited by J. Lindquist. Washington: Council for the Advancement of Small Colleges.

Bergquist, W. and S. Phillips. 1975. *A Handbook for Faculty Development*. Washington, D.C.: Council for the Advancement of Small Colleges.

Bhavsar, V.M. et al. 2000. "Peer Review of Teaching: Lessons Learned from the University of Kentucky." *Journal of Natural Resources and Life Sciences Education* 29: 36-40

Biggs, John. 2001. The reflective institution: Assuring and enhancing the quality of teaching and learning. *Higher Education* 41: 221-238.

Bingham, R. and R. Ottewill. 2001. "Whatever happened to peer review? Revitalising the contribution of tutors to course evaluation" *Quality Assurance in Education* 9:32-39.

Black, L. 1994. *New Directions in Portfolio Assessment*. Portsmouth, NH: Boynton/Cook Publishers.

Black, L. and Cessna, M. A. 2002. "Teaching Circles: Making Inquiry Safe for Faculty." *Teaching Excellence* POD Network, Ft. Collins, CO Vol 14, No 3.

Blackburn, R.T., and M.T. Clark. 1975. "An Assessment of Faculty Performance: Some Correlates Between Administrator, Colleague, Student, and Self-Ratings." *Sociology of Education* 48:342-56.

Blackburn, R.T., J.H. Lawrence, and J.P Bieber, and L. Trautvetter. 1991. "Faculty At Work: Focus on Teaching." *Research in Higher Education* 32:363-81.

Blau, Peter M. 1973. *The Organization of Academic Work*. New York: Wiley.

Bok, Derek. 1986. *Higher Learning*. Cambridge: Harvard University Press.

--------. 2006. *Our Underachieving Colleges: A Candid Look at How Much Students Learn and Why They Should Be Learning More*. Princeton, NJ: Princeton University Press.

Bolander Laksov, Klara, Sarah Mann, and Lars Owe Dahlgren. 2008. "Developing a Community of Practice Around Teaching: A Case Study" *Higher Education Research and Development* 27(2):121-132.

Bowser, B. (1997). *UNC Intercampus Dialogues on Peer Review of Teaching: Results and Recommendations.* World Wide Web. http://cte.uncwil.edu/et/prev1.htm.

Boyer, E. 1990. *Scholarship Reconsidered: New Priorities for the Professoriate.* Princeton: The Carnegie Foundation for the Advancement of Teaching.

Brandenburg, D.C., L.A. Braskamp, and J.C. Ory. Winter 1979. "Considerations for an Evaluation Program of Instructional Quality." *CEDR Quarterly.* 12:8-12.

Braskamp, L.A. 1978. "Colleague Evaluation of Instruction." *Faculty Development and Evaluation in Higher Education* 4:1-9.

Braskamp, L.A. and J.C. Ory. 1994. *Assessing Faculty Work: Enhancing Individual and Institutional Performance.* San Francisco: Jossey-Bass.

Braxton, J. M. 2008. "Toward a Theory of Faculty Professional Choices in Teaching that Foster College Student Success." Pp. 181-208 in J. C. Smart (ed). *Higher Education: Handbook of Theory and Research*, Springer

Brinko, K.T. 1993. "The Practice of Giving Feedback to Improve Teaching: What is Effective?" *Journal of Higher Education* 64(5):574-93.

Briggs, Charlotte L.. 2007. "Curriculum Collaboration: A Key to Continuous Program Renewal" *The Journal of Higher Education* 78(6):676-711.

Britt, N. Jr. 1982. "Faculty Attitudes About Colleague Evaluation of Teaching." *Dissertation Abstracts International* 42:5034A (University Microfilms, No. 82-09886)

Brock, S.C. 1981. "Evaluation-Based Teacher Development." *Handbook of Teacher Evaluation*, edited by J. Millman. Beverly Hills: Sage.

Brooks, Michael. 1987. "Building Commitment to Undergraduate Education: A Structural Response." *Teaching Sociology* 15:376-383.

Bruff, D. 2007. "Valuing and Evaluating Teaching in the Mathematics Hiring Process." *Notices of the American Mathematical Society.* 54 (120): 1308-1315.

Bruffee, Kenneth A. 1993. *Collaborative Learning: Higher Education, Interdependence, and the Authority of Knowledge.* Baltimore: Johns Hopkins University Press.

Buckridge, M. 2008. "Teaching Portfolios: Their Role in Teaching and Learning Policy." *International Journal for Academic Development* 13(2):117-127.

Buschman, L. 2001.-"Using Student Interviews To Guide Classroom Instruction: An Action Research Project." *Teaching Children Mathematics*, Vol 8, No 4: 222-227.

Cambridge, B.L. 1996. "The Paradigm Shifts: Examining Quality of Teaching Through Assessment of Student Learning." *Innovative Higher Education* 20(4):287-298.

Cameron, Jeanne, Tina Stavenhaven-Helgren, Philip Walsh, and Barbara Kobritz. 2002. Assessment as Critical Praxis: A Community College Experience" *Teaching Sociology* 30(4): 414-429.

Campbell, Dorothy, et al. 1997. *How to Develop a Professional Portfolio: A Manual for Teachers.* Boston, MA: Allyn & Bacon.

Campbell, Frederick L. 1985. "Turning toward Teaching." In *Teaching Sociology: The Quest for Excellence*, edited by Frederick L. Campbell, Hubert M. Blalock, Jr., and Reece. Chicago: Nelson-Hall: 3-22.

Carroll, J.G. and S.R. Goldberg. 1989. "Teaching Consultants: A Collegial Approach to Better Teaching." *College Teaching* 37:143-46.

Carroll, M.A. and J.C. Tyson. 1981. "Good Teachers Can Become Better." *Improving College and University Teaching* 29(2):92-94.

Carter, V.K. 2008. "Five Steps to Becoming a Better Peer Reviewer." *College Teaching* 56(2):85-88.

Carton, A.S. 1988. "Linguistics 111." *Turning Professors Into Teachers: A New Approach to Faculty Development and Student Learning*, edited by J. Katz and M. Henry. New York: American Council on Education/Macmillan.

Cashin, William E. 1989: "Defining and Evaluating College Teaching" IDEA Paper No. 21. *Center for Faculty Evaluation and Development*, Kansas State University.

Cavanagh, Ronald R. 1996. "Formative and Summative Evaluation in the Faculty Peer Review of Teaching." *Innovative Higher Education* 20(4):235-240.

Centra, J.A. 1986. "Colleague Evaluation: The Critical Link." Paper presented at the Annual Meeting of the American Educational Research Association, San Francisco. ED 275 722. 6 pp. MF-01; PC-01.

----------. May/June 1975. "Colleagues as Raters of Classroom Instruction." *Journal of Higher Education* 46:327-37.

----------. 1980. *Determining Faculty Effectiveness*. San Francisco: Jossey-Bass Publishers.

----------. 1993. *Reflective Faculty Evaluation: Enhancing Teaching and Determining Faculty Effectiveness*. San Francisco: Jossey-Bass.

----------. 1994 "The Use of the Teaching Portfolio and Student Evaluations for Summative Evaluation." *Journal of Higher Education* 65(5):555-570.

----------. 2000. *Evaluating the Teaching Portfolio: A Role for Colleagues.* New Directions for Teaching & Learning, no. 83: 87-94.

Cerbin, W. 1994. "The Course Portfolio as a Tool for Continuous Improvement of Teaching and Learning." *Journal on Excellence in College Teaching* 5:1.

Cessna, M. A. and Graf, D. 2000. "The Benefits of Teaching Circles."
NEA Higher Education Advocate. 17(6): 4-8

Chen, Y. and Hoshower, L. B. 2003. "Student Evaluation of Teaching
Effectiveness: An Assessment of Student Perception and
Motivation" *Assessment & Evaluation in Higher Education*, Vol 28,
No 1: 71-88.

Chenoweth, T. 1991. "Evaluating Exemplary Teaching." *Journal of
Personnel Evaluation in Education* 4:359-66.

Chickering, A.W. 1984. "Faculty Evaluation: Problems and
Solutions." *Changing Practices in Faculty Evaluations*, edited by P.
Seldin. San Francisco: Jossey-Bass.

Chickering, Arthur, and Zelda Gamson, editors. 1991: *Applying the
Seven Principles for Good Practice in Undergraduate Education.*
San Francisco: Jossey-Bass.

Chism, Nancy Van Note. 1999. *Peer Review of Teaching: A
Sourcebook.* Bolton, MA: Anker Publishing.

----------. 2007. *Peer Review of Teaching: A Sourcebook*, Second
Edition. Anker Publishing.

Chism, N.V.N, W.J. McKeachie, and G.W. Chism. 2007. *Peer Review of
Teaching: A Sourcebook*. Bolton, MA: Anker.

Clark, L., et al. 1991. *Project 30 and the Pedagogy Seminars: A
Report to the Administration and Faculty*. ERIC Document No. 368
687.

Coffman, S.J. 1991. "Improving Your Teaching Through Small-
Group Diagnosis." *College Teaching* 39(2):80-82.

Cohen, P.A. and W.J. McKeachie. 1980. "The Role of Colleagues in
the Evaluation of College Teaching." *Improving College and
University Teaching* 28: 147-54.

Cooke, N., J. Passe, and M. Yon. 1997. "Revisiting and Evaluating the
Peer Observation Process: Perceptions of the Observer and
Observed." Presented at the AAHE Peer Review of Teaching All-
Project Meeting, June 20, Albuquerque, NM.

Cooperrider, D. and D. Whitney. 2005. *Appreciative Inquiry.* San Francisco: Barrett-Koehler Publishers

Copeland, W.D. and R. Jamgochian. March/April 1985. "Colleague Training and Peer Review." *Journal of Teacher Education* 36:18-21.

Coppola, B.P. 1997. "Assessing Student Learning: New Tools and How They Can Inform Our Understanding of Teaching and the Scholarship of Teaching." Presented at the AAHE Peer Review of Teaching All-Project Meeting, June 20, Albuquerque, NM.

Corcoran, K. and S.A. Kirk. 1995. "School Rankings: Mindless Narcissism or Do They Tell Us Something." *Journal of Social Work Education* 31(3):408-14.

Cosser, Michael. 1996. "Introducing the Teaching Portfolio in the University: A Preliminary Investigation." *South African Journal of Higher Education.* 10(2):130-137.

----------. 1998. "Towards the Design of a System of Peer Review of Teaching for the Advancement of the Individual Within the University." *Higher Education.* 35:143-162.

Costantino, P.M., M.N. De Lorenzo, and C. Tirrell-Corbin. 2008. *Developing a Professional Teaching Portfolio: A Guide for Success* (3rd ed.). Princeton: Allyn & Bacon.

Courneya, C., D.D. Pratt, and J. Collins. 2008. "Through What Perspective Do We Judge the Teaching of Peers?" *Teaching and Teacher Education: An International Journal of Research and Studies* 24(1):69-79.

Cox, M.C., ed. 1996. *A Department-Based Approach to Developing Teaching Portfolios: Perspectives for Faculty Developers.* Vol. 15. Stillwater, OK: New Forums Press and the Professional and Organizational Development Network in Higher Education.

Cox, Rebecca D.. 2009. *The College Fear Factor: How Students and Professors Misunderstand One Another.* Cambridge: Harvard University Press.

Creamer, D. G. and Creamer, E. G. 1990. "Use of a Planned Change Model to Modify Student Affairs Programs" in D. Creamer, (Ed.),

College Student Development: Theory and Practice for the 1990s
Alexandria, VA: American College Personnel Assoc. 181-192.

Cross, K. Patricia. 1990. "Teachers as Scholars." *AAHE Bulletin*
43(4):3-5.
D'Andrea, V. & D. Gosling (2005) *Improving Teaching and
Learning: a whole institution approach*, Buckinghamshire:
McGraw Hill/Open University/SRHE Press.

D'Andrea, V. & D. Gosling (2005) *Improving Teaching and Learning:
a whole institution approach*, Buckinghamshire: McGraw
Hill/Open University/SRHE Press.

Danielson, C. 1996. *Performance Assessment: A Collection of Tasks.*
Princeton, NJ; Eye on Education.

Davis, B. G. 2009. *Tools for Teaching*, 2nd Edition. San Francisco:
Jossey-Bass.

Dennis, L.J. 1976. "Teacher Evaluation in Higher Education." *Liberal
Education* 62:437-43.

D'Andrea, V. and D. Gosling. 2005. *Improving Teaching and
Learning: a whole institution approach*, Buckinghamshire: Open
University/SRHE Press

De Rijdt, C., E. Tiquet, F. Dochy, and M. Devolder. 2006. "Teaching
Portfolios in Higher Education and Their Effects: An Exploratory
Study." *Teaching and Teacher Education* 22:1084-1093.

DeZure, Deborah. 1993. "Opening the Classroom Door." *Academe*
Sept-Oct:27-28.

----------. 1999. "Evaluating Teaching Through Peer Classroom
Observation." Pp. 70-96 in *Changing Practices in Evaluating
Teaching,* edited by Peter Seldin. Bolton, MA: Anker Publishing.

Dienst, E.R. 1981. *Evaluation by Colleagues.* San Francisco:
University of California. ED 309 341. 6 pp. MF-01; PC-01.

Discoll, M.P. 2002. *How People Learn and What Technology Might
have to do with It.* ERIC Clearinghouse on Information and
Technology, Syracuse, NY.

Dornbusch, S.M. 1975. *Evaluation and the Exercise of Authority*. San Francisco: Jossey-Bass.

Douglas, J. and Douglas, A. 2006. *Evaluating Teaching Quality* (April) 12 (1): 3–13.

Doyle, K.O. Jr., and L.I. Crichton. 1978. "Student, Peer, and Self Evaluations of College Instruction." *Journal of Educational Psychology* 70:815-26.

Dressel, P.L. 1976. "Faculty." *Handbook of Academic Evaluation,* by P.L. Dressel, 331-75. San Francisco: Jossey-Bass.

Driscoll, Amy and Ernest Lynton, eds. 1999 . *Making Outreach Visible: A Workbook on Documenting Professional Service and Outreach.* Washington, DC: American Association for Higher Education.

Dziech, B. W, and L. Weiner, 1990. *The Lecherous Professor: Sexual Harassment on Campus, 2nd Edition.* University of Illinois Press, Urbana and Chicago, IL

Eble, K.E. 1972a. *Professors as Teachers*. San Francisco: Jossey-Bass

----------. 1972b. *The Recognition and Evaluation of Teaching.* Washington: American Association of University Professors.

----------. 1988. *The Craft of Teaching*. 2d ed. San Francisco: Jossey-Bass

Eckert. R.E. 1950. "Ways of Evaluating College Teaching." *School and Society* 71:65-69.

Edgerton, R., P. Hutchings, and K.M. Quinlan. 1992. *The Teaching Portfolio: Capturing the Scholarship in Teaching*. Washington: American Association for Higher Education.

Edgerton, R., Hutchings, P., Quinlan, P. & Schulman, L.. 1995. "From Idea to Prototype: The Peer Review of Teaching – Starting the Conversation. *From Idea to Prototype: The Peer Review of Teaching* by Pat Hutchings. Washington, DC: AAHE.

Edgerton, R. 1993. "The Reexamination of Faculty Priorities Fourteen Points." *Change* July/August:10-25.

----------. 1988. "All Roads Lead to Teaching." *AAHE Bulletin* 40(8):3-9.

----------. 1994. "A National Market for Teaching Excellence." *Change.* Sept/Oct.

Edwards, Richard. 1997. "Can Post-Tenure Review Help Us Save the Tenure System?" *Academe* 83(3): 26-31.

Edwards, S. 1974. "A Modest Proposal for the Evaluation of Teaching." *Liberal Education* 60 316-26.

Elbow, P. 1980. "One-to-One Faculty Development." *Learning About Teaching*, edited by J.F. Noonan. New Directions for Teaching and Learning No.4. San Francisco: Jossey-Bass.

----------. 1986. *Embracing Contraries: Explorations in Learning and Teaching.* New York: Oxford.

----------. 1992. "Making Better Use of Student Evaluations of Teachers." *Association of Departments of English Bulletin.* Spring.

El Hassan, K. 2009. "Investigating Substantive and Consequential Validity of Student Ratings of Instruction." *Higher Education Research & Development* 28(3):319-333.

Emery, C. R., Kramer, T. R. and Tian,R. G. 2003. "Return to Academic Standards: a Critique of Student Evaluations of Teaching Effectiveness", *Quality Assurance in Education*, Vol 11, No 1: 37-46.

England, J. 1996. "How Evaluations of Teaching are Used in Personnel decisions." In England, J, Hutchings, P. and McKeachie, W. *The Professional Evaluation of Teaching*, Occasional Paper 33, American Council of Learned Societies.

Erickson, G.R., and B.L. Erickson. 1979. "Improving College Teaching: An Evaluation of Teaching Consultation Procedure." *Journal of Higher Education* 50(5):670-683.

Evans, Lynn and Shelia Chauvin. 1993. "Faculty Developers as Change Facilitators: The Concerns-Based Adoption Model." *To Improve the Academy: Resources for Student, Faculty and Institutional Development*. 165-178.

Evans, S. 1994. *Changing the Process of Teaching & Learning: Essays by Notre Dame Faculty*. South Bend: University of Notre Dame.

Fairweather, J.S. 1993. "Academic Values and Faculty Rewards." *Review of Higher Education* 17(1):43-68.

Fairweather, J.S. 2002. "The Ultimate Faculty Evaluation: Promotion and Tenure Decisions." *New Directions for Institutional* Research 2002 (114):97-108.

Farmer, C.H. 1976. "Colleague Evaluation: The Silence Is Deafening." *Liberal Education* 62:432-36.

Feldman, K. A. 1988: Effective College Teaching From the Students' and Faculty's View: Matched or Mismatched Priorities?" *Research in Higher Education*. 30: 291-344.

Fitzgerald, M.J., and C.L. Grafton. 1981. "Comparisons and Implications of Peer and Student Evaluations for a Community College Faculty." *Community/Junior College Research Quarterly* 5:331-37.

FitzPatrick, M.A. and D. Spiller. 2010. "The Teaching Portfolio: Institutional Imperative or Teacher's Personal Journey?" *Higher Education Research & Development* 29(2):167-178.

Flanigan, Michael. 1970. "Observing and Developing the Individual's Teaching Style." *Writing Program Administration* Winter.

Fleak, S.K. et al. 2003. "Portfolio Peer Review: A Tool for Program Change." *Journal of Education for Business* 78(3): 139-146.

Flexner, Abraham. 1908. *The American College: a Criticism*. New York: The Century Co..

Fortune, J.C., J.M. Cooper and D.W. Allen. 1967. "The Stanford Summer Micro-teaching Clinic, 1965," *Journal of Teacher Education*, 18: 389-393.

Franse, Steven R. 1994. "Portfolios and Professors." *Contemporary Education.* 66, Fall, pp.18-19.

Freer, M., and J. Dawson. 1985. "DON'T Evaluate Your Teachers." *Phi Delta Kappan* 66:720-22.

French-Lazovik, G. 1981. "Peer Review: Documentary Evidence in the Evaluation of Teaching." *Handbook of Teacher Evaluation*, edited by J. Millman. Beverly Hills, CA: Sage.

----------. 1975. "Evaluation of College Teaching: Guidelines for Summative and Formative Procedures." Washington, DC: Association of American Colleges.

Fullan, M. G. 1991. *The New Meaning of Educational Change.* Teachers College Press.

Fullan, Michael. 1994. *Change Forces.* San Francisco: Jossey-Bass.

Gabelnick, F., J. MacGregor, R.S. Matthews, and B.L.Smith. 1990. *Learning Communities: Creating Connections Among Students, Faculty, and Disciplines.* New Directions for Teaching and Learning, no. 41. San Francisco: Jossey-Bass Publications.

Gaff, J.G. 2009. "Academic Freedom, Peer Review, and Shared Governance in the Face of New Realities." Pp. 19-36 in *The Future of the Professoriate: Academic Freedom, Peer Review, and Shared Governance*, edited by N.W. Hamilton and J.G. Gaff. Washington DC: Association of American Colleges and Universities.

Gage, N.L. January/February 1961. "The Appraisal of College Teaching." *Journal of Higher Education* 32(1):17-22.

Galle, W.P. et al. 1993. "Tenure and Promotion after Penn vs. EEOC." *Academe* 79(5):19-26.

Galm, J.A. 1985. "Welcome to Post-Tenure Review." *College Teaching* 33:65-67.

Gardner, Howard. 1991. *The Unschooled Mind: How Children Think and How Schools Should Teach.* Basic Books.

Garland, J.K.. 1969. "Training for Teaching Assistants: Trial Classes and IV Taping," *Journal of Chemical Education,* 46: 621.

Geis, G.L. 1991. "The Moment of Truth: Feeding Back Information about Teaching." In M. Theall and J. Franklin *Effective Practices for Improving Teaching and Learning: New Directions for Teaching and Learning,* 48, San Francisco, VA: Jossey-Bass.

Gerstman, B. B. 1995. "Student Evaluations of Teaching Effectiveness: The Interpretation of Observational Data and the Principle of *Faute de Mieux." Journal on Excellence in College Teaching* 6(3):115-124.

Gibbs, G. 1995. "How can Promoting Excellent Teachers Promote Excellent Teaching? *Innovations in Education and Training International* 32:74-84.

Goldhammer, R. 1969. *Clinical Supervision.* New York: Holt, Rinehart, and Winston.

Goldner, Fred H., Ritti, Richard R., and Ference, Thomas P. 1977. "The Production of Cynical Knowledge in Organizations." *American Sociological Review* 42(4):539-551.

Goldstein, R.J.. 1993. "Some Thoughts about Standardized Teaching Evaluations." *Perspectives on Political Science* 22(1):8-11.

Golin, S. 1990. "Four Arguments for Peer Collaboration & Student Interviewing: Master Faculty Program." *AAHE Bulletin* December.

Goroff, D.L. and J. Wilkinson. 1994. "Force and Inertia: A Case about Teaching Introductory Physics." *Change* Nov/Dec.

Gray, P.J. 1991. "Using Assessment Data to Improve Teaching." *Effective Practices for Improving Teaching,* edited by M. The all and J. Franklin. New Directions for Teaching and Learning No. 48. San Francisco: Jossey-Bass.

Greenwood, G.E. and H.J. Ramagli Jr. November/December 1980. "Alternatives to Student Ratings of College Teaching." *Journal of Higher Education* 51:673-84.

Guernsey, L. 1999. "With Web Skills–and Now Tenure–A Professor Promotes Improved Teaching." *Chronicle of Higher Education* February 26:A24.

Gunn, B. 1982. "Evaluating Faculty Performance: A Holistic Approach." *Journal of the College and University Personnel Association* 34(4):23-30.

Guthrie, E.R. 1949. "The Evaluation of Teaching." *The Educational Record* 30:109-15.

Hacker, A. and C. Dreifus. 2010. Higher Education? *How Colleges are Wasting Our Money and Failing Our Kids—and What We Can Do About It.* New York: Times Books.

Hagerty, P., Wolf, K., and Whinery, B. 1997. "Improving Teaching through Faculty Portfolio Conversations." Pp. 317-334 in *To Improve the Academy: Resources for Student, Faculty and Institutional Development,* edited by D. DeZure. Vol. 16. Stillwater, OK: New Forums Press.

Halpern, D F. 1994. "Rethinking College Instruction for a Changing World." Pp 1-12 in *Changing College Classrooms,* edited by D.F. Halpern and Associate. San Francisco: Jossey-Bass.

Hamilton, N. W. 2007. "Faculty Autonomy and Obligation". *Academe* 93(1): 36–43.

----------, N.W. 2009. "Proactively Justifying the Academic Profession's Social Contract."Pp. 1-18 in *The Future of the Professoriate: Academic Freedom, Peer Review, and Shared Governance,* edited by N.W. Hamilton and J.G. Gaff. Washington DC: Association of American Colleges and Universities.

Hamilton, N. W. and Gaff, J. G.. 2009. *The Future of the Professoriate: Academic Freedom, Peer Review, and Shared Governance.* Washington, DC: Association of American Colleges and Universities.

Hammersley-Fletcher, Linda, and Paul Orsmond. 2004. "Evaluating our Peers: Is Peer Observation a Meaningful Process?" *Studies in Higher Education* 29:489-503.

Harper, Victoria. 1996. "Establishing a Community of Conversation: Creating a Context for Self-Reflection Among Teacher Scholars." Pp. 251-266 in *To Improve the Academy: Resources for Student, Faculty and Institutional Development*, edited by D. DeZure. Stillwater, OK: New Forums Press.

Harrison, P.D., D.K. Douglas, and C.A. Burdsal. 2004. "The Relative Merits of Different Types of Overall Evaluations of Teaching Effectiveness" *Research in Higher Education* 45:311-323.

Hart, F.R. 1987. "Teachers Observing Teachers." *Teaching at an Urban University*, edited by J.H. Broderick. Boston: University of Massachusetts at Boston. ED 290 704. 77 pp. MF 01; PC-01.

Heller, D.A. 1989. *Peer Supervision: A Way of Professionalizing Teaching*. Bloomington: Phi Delta Kappa.

Helling, B.B. 1988. "Looking for Good Teaching: A Guide to Peer Observation." *Journal of Staff, Program, and Organization Development* 6(4):1-12.

Helms, M. M., Williams, A. B., Nixon, J. C. 2001. "TQM Principles and their Relevance to Higher Education: the Question of Tenure and Post-tenure Review", *International Journal of Educational Management*, Vol 15, No 7: 322-331.

Hewitt, John P. and Randall Stokes. 1978. "Disclaimers." In *Symbolic Interaction: A Reader in Social Psychology*, edited Jerome G. Manis and Bernard N. Meltzer. Boston: Allyn and Bacon.

Higgerson, Mary Lou. 1999. "Building a Climate Conducive to Effective Teaching Evaluation." Pp. 194-212 in Peter Seldin et al., *Changing Practices in Evaluating Teaching*. Bolton MA: Anker Publishing.

Higgerson, Mary Lou, and Susan S. Rehwaldt. Summer 1992. "The Mandate for Assessment: Institutional Expectations and Departmental Perspectives." *The Department Chair* 1: 5-6.

Hilsen, Linda and LeAne Rutherford. 1991. "Front Line Faculty Development: Chairs Constructively Critiquing Colleagues in the Classroom." Pp. 251-269 in *To Improve the Academy: Resources for Student, Faculty and Institutional Development*, edited by D. DeZure. Stillwater, OK: New Forums Press.

Hind, R.R., S.M. Dornbusch, and W.R. Scott. 1974. "A Theory of Evaluation Applied to a University Faculty." *Sociology of Education* 47:114-28.

Hoban, G. 2000. "Making Practice Problematic: Listening to Student Interviews as a Catalyst for Teacher Reflection." *Asia-Pacific Journal of Teacher Education*, Vol 28, No 2: 133-147.

Hockey, John. 1993. "Research Methods—Research Peers and Familiar Settings." *Research Papers and Education* 8(2):199-225.

Hodgkinson, H. 1974. "Adult Development: Implications for Faculty and Administrators." *Educational Record* 55:263-74.

----------. 1972. "Unlock the Doors, Let Your Colleagues In: Faculty Reward and Assessment Systems." *The Academic Department and Division Chairmen*, edited by J. Braun and T.A. Emmet. Detroit: Balamp.

Horowitz, D. 2004. "In Defense of Intellectual Diversity." *The Chronicle of Higher Education.* February, 13, Retrieved 12/10/2004. (http://chronicle.com/).

Howery, C., Van Valey, T. and T.C. Wagenaar (Eds). 1998. Peer *Review of Teaching: Departmental Resources Group Training Session Handbook.* Washington, D.C. American Sociological Association.

Howery, C. 1997. *Enhancing Peer Collaboration in Teaching Sociology*: a proposal to the American Association for Higher Education. Washington, DC. American Sociological Association.

----------. 1998 "Making Teaching and Small College Faculty More Cosmopolitan." In Godfrey, E. (ed), *Teaching Sociology in Small Institutions*, American Sociological Association, 1998.:253-266

----------.. 1998. Recognizing *and Rewarding the Professional and Scholarly Work of Sociologists.* A report of the Task Force of the American Sociological Association. Washington, D.C.: American Sociological Association

Hoyt, D.P. and G.S. Howard. 1978. "The Evaluation of Faculty Development Programs." *Research in Higher Education* 8:25-38.

Huba, M.E., and J.E. Freed. 2000. *Learner-Centered Assessment on College Campuses: Shifting the Focus from Teaching to Learning.* Needham Heights, MA: Allyn and Bacon.

Huber, Mary Taylor. 2001. "Balancing Acts: Designing Careers Around The Scholarship Of Teaching" *Change* 33(4): 21-30.

Huber, Mary Taylor and Pat Hutchings. 2006. "Building the Teaching Commons." *Change* 38(3):25-31

Huston, Therese, and Carol L. Weaver. 2008. "Peer Coaching: Professional Development for Experienced Faculty." *Innovative Higher Education* 33:5-20.

Hutchings, P. 1993a. "Introducing Faculty Portfolios: Early Lessons From CUNY York College." *AAHE Bulletin* 45 (9):14-17.

----------. 1993b. *Using Cases to Improve College Teaching: A Guide to More Reflective Practice.* Washington, DC: AAHE.

----------. 1994. "Breaking the Solitude of Teaching." *Metropolitan Universities: An International Forum* 5(1):19-25.

----------. 1994. "Peer Review of Teaching: From Idea to Prototype: lessons from a current AAHE teaching initiative project." *AAHE Bulletin* 47 (3):3-7.

----------. 1995. "Peer Review of Teaching: From Idea to Prototype." *AAHE Bulletin* 47(3):3-7.

----------. 1995. *From Idea to Prototype: The Peer Review of Teaching, A Project Workbook.* Washington DC: AAHE Publications.

----------. 1996. "The Peer Review of Teaching: Progress, Issues and Prospects." *Innovative Higher Education* 20(4):221-234.

----------. 1996. *Making Teaching Community Property: Menu for Peer Collaboration and Peer Review.* Washington DC: AAHE Publications.

----------. 1997. "The Pedagogical Colloquium: Taking Teaching
Seriously in the Faculty Hiring Process." Pp. 271-294 in *To
Improve the Academy*, edited by D. DeZure. Vol. 16. Stillwater, OK:
New Forums Press.

Hutchings, P., ed. 1999. *The Course Portfolio.* Washington, DC:
American Association for Higher Education.

Hutchings, P., L. Schulman and H. Byrnes. 1995. "Faculty Hiring: A
Pivotal Opportunity to Foster a Culture of Teaching." *AAHE
Bulletin* 48(2):7-12.

Hynes, J. 1997. *Publish and Perish: Three Tales of Tenure and
Terror.* New York: St. Martin's Press

Irby, D M. 1983. "Peer Review of Teaching in Medicine." *Journal of
Medical Education.* Vol 58 No 6: 457-461.

Ives, S.M. 1997. "The Virtual Geography Department: A Disciplinary
Attempt to Develop Mechanisms for the Peer Review of
Teaching." Prepared for the AAHE Peer Review of Teaching
Project Meeting, June 20-22, Albuquerque, NM.

Jacoby, R. 1987. *The Last Intellectuals: American Culture in the Age
of Academe.* New York: Basic Books

Johnson, D.W., Johnson, R.T. and K.A. Smith. 1991. *Cooperative
Learning: Increasing College Faculty Productivity.* ASHE-ERIC
Higher Education Report No.4. Washington: Association for the
Study of Higher Education. ED 343 465. 168 pp. MF-01; PC-07.

Johnson, T., and Ryan, K. 2000. "A Comprehensive Approach to the
Evaluation of College Teaching." In K. E. Ryan (ed.), *Evaluating
Teaching in Higher Education: A Vision for the Future.* New
Directions for Teaching and Learning, no. 83. San Francisco:
Jossey-Bass,

Johnson, T. D. and Katherine E. Ryan. 2001. "A Comprehensive
Approach to the Evaluation of College Teaching" pp. 109-133. in
Christopher Knapper and Patricia Cranton., eds.
2001. *Fresh Approaches to the Evaluation of Teaching. New
Directions for Teaching and Learning.* No 88, Winter. : San
Francisco, CA: Jossey Bass.

Jones, M.A. 1986. "Participatory Evaluation of a Departmental Peer Review Process for Awarding Merit Pay to University Faculty." *Dissertation Abstracts International* 48:0316A. (University Microfilms, No. 87-11724.)

Kahn, S. 1995. "Better Teaching Through Better Evaluation: A Guide for Faculty and Institutions." *To Improve the Academy* 12:111-125.

Kain, Edward L. 2006. "Bridging the Gap between Cultures of Teaching and Cultures of Research." *Teaching Sociology* 34(4):325-340.

Katz, J. and M. Henry. 1988. *Turning Professors Into Teachers: A New Approach to Faculty Development and Student Learning.* New York: Macmillan.

Katz, S.N. 1994. "Defining Educational Quality and Accountability." *The Chronicle of Higher Education* November 16.

Keig, L.W. 1989. *Faculty Evaluation: Iowa Association of Independent Colleges and Universities.* Unpublished manuscript.

----------. 1991. "A Study of Peer Involvement in the Formative Evaluation of Instruction in Higher Education." *Dissertation Abstracts International* 52: 5-1, 593A (University Microfilms No.91-31189.)

Keig, L. and M.D. Waggoner. 1994. *Collaborative Peer Review. The Role of Faculty in Improving College Teaching.* ERIC Digest. Washington DC: ERIC Clearinghouse on Higher Education.

----------. 1995. "Peer Review of Teaching: Improving College Instruction Through Formative Assessment." *Journal on Excellence in College Teaching* 6(3):51-93.

----------. 2000. "Formative Peer Review of Teaching: Attitudes of Faculty at Liberal Arts Colleges toward College Assessment." *Educational Administration Abstracts* 35 (4).

Keith, Bruce and Nicholas Babchuk. 1998. "The Quest for Institutional Recognition: A Longitudinal Study of Scholarly Productivity and Academic Prestige among Sociology Departments." *Social Forces* 76(4): 1495-1533.

Kell, C. and S. Annetts. 2009. "Peer Review of Teaching: Embedded Practice or Policy-Holding Complacency?" *Innovations in Education and Teaching International* 46(1):61-70.

Kember, D., D.Y.P. Leung & K.P. Kwan. 2002. "Does the Use of Student Feedback Questionnaires Improve the Overall quality of Teaching?" *Assessment & Evaluation in College Teaching.* Vol 27. No. 5: 411-425.

Kern, V.M., Saraiva, L.M., and R.C. dos Santos Pacheco. 2003. :Peer Review in Education: Promoting Collaboration, Written Expression, Critical Thinking, and Professional Responsibility" *Education and Information Technologies* 8:37-46.

Killen, Roy. 1995. "Improving Teaching Through Reflective Partnerships." Pp. 125-141 in *To Improve the Academy: Resources for Student, Faculty and Institutional Development*, edited by D. DeZure. Stillwater, OK: New Forums Press.

Klingstedt, J.L.. 1976. "Video Taped Microteaching: Students Rate It Great," *Improving College and University Teaching*, 24: 20-21.

Knapper, Christopher and Patricia Cranton., eds. 2001. "Fresh Approaches to the Evaluation of Teaching." *New Directions for Teaching and Learning.* No 88, Winter. Jossey Bass: San Francisco, CA

Knapper, Christopher and W. Alan Wright. 2001. "Using Portfolios to Document Good Teaching: Premises, Purposes, Practices." Pp. 19-30 in *New Directions for Teaching and Learning.* No. 88, Winter. Edited by Christopher Knapper and Patricia Cranton. San Francisco, CA: Jossey Bass.

Kohut, G.F., C. Burnap, and M.G. Yon. 2007. "Peer Observation of Teaching: Perceptions of the Observer and the Observed." *College Teaching* 55(1):19-25.

Kremer, John F. 1990. "Construct Validity of Multiple Measures in Teaching, Research, and Service and Reliability of Peer Ratings." *Journal of Educational Psychology* 82(2):213-218.

Kuh, George D. "Designing an Institutional Renewal Strategy to Create Seamless Learning Environments for Undergraduates". *Journal of College Student Development* 37. 135 – 148.

Kulski, M.M. and A. Radloff. 1998. "Adding Value to Teaching: A Framework for Institutional Use of the Teaching Portfolio." *South African Journal of Higher Education* 12:179-185.

Kumaravadivelu, B. 1995. "A Multidimensional Model for Peer Evaluation of Teaching Effectiveness." *Journal on Excellence in College Teaching* 6(3):95-113.

Kurz, T.L., G. Llama, and W. Savenye. 2005. *TechTrends*, 49 (4), 67-73.

Lacey, P.A. 1988. "Faculty Development and the Future of College Teaching." *College Teaching and Learning: Preparing for New Commitments*, edited by R.E. Young and K.E. Eble. New Directions for Teaching and Learning No.33. San Francisco: Jossey-Bass.

Ladd, E.C. Jr. 1979. "The Work Experience of American College Professors: Some Data and an Argument." *Current Issues in Higher Education* No.2. Washington, DC: American Association for Higher Education.

Lamont, M. 2009. *How Professors Think: Inside the Curious World of Academic Judgment.* Cambridge: Harvard University Press

Lang, J. 2010. "4 Steps to a Memorable Teaching Philosophy." *Chronicle of Higher Education* Aug. 29:online.

Langenberg, D.N. 1992. "Team Scholarship Could Help Strengthen Scholarly Traditions." The Chronicle of Higher Education, September 2, A64.

Lawrence, J., and R. Blackburn. 1985. "Faculty Careers: Maturation, Demographic, and Historical Effects." *Research in Higher Education* 22:135-54.

Lawrence, Paul R., and Jay W. Lorsch. 1967. *Organization and Environment: Managing Differentiation and Integration.* Boston: Harvard Business School Press.

Leaming, D.R. 1998. *Academic Leadership: A Practical Guide to Chairing the Department.* Bolton, MA: Anker.

Lee, B.A. 1982. "Balancing Confidentiality and Disclosure in Faculty Peer Review: Impact on Title VII Litigation." *Journal of College and University Law* 9:279-314.

Leggett, M. and Bunker, A. 2006. "Teaching Portfolios and University Culture." *Journal of Further and Higher Education* 30:269-282.

Leve, J and E. Wenger. 1991. *.Situated Learning: Legitimate Peripheral Participation.* Cambridge: Cambridge University Press

Levinson-Rose, J., and R.J. Menges. 1981. "Improving College Teaching: A Critical Review of Research." *Review of Educational Research* 3:403-34.

Lewis, M. 1997. *Poisoning the Ivy: The Seven Deadly Sins and Other Vices of Higher Education in America.* Armonk, NY: M. E. Sharpe, Inc

Licata, C.M. 1986. *Post-Tenure Faculty Evaluation: Opportunity of Threat?* ASHE-ERIC Higher Education Report No.1. Washington: Association for the Study of Higher Education. ED 270 009. 118 pp. MF 01; PC-05.

--------. 2004. "Post-Tenure Faculty Review Practices: Context and Framework." Pp. 6-11 in *Post-Tenure Faculty Review and Renewal II: Reporting Results and Shaping Policy*, edited by Christine M. Licata and Betsy Brown. Bolton, MA: Anker Publishing Company, Inc.

Licata, C.M. and J. Morreale. 1999. "Post-tenure Review: National Trends, Questions, and Concerns" *Innovative Higher Education.* 24:

--------. 2006. *Post-Tenure Faculty Review and Renewal III: Outcomes and Impact.* Bolton, MA: Anker Publishing Company, Inc.

Lichty, R.W. and J.M. Peterson. 1979. *Peer Evaluations--A Necessary Part of Evaluating Teaching Effectiveness.* Duluth: University of Minnesota. ED 175 352. 7 pp. MF-01: PC-01.

Lindholm, Jennifer A.. 2004. "Pathways to the Professoriate: The Role of Self, Others, and Environment in Shaping Academic Career Aspirations" *The Journal of Higher Education* 75(6): 603-635.

Liston, D.D., C.A. Hansman, S.L. Kenney, and C.C. Brewton. 1998. "Teaching Portfolio Use in the Absence of Institutional Support. *Journal on Excellence in College Teaching* 9:121-134.

Lomas, Laurie and Nicholls, Gill. 2005. "Enhancing Teaching Quality Through Peer Review of Teaching" *Quality in Higher Education* 11:137-149.

Lord, T. 2009. "What? Professors Evaluating Themselves? Are You out of Your Mind?: In Defense of Faculty Self – Evaluation." *Journal of College Science Teaching* 38(4):72-74.

Love, K.G. 1981. "Comparison of Peer Assessment Methods: Reliability, Validity, Friendship Bias, and User Reaction." *Journal of Applied Psychology* 66:451-457.

Lowry, Janet Huber, et al. 2005. *Creating an Effective Assessment Plan for the Sociology Major.* Washington, DC: American Sociological Association.

Lucal, B. et al. 2003 "Assessment of Faculty and the Scholarship of Teaching and Learning: Knowledge Available/Knowledge Needed." *Teaching Sociology* 31(2): 146-161.

Lynton, E.A. 1998. "Reversing the Telescope: Fitting Individual Tasks to Common Organizational Ends." *AAHE Bulletin* 50(7) March: 8-10.

Lyons, Richard E., Meggin McIntosh, and Marcella L. Kysilka. 2003. "Evaluating the Effectiveness of Your Teaching" in *Teaching College in an Age of Accountability.*
Boston, MA: Allyn and Bacon.

Macdonald, R.H. and K.M. Kemp. 1996. "Teaching Portfolios and Their Use in Assessment." *Journal of Geoscience Education* 44:395-400.

Maehr, M. and C. Midgley. 1996. *Transforming School Cultures.* Westview.

Mahaffy, Kimberly A., and Elizabeth M. Caffrey. 2003. "Are Requests for Teaching Credentials Customary? A Content Analysis of the 1999 *Employment Bulletin*." *Teaching Sociology* 31(2):203-211.

Malik, D. J. 1996. "Peer Review of Teaching: External Review of Course Content." *Innovative Higher Education* 20(4): 277-286.

Mangan, K.. 1992. "Colleges Expand Efforts to Help Teaching Assistants Learn to Teach," *The Chronicle Of Higher Education*, (March 4): A17-A18.

Manus, D.A. 2001. "The Two Paradigms of Education and the Peer Review of Teaching." *Journal of Geoscience Education* 49(5): 423-34.

Marques, T.E., D.M. Lane, and P.W. Dorfman. 1979. "Toward the Development of a System for Instructional Evaluation: Is There a Consensus Regarding What Constitutes Effective Teaching?" *Journal of Educational Psychology*. 71:840-49.

Marshall, M. J. 2008 "Teaching Circles: Supporting Shared Work and Professional Development." *Pedagogy* Vol 8, No 3: 413-431

Maslow, A.H., and W. Zimmerman. 1956. "College Teaching Ability, Scholarly Activity and Personality." *The Journal of Educational Psychology* 47:185-89.

Massy, W. F. and A.K. Wilger and C. Colbeck. 1994. "Overcoming 'Hollowed Collegiality': Departmental Culture and Teaching Quality." *Change* July/August 26(4):11-20..

Mathis, B.C. 1974. *Persuading the Institution to Experiment: Strategies for Seduction*. Occasional Paper No.9, Center for the Teaching Professions. Evanston: Northwestern University.

----------. 1979a. "Academic Careers and Adult Development." *Current Issues in Higher Education* No.2, edited by R. Edgerton. Washington: American Association for Higher Education.

----------. 1979b. "The University Center." *Designing Teaching Improvement Programs*, edited by L. Lindquist. Washington: Council for the Advancement of Small Colleges.

Mauksch, H.O. 1980. "What are the Obstacles to Improving Quality Teaching?" *Current Issues in Higher Education* No.1:49-56.

McCarthey, S.J., and K.D. Peterson. 1988. "Peer Review of Materials in Public School Teacher Evaluation." *Journal of Personnel Evaluation in Education* 1:259-67.

McColgan, K. and B. Blackwood. 2009. "A Systematic Review Protocol on the Use of Teaching Portfolios for Educators in Further and Higher Education." *Journal of Advanced Nursing* 65(12):2500-2507.

McDaniel, E.A. 1987. "Faculty Collaboration for Better Teaching: Adult Learning Principles Applied to Teaching Improvement." Pp. 94-102 in *To Improve the Academy: Resources for Student, Faculty, and Institutional Development*, edited by Joanne Kurfiss. Stillwater: New Forums Press.

McEnerney, K. and J. L. Webb. "The View From the Back of the Classroom: Faculty Based Peer Observation Program." *Journal of Excellence in College Teaching* in press.

McGee, Reece. 1985. "Lies We Live By: Some Academic Myths and Their Functions." *Teaching Sociology*, 12:477-490.

McIntosh, T.H., and T.E. Van Koevering. 1986. "Six-Year Case Study of Faculty Peer Review, Merit Ratings, and Pay Awards in a Multidisciplinary Department." *Journal of the College and University Personnel Association* 37:5-14.

McIntyre, C.J. 1978. *Peer Evaluation of Teaching* Urbana-Champaign: University of Illinois. ED 180 295. 7 pp. MF-01; PC-01.

McIntyre, K.E. 1986. *Using Classroom Observation Data for Diagnosis Purposes.* Paper presented at the annual meeting of the American Educational Research Association, San Francisco, ED 275 731. 12 pp. MF-01; PC-01.

McKeachie, W.J. 1982. "The Reward of Teaching." *Motivating Professors to Teach Effectively*, edited by J.L. Bess. New Directions for Teaching and Learning, No. 10. San Francisco: Jossey-Bass.

McKeachie, W.J. 1987. "Can Evaluating Instruction Improve Teaching?" *Techniques for Evaluating and Improving Instruction*, edited by L.M. Aleamoni. New Directions for Teaching and Learning, No.31. San Francisco: Jossey-Bass.

McKeachie, W.J. 1994. *Teaching Tips: Strategies, Research, and Theory for College and University Teachers*. 9th ed. Lexington: D.C. Heath and Company.

McKeachie, W. J. 1996. Student ratings of teaching. In England, J., Hutchings, P., and McKeachie, W. J., *The Professional Evaluation of Teaching*. New York: American Council of Learned Societies, Occasional Paper No. 33, 1-7.

McKinney, Kathleen, Carla B. Howery, Kerry J. Strand, Edward L. Kain, and Catherine White Berheide. 2004. *Liberal Learning and the Sociology Major Updated: Meeting the Challenge of Teaching Sociology in the Twenty-First Century*. Washington, DC: American Sociological Association.

Menges, R. 1980. "Teaching Improvement Strategies: How Effective Are They?" *Current Issues in Higher Education* 1:25-31.

----------. 1985. "Career-Span Faculty Development." *College Teaching* 33:181-84.

----------. 1987. "Colleagues as Catalysts for Change in Teaching." Pp. 83-93 in *To Improve the Academy: Resources for Student, Faculty and Institutional Development*, edited by Joanne Kurfiss. Stillwater: New Forums Press.

----------. 1990. "Using Evaluation Information to Improve Instruction." *How Administrators Can Improve Teaching*, by P. Seldin. San Francisco: Jossey-Bass.

----------. 1991. "The Real World of Teaching Improvement: A Faculty Perspective." *Effective Practices for Improving Teaching*, edited by M. Theall and J. Franklin. New Directions for Teaching and Learning, No.48. San Francisco: Jossey-Bass.

----------. 1991. "Why Hasn't Peer Evaluation of College Teaching Caught On?" Presented at the meeting of the American Educational Research Association, Chicago, IL.

Menges, R.J., and B.C. Mathis. 1988. *Key Resources on Teaching, Learning, Curriculum, and Faculty Development.* San Francisco: Jossey-Bass.

Meyer, Luanna H. and Ian M. Evans. 2003. "Motivating the Professoriate: Why Sticks and Carrots are only for Donkeys." *Higher Education Management and Policy* 15(3):151-167.

Mezeske, B. A. 2006 "Teaching Circles: Low-Cost, High-Impact Faculty Development" *Academic Leader*: 8

Mignon, Charles and Deborah Langsam. 1999. "Peer Review and Post-Tenure Review." *Innovative Higher Education* 24(1): 49-59.

Mikula, A.R. 1979. *Using Peers in Instructional Development.* Altoona: The Pennsylvania State University. ED 172 599. 14 pp. MF-01; PC-01.

Miller, L.H. Jr. September/October 1990. "Hubris in the Academy." *Change.* 22 (5): 9+

Millis, B.J. 1992. "Conducting Effective Peer Classroom Observations." *To Improve the Academy* 11:189-201.

----------. 1996. "The Peer Review of Teaching: Progress, Issues, and Prospects." *Innovative Higher Education.* 20 (4), 221-234.

----------. 1999. "Three Practical Strategies for Peer Consultation." *New Directions for Teaching and Learning* 79 (Fall):19-28.

Millis, B.J., and B.B. Kaplan. 1995. "Enhancing Teaching Through Peer Classroom Observations." Pp. 137-149 in *Improving College Teaching*, edited by Peter Seldin Bolton: Anker Publishing.

Millis, B.J., and L. Richlin. 1994. "Three-Year Evaluation of Peer Consultation Program: The University of Maryland University College." University of Maryland College Park. Manuscript.

Mills, C. Wright. 1978. "Situated Actions and Vocabularies of Motive." In *Symbolic Interaction: A Reader in Social Psychology*, edited by Jerome G. Manis and Bernard N. Meltzer. Boston: Allyn and Bacon.

Misra, J. 2000. "Integrating 'The Real World' Into Introduction to
Sociology: Making Sociological Concepts Real." *Teaching
Sociology* 28:346-363.

Monroe-Baillargeon, A. 2002. "Talking about our Work: Teachers
Use of Video as a Problem Solving Tool." In R. Griffin, J. Lee, and
V. Williams *Visual Literacy in Message Design*. Rochester, NY:
International Visual Literacy Association, pp.2-6.

Montell, Gabriela. 2002. "The Fallout from Post-Tenure Review."
Chronicle of Higher Education.
(http://chronicle.com/article/The-Fallout-From-Post-
Tenure/46063/)

Mooney, L.A., and B. Edwards. "Experiential Learning in Sociology:
Service Learning and Other Community-Based Learning
Initiatives." *Teaching Sociology* 29:181-194.

Moran, T.P. 1999. "Versifying Your Reading List: Using Poetry to
Teach Inequality." *Teaching Sociology* 27:110-125.

Morehead, J.W., and P.J. Shedd. 1996. "Student Interviews: A Vital
Role in the Scholarship of Teaching." *Innovative Higher Education*
20(4):261-270.

----------. 1997. "Utilizing Summative Evaluation Through External
Peer Review of Teaching." *Innovative Higher Education* 22(1):37-
44

Morreale, Joseph C. 1999. "Post-Tenure Review: Evaluating
Teaching." Pp. 166-138 in *Changing Practices in Evaluating
Teaching*, edited by Peter Seldin. Bolton, MA: Anker Publishing.

Mosteller, F.. 1989. "The Muddiest Point in the Lecture' as a
Feedback Device." *Teaching and Learning: The Journal of The
Harvard-Danforth Center* 3:10-21.

Muchinsky, P.M. 1995. "Peer Review of Teaching: Lessons Learned
from Military and Industrial Research on Peer Assessment.
Journal of Excellence in College Teaching 6(3):17-30.

Murray, H. E. Gillese, M. Lennon, P. Mercer, and M. Robinson. 1996.
Ethical Principles for College and University Teaching, Society for
Teaching and Learning in Higher Education, York University:

Reprinted in *AAHE Bulletin* Volume 49, Number 4, (December, 1996): 3-6.

Murray, H.G. 1975. "Predicting Student Ratings of College Teaching from Peer Ratings of Personality Types." *Teaching of Psychology* 2(2):66-69. New Jersey Institute for Collegiate Teaching and Learning. 1991. *Partners in Learning.* South Orange: NJICTL, Seton Hall University.

Murray, Harry G. 1987. ΛAcquiring Student Feedback that Improves Instruction.@ Pp. 93 in *New Directions for Teaching and Learning*, 32 (Winter). San Francisco: Jossey-Bass.

Murray, J.P. 1995. "The Teaching Portfolio: A Tool for Department Chairpersons to Create a Climate of Teaching Excellence." *Innovative Higher Education* 19:63-175.

----------. 1997. *Successful Faculty Development and Evaulation: The Complete Teaching Portfolio.* ASHE-ERIC Higher Education Report, no. 8. Washington, DC The George Washington University, Graduate School of Education and Human Development.

Myers, J. 1998. "Videotaping: A Tool for Teachers" GSAS Bulletin 27:6 January. Derek Bok Center for Teaching and Learning, Harvard University.

Naumes, W. and J.J. Naumes. 1999. *The Art and Craft of Case Writing.* Thousand Oaks, CA: Sage Publications.

Neal, Anne D. 2008. "Reviewing Post-Tenure Review." *Academe Online* 94 (5). Retrieved March 10, 2010 (AAUP.org).

Newmann, Fred. 1996. *Authentic Achievement: Restructuring Schools for Intellectual Quality.* Jossey-Bass.

Nilson, L. B. 2010. *Teaching at its Best: a Research-Based Resource for College Instructors*, 3rd Edition. San Francisco: Jossey-Bass.

Nolinkse, T. 1997. "Preparing and Developing faculty Through Faculty Development Initiatives." *The American Journal of Occupational Therapy.* 53(1): 9-13

Nordstrom, K.F. 1995. "Multiple-Purpose Use of a Peer Review of Course Instruction Program in a Multidisciplinary University Department." *Journal on Excellence in College Teaching* 6(3):125-144.

North, Joan DeGuire. 1999. "Administrative Courage to Evaluate the Complexities of Teaching" Pp. 183-193 in Peter Seldin et al., *Changing Practices in Evaluating Teaching*. Bolton MA: Anker Publishing.

Ory, John C. 1991. "Changes in Evaluating Teaching in Higher Education." *Theory into Practice* 30(1):30-36.

Osborne, J.L. 1998. "Integrating Student and Peer Evaluation of Teaching." *College Teaching* 46: 36-8.

Ottaway, R.N. 1991. "How Students Learn in a Management Class." *Teaching Portfolio: Capturing the Scholarship of Teaching*, edited by R. Edgerton, P. Hutchings, and K. Quinlan. Washington: American Association for Higher Education.

Page, B. 1992. "Evaluating, Improving, and Rewarding Teaching: A Case for Collaboration." *ADE Bulletin* 101:15-18.

Palmer, P. 1993. "Good Talk about Good Teaching: Improving teaching through conversation and community." *Change* Nov/Dec., 8-13.

----------. 1998. *The Courage to Teach: Exploring the Inner Landscape of a Teacher's Life.* San Francisco: Jossey-Bass.

Pascale, R.T. 1978. "Zen and the Art of Management," *Harvard Business Review*, March-April: 153-162.

Paulsen, M. B. 2001. "The Relation Between Research and the Scholarship of Teaching." In C. Kreber, (ed.), *Scholarship Revisited: Defining and Implementing the Scholarship of Teaching*. New Directions for Teaching and Learning, no. 86. San Francisco: Jossey-Bass: 19-29.

Paulsen, M. B. 2002. "Evaluating Teaching Performance." *New Directions for Institutional Research*, no. 114. Wiley Periodicals: 5-18.

Perkins, David. 1992. *Smart Schools: From Training Memories to Educating Minds.* Free Press.

Perlberg, A. 1983. "When Professors Confront Themselves: Toward a Theoretical Conceptualization of Video Self-Confrontation in Higher Education." *Higher Education* 12:633-63.

Perry, G. and S. Talley. 2001. "Online Video Case Studies and Teacher Education: A New Tool for Preservice Education." *Journal of Computing in Teaching Education.* 17 (4), pp. 26-31.

Peterson, K. and D. Kaucheck. 1982. *Teacher Evaluation: Perspectives, Practices, and Promises.* Salt Lake City: Center for Professional Practice, University of Utah. ED 233 996. 53 pp. MF-01; PC-03.

Peterson, M.W., and R. Blackburn. 1985. "Faculty Effectiveness: Meeting Institutional Needs and Expectations." *Review of Higher Education* 9:21-34.

Pew Higher Education Research Program. May 1989. "The Business of the Business." *Policy Perspectives* 1:1-7.

----------. September 1990. "Back to Business." *Policy Perspectives* 3:108.

----------. September 1992. "Testimony From the Belly of the Whale." *Policy Perspectives* 4(3):1-8.

Pew Higher Education Roundtable. "1996. "Double Agent." *Policy Perspectives* 6(3):1-11.

Piker-King, Kathleen, Edward L. Kain, Keith A. Roberts, and Gregory L. Weiss. 2006. *Applying for a Faculty Position in a Teaching-Oriented Institution* (2nd Edition). Washington, DC: ASA Teaching Resources Center.

Pittman, R.B. and J.R. Slate. 1989. "Faculty Evaluation: Some Conceptual Considerations." *Journal of Personnel Evaluations in Education* 3:39-51.

Prezas, R., M. Shaver, T. Carlson, J.S. Taylor, and R. Scudder. 2009. "Peer Review of Teaching: Multiple Raters." *Perspectives on Issues in Higher Education* 12:59-63.

Pritchard, R.D., M.D. Watson, K. Kelly, and A.R. Paquin, *Helping Teachers Teach Well.* San Francisco: New Lexington Press, see pages 170-193.

Pulakos, E.D. 1986. "The Development of Training Programs to Increase Accuracy with Different Rating Tasks." *Organizational Behavior and Human Decision Processes* 38:76-91.

Quinlan, Kathleen M. 1995. "Faculty Perspectives on Peer Review." *Thought and Action* 11:5-22.

----------. 1996. "Involving Peers in the Evaluation and Improvement of Teaching: A Menu of Strategies." *Innovative Higher Education* 20(4):299-308.

----------. 1998. "Promoting Faculty Learning About Collaborative Teaching." *College Teaching* 46(2):43-47.

----------. 2002. "Inside the Peer Review Process: How Academics Review a
Colleague's Teaching Portfolio." *Teaching and Teacher Education* 18(8): 1035-49

Quinlan, Kathleen M. and Gerlese S. Akerlind. 2000. "Factors Affecting Departmental Peer Collaboration for Faculty Development: Two Cases in Context." *Higher Education* 40:23-52.

Quinlan, K.M. et al. 2000. "Factors Affecting Departmental Peer Collaboration for Faculty Development: Two Cases in Context." *Higher Education* 40(1): 23-52.

Rau, William and Baker, Paul J. 1989. "The Organized Contradictions of Academe: Barriers Facing the Next Academic Revolution." *Teaching Sociology* 17:161-175.

Razor, J. E. 1979. *The Evaluation of Administrators and Faculty Members—Or Evaluation of the "Boss" or Each Other.* Normal: Illinois State University. ED 180 355.

Reder, M. 2007. "Does Your College *Really* Support Teaching and Learning?". *Peer Review* 9: 9–13.

Reder, Michael and Eugene V. Gallagher. "Transforming a Teaching

Culture Through Peer Mentoring: Connecticut College's Johnson Teaching Seminar for Incoming Faculty." Pp. 280-297 in *To Improve the Academy*, edited by Douglas Reimondo Robertson and Linda B. Nilson. Bolton, MA: Anker Publishing.

Renfrew, D. (ed) 2009 . *Teaching Portfolios Within the Discipline*. Washington, DC: American Sociological Association.

Rhem, J. 1993. "Peers and Teaching." *National Teaching & Learning Forum* 2(4):9-11.

Rhode, Deborah L. 2006. *In Pursuit of Knowledge: Scholars, Status, and Academic Culture*. Stanford: Stanford University Press.

Rice, R.E., and S.I. Cheldolin. 1989. "The Knower and the Known: Making the Connection: Evaluation of the New Jersey Master Faculty Program." South Orange: New Jersey Institute for Collegiate Teaching and Learning, Seton Hall University.

Rice, R.E. (1992) 'Toward a Broader Conception of Scholarship: the American context', in Whiston, T.G. and Geiger, R.L. (eds), *Research and Higher Education: the United Kingdom and the United States*, Buckingham: Open University Press, 117-129.

Rice, R. E. 2002. "Beyond *Scholarship Reconsidered*: Toward an Enlarged Vision of the Scholarly Work of Faculty Members" *New Directions for Teaching and Learning* 90: 7-17.

Rice, R. E. 2006. "From Athens and Berlin to LA: Faculty Work and the New Academy." *Liberal Education* 92 (4):6]–13.

Richlin, L. 1995. "A Different View on Developing Teaching Portfolios: Ensuring Safety While Honoring Practice." *Journal of Excellence in College Teaching* 6:161-178.

_____. and B. Manning. 1995. "Evaluating College and University Teaching: Principles and Decisions for Designing a Workable System." *Journal of Excellence in College Teaching* 6:3-15.

Riegle, R.P., and D.M. Rhodes. 1986. "Avoiding Mixed Metaphors in Faculty Evaluation." *College Teaching* 34:123-28.

Roberts, Keith A. and Karen A. Donahue. 2000. "Professing Professionalism: Bureaucratization and Deprofessionalization in the Academy" *Sociological Focus.* 33: 365-83.

Romberg, E. 1985. "Description of Peer Evaluation within a Comprehensive Evaluation Program in a Dental School." *Instructional Evaluation* 8(1):10-16.

Root, L.S. 1987. "Faculty Evaluation: Reliability of Peer Assessment of Research, Teaching, and Service." *Research in Higher Education* 26:71-84.

Roper, S.S., T.E. Deal, and S. Dornbusch. 1976. "Collegial Evaluation of Classroom Teaching: Does it Work?" *Educational Research Quarterly.* 1(1):56-66

Rorschach, E., and R. Whitney. 1986. "Relearning to Teach: Peer Observation as a Means of Professional Development for Teacher." *English Education.* 18:159-72.

Rose, S. 2007. "Perfecting Your Portfolio: Preparing for Promotion." *FASEB Journal* 21(5):A33-A34.

Ross, D., E. Bondy, L. Hartle, L. Lamme, and R. Webb. 1995. "Guidelines for Portfolio Preparation: Implications from an Analysis of Teaching Portfolios at the University of Florida." *Innovative Higher Education* 20:45-62.

Russell, G, and A. Ng. 2009. "Observation and Learning in Family Practice" *Can Fam Physician* Vol. 55, No. 9: 948 - 950

Rutland, P. 1990. "Some Considerations Regarding Teaching Evaluations." *Political Science Teacher.* 3(4):1-2.

Salmon, Victoria N. 2008. "Preparing Future Teacher-Scholars" Pp 184-192 in Sean P. Murphy, ed., *Academic Cultures: Professional Preparation and the Teaching Life.* New York: Modern Language Association.

Sauter, R.C., and J.K. Walker. 1976. "A Theoretical Model for Faculty 'Peer' Evaluation." *American Journal of Pharmaceutical Education* 40:165-66.

Scharff, L. F. V. 2003. "Organizing and Maintaining University-wide Teaching Circles. In W. Buskist, V. Hevern, & G. W. Hill, IV, (Eds.). *Essays from E-xcellence in teaching, 2002* (Chap. 8). Society for the Teaching of Psychology

Schiller, S.A., M.M. Taylor, and P.S. Gates. 2004. "Teacher Evaluation Within a Community of Truth: Testing the Ideas of Parker Palmer" *Innovative Higher Education* 28:263-186.

Schmitt, N. and M. Lappin. 1980. "Race and Sex as Determinants of the Mean and Variance of Performance Ratings." *Journal of Applied Psychology* 65:428-435.

Schneider, L.S. 1975. *Faculty Opinion of the Spring 1974 Peer Evaluation.* Los Angeles: Los Angeles City College. ED 104 493. 24 pp. MF-01; PC-01.

----------. 1988. "A Union of Insufficiencies: Strategies for Teacher Assessment in a Period of Educational Reform." *Educational Leadership* (November):36-41.

----------. 1993. "Teaching as Community Property: Putting an End to Pedagogical Solitude." *Change* (November/December):6-7.

Schweizer, Bernard. 2009. "The Dreaded Peer-Teaching Observation." *The Chronicle of Higher Education.* December 10, 2009. http://chronicle.com/article/The-Dreaded-Peer-Teaching-0/49356/

Scriven, M.S. 1980. *The Evaluation of College Teaching.* Syracuse: National Council on States Inservice Education. ED 203 729. 22 pp. MF-01; PC-01.

----------. 1983. "Evaluation Ideologies." *Evaluation Models: Viewpoints on Educational and Human Services Evaluation,* edited by G.R. Madaus, M.S. Scriven, and D.L. Stufflebeam. Boston: Kluver-Nijhof.

Seldin, P. 1980. *Successful Faculty Evaluation Programs.* Crugers: Coventry Press.

----------.. 1984. *Changing Practices in Faculty Evaluation.* San Francisco: Jossey-Bass.

----------. 1990. *How Administrators Can Improve Teaching.* San Francisco: Jossey-Bass.

----------. 1991. *The Teaching Portfolio: A Practical Guide to Improved Performance and Promotion/Tenure Decisions.* Bolton: Anker.

----------. 1997. *The Teaching Portfolio: A Practical guide to Improved Performance and Promotion/Tenure Decisions* (Second Edition). Bolton, MA: Anker

----------. 1993. "How Colleges Evaluate Professors." *AAHE Bulletin* 46(2):6+.

----------. 1998. "How Colleges Evaluate Teaching: 1988 vs. 1998." *AAHE Bulletin* March 50(2):3-7.

----------. 2006. *Evaluating Faculty Performance: A Practical Guide to Assessing Teaching, Research, and Service.* Bolton, MA: Anker.

Seldin, P. and Associates. 1993. *Successful Use of Teaching Portfolios.* Bolton: Anker Publishing.

Seldin, P. et al. 1995. *Improving College Teaching.* Bolton: Anker Publishing Co., Inc.

Seldin, P. and J.E. Miller. 2008. *The Academic Portfolio: A Practical Guide to Documenting Teaching, Research, and Service.* San Francisco: Jossey Bass.

Seldin, P., J.E. Miller, C.A. Seldin, and W. McKeachie. 2010. *The Teaching Portfolio: A Practical Guide to Improved Performance and Promotion/Tenure Decisions* (4th ed.). San Francisco: Jossey Bass.

Shaughnessy, Michael F. 1994. "Peer Review of Teaching" ERIC. Acc. No. ED371689.

Shaw D, Belcastro S, Thiessen D. 2002. "A Teaching Discussion Group in your Department – It Can Happen!" *College Teaching.* Vol 50, No 1: 29-33

Sheppard, Sherri, Leifer, L. and Carryer, J. E. 1996. "Commentary on Student Interviews" *Innovative Higher Education* 20: 271-276.

Shevlin, M. Banyard, P. Davies, M. and Griffiths, M. 2000. "The Validity of Student Evaluation of Teaching in Higher Education: Love me, love my lectures?" *Assessment & Evaluation in Higher Education*, Vol 25, No 4: 397-405.

Shortland, S. 2004. "Peer Observation: A Tool for Staff Development or Compliance?" *Journal of Further and Higher Education* 28:219-228.

Shulman, L.S. 1987. "Knowledge and Teaching: Foundations of the New Reforms." *Harvard Educational Review* 57(1): 1-22.

----------. 1988. "A Union of Insufficiencies: Strategies for Teacher Assessment in a Period of Education Reform." *Educational Leadership* 46(3):36-41.

----------. 1988. "Teaching Alone, Learning Together: Needed Agendas for the New Reforms." *Schooling for Tomorrow: Directing Reform to Issues that Count.* Boston: Allyn and Bacon.

----------. 1989. "Toward a Pedagogy of Substance." *AAHE Bulletin.* 41(10):8-13.

----------. 1993. "Teaching as Community Property." *Change* Nov/Dec. 20(6):6-7.

----------. 1993. "Displaying Teaching to a Community of Peers." Presented at The American Association for Higher Education National Conference on Faculty Roles and Rewards, January 30.

----------. 1995. "Faculty Hiring: The Pedagogical Colloquium: Three Models." *AAHE Bulletin* 47(9):6-9.

----------. 1997."Promoting a Culture of Teaching: The Pedagogical Colloquium." *Speaking of Teaching.* Stanford University Newsletter on Teaching, Spring: 1-4

Shulman, L.S., Steven Dunbar and Gary Sandefur. 1996. "Capturing the Scholarship in Teaching: The Course Portfolio." Presentation at the AAHE Conference on Faculty Roles and Rewards, Atlanta, January.

Silverman, R. and W. Welty. 1992. "The Case of Edwina Armstrong."

To Improve the Academy, 11, pp. 265-270.

Singer, Benjamin. 1989. "The Criterial Crisis of the Academic World." *Sociological Inquiry* 59(2):127-143.

Singh, R. 1984. "Peer-Evaluation: A Process That Could Enhance the Self-Esteem and Professional Growth of Teachers." *Education* 105(1):73-75.

Sizer, Theodore. 1992. *Horace's School: Redesigning the American High School*. Houghton Mifflin.

Skinner, M.E. and R. C. Welch. 1996. "Peer Coaching for Better Teaching," *College Teaching* 44(4):153-156.

Skoog, G. March/April 1980. "Improving College Teaching Through Peer Observation." *Journal of Teacher Education* 31:23-25.

Smith, A. 1985. "The Challenge of Peer Evaluation." *Instructional Evaluation* 8(1):2-3.

Smith, G. 1987. "The Practitioners of Staff Development." *Journal for Higher Education* 1(1):58-67.

Smith, H.L. and B.E. Walvoord. 1993. "Certifying Teaching Excellence: AN Alternative Paradigm to the Teaching Award." *AAHE Bulletin* 46(2):3+.

Smith, K. and H. Tilema. 2007. "Use of Criteria in Assessing Teaching Portfolios: Judgemental Practices in Summative Evaluation." *Scandinavian Journal of Educational Research* 51(1):103-117.

Smith, M.J. and M. LaCelle-Peterson. 1991. "The Professor as Active Learner: Lessons from the New Jersey Master Faculty Plan." *To Improve the Academy* 10:271-78.

Smith, M.R. 1981. "Protecting the Confidentiality of Faculty Peer Review Records: Department of Labor v. The University of California." *Journal of College and University Law* 8:20-53.

Smith, P., C. Hausken, H. Kovacevich, and M. McGuire. 1988. *Alternatives for Developing Teacher Effectiveness.* Seattle: School of Education, Seattle Pacific University. Ed 301 115. 22 pp. MF-01; PC-01.

Smith, R.A. 1995. "Creating a Culture of Teaching Through the Teaching Portfolio." *Journal of Excellence in College Teaching* 6:75-99.

Smith, Ronald. 2001. "Formative Evaluation and the Scholarship of Teaching and Learning." Pp. 51-62 in *New Directions for Teaching and Learning.* No. 88, Winter. Edited by Christopher Knapper and Patricia Cranton. San Francisco, CA: Jossey Bass

Soderberg, L.O. 1985. "Dominance of Research and Publications: An Unrelenting Tyranny." *College Teaching.* 33:168-72.

----------. March 1986, "A Credible Model: Evaluating Classroom Teaching in Higher Education." *Instructional Evaluation* 8:13-27.

Solem, Michael N. and Kenneth E. Foote. 2006. "Concerns, Attitudes, and Abilities of Early-Career Geography Faculty" *Journal of Geography in Higher Education* 30(2):199-234.

Somervell, Hugh. 1993. "Issues in Assessment, Enterprise and Higher Education: The Case for Self-, Peer and Collaborative Assessment." *Assessment and Evaluation in Higher Education* 18(3):221-33.

Sorcinelli, M.D. 1984. "An Approach to Colleague Evaluation of Classroom Instruction." *Journal of Instructional Development* 7:11-17.

----------. 2007. "Faculty Development: The Challenge Going Forward". *Peer Review* 9: 4–8.

Sorcinelli, Mary Deane, Mei-Yau Shih, Mathew L. Ouellett, and Marjory Stewart. "How Post-Tenure Review Can Support the Teaching Development of Senior Faculty." Pp. 280-297 in *To Improve the Academy*, edited by Douglas Reimondo Robertson and Linda B. Nilson. Bolton, MA: Anker Publishing.

Sorcinelli, Mary Deane, Ann E. Austin, Pamela L. Eddy, and Andrea L. Beach. 2006. *Creating the Future of Faculty Development.* Boston: Anker.

Spaights, E., and E. Bridges. 1986. "Peer Evaluations for Salary Increases and Promotions Among College and University Faculty Members." *North Central Association Quarterly* 60:403-10.

Steinert, Yvonne. 2004. "Student Perceptions of Effective Small Group Teaching" *Medical Education* 38 (3), 286-293.

Stenson, N., J. Smith, and W. Perry. 1983. "Facilitating Teacher Growth: An Approach to Training and Evaluation." *The MinneTESOL Journal* 3:42-55.

Stevens, E. 1988. "Tinkering With Teaching." *Review of Higher Education* 12:63-78.

Stevens, J.J. 1985. "Legal Issues in the Use of Peer Evaluation." *Instructional Evaluation* 8(1):17-21.

Stevens, J.J., and L.M. Aleamoni. 1985. "Issues in the Development of Peer Evaluation Systems." *Instructional Evaluation* 8(1):4-9.

Stodolsky, S.S. November 1984. "Teacher Evaluation: The Limits of Looking." *Educational Researcher* 13:11-18.

Stoner, M., and L. Martin. 1993. *Talking About Teaching Across the Disciplines: How Cognitive Peer Coaching Makes It Happen.* Paper presented at the 79th annual meeting of the Speech Communication Association, Miami.

Stoner, Mark. "The Peer Coaching Program at California State University, Sacramento." *Peer Review as Peer Support: Proceeding of the California State University Peer Review Conference*, Vincent J. Buck ed., Long Beach: California State University.

Strand, K., S. Marullo, N. Cutforth, R. Stoecker, and P. Donohue. 2003. *Community – Based Research and Higher Education.* San Francisco: Jossey Bass.

Study Group on the Conditions of Excellence in American Higher Education. 1984. *Involvement in Learning: Realizing the Potential of American Higher Education.* Study Group on the Conditions of

Excellence in American Higher Education. Washington, DC: National Institute of Education.

Stumpf, W.E. 1980. "Peer Review." *Science* 207:822-23.

Sudzina, M.R. 2003. *Creating and Producing a Video Tape on Facilitating Case Discussions.* International Conference for the World Association for Case Method Research and Case Method Application, Bordeaux, France.

Sullivan, Teresa, A. 1995. "Teaching Evaluations by Peers." *Teaching Sociology* 23 (1):61-63.

Sung, Y.T., K.E. Chang, W.C. Yu, and T.H. Chang. 2009. "Supporting Teachers' Reflection and Learning through Structured Digital Teaching Portfolios." *Journal of Computer Assisted Learning* 25(4):375-385.

Swanson, F.A. and D.J. Sisson. 1971. "The Development, Evaluation, and Utilization of Departmental Faculty Appraisal System." *Journal of Industrial Teacher Education* 9(1):64-79.

Sweeney, J.M., and A.F. Grasha. 1979. "Improving Teaching Through Faculty Development Triads." *Educational Technology* 19:54-57.

Sweeney, J.M.W. 1976. "A Report on the Development and Use of a Faculty Peer Evaluation/Development Program." *Dissertation Abstracts International.* 37: 5458A. (University Microfilms No 76-30408).

Switkes, E.1999. "University of California Peer Review System and Post-tenure Evaluation". *Innovative Higher Education* 24 (1): 39–48.

Sykes, Charles J. 1998. *Profscam: Professors and the Demise of Higher* Education. Washington, DC: Regnery Gateway.

Taylor, J.W. 1999. "Lessons Learned about Post-Tenure Review from the AAHE Peer Review of Teaching Project." *Innovative Higher Education* 24(1): 73-80.

Taylor, M. 2010. *Crisis On Campus: A Bold Plan for Reforming Our Colleges and Universities.* New York: Knopf.

Tharp, Roland and Ronald Gallimore. 1991. *Rousing Minds to Life.* Cambridge.

Theall, M. 1999. "Motivation from Within: Approaches for Encouraging Faculty and Students to Excel." *New Directions for Teaching and Learning.* Jossey-Bass.

Tierney, William G. 1997. "Academic Community and Post-Tenure Review." *Academe* 83(5): 23-25.

----------. 2000. "Dealing with Deadwood." *The Department Chair,* Vol 10, No 3: 1-3.

----------. 2008. *The Impact of Culture on Organizational Decision Making: Theory and Practice in Higher Education.* Sterling, VA: Stylus.

Tigelaar, D.E.H., D.H.J.M. Dolmans, I.H.A. Wolfhagen, and C.P.M. van der Vleuten. 2005. Quality Issues in Judging Portfolios: Implications for Organizing Teaching Portfolio Assessment Procedures." *Studies in Higher Education* 30:595-610.

Tinto, Vincent. 1987. *Leaving College: Rethinking the Causes and Cures of Student Attrition.* Chicago: The University of Chicago Press, 1987.

----------. 1997. "Universities as Learning Organizations" *About Campus* Jan/Feb pp. 2-4.

Tobias, S. March/April 1986. "Peer Perspectives on the Teaching of Science." *Change* 18(2):36-41.

Toth, K.E. and C.A. McKey. 2010. "Identifying the Potential Organizational Impact of an Educational Peer Review Program." *International Journal for Academic Development* 15(1):73-83.

Travers, R.M.W. (ed) 1973. *Second Handbook or Research on Teaching.* Chicago: Rand McNally and Company.

Tynes, S.R. 2001. "Bringing Social Class Home: The Social Class Genealogy and Poverty Lunch Projects." *Teaching Sociology* 29:286-298.

Uguroglu, M.E., and M.M. Dwyer. 1981. "Staff Review System." *Improving College and University Teaching.* 29:121-24.

Urbach, F. 1992. "Developing a Teaching Portfolio." *College Teaching* 40:71-74.

van den Berg, Ineke and Wilfried Admiraal and Albert Pilot. 2006. "Peer Assessment in   University Teaching: Evaluating Seven Course Designs" *Assessment & Evaluation in Higher Education* 31: 19-36.

Van Valey, T. L. and Hillsman, S. 2007. "The Code of Ethics of the American Sociological Association" *Bulletin of the Swiss Society of Sociology*, 132: 11-15

Vaught-Alexander, Karen. 1997. *A Practical Guide to Course Portfolios: Writing, Thinking and Learning Across the Curriculum.* Pencil Point Press.

Van der Schaaf, M.F. and K. M. Stokking. 2008. "Developing and Validating a Design for Teacher Portfolio Assessment." *Assessment and Evaluation in Higher* Education 33(3):245-262.

Van Tartwijk, J., E. Driessen, C. van der Vleuten, and K. Stokking. 2007. "Factors Influencing the Successful Introduction of Portfolios." *Quality of Education* 13:69-79.

Wagenaar, Theodore C. 1995. "Student Evaluation of Teaching: Some Cautions and Suggestions." *Teaching Sociology* 23(10:64-68.

Ward, M.D., D.C. Clark, and G.V. Harrison. 1981. *The Observation Effect in Classroom Visitation.* Macomb: Western Illinois University. ED 204 384. 21 pp. MF-01; PC-01.

Webb, J. and K. McEnerney. 1995. "The View from the Back of the Classroom: A Faculty-Based Peer Observation Program." *Journal on Excellence in College Teaching* 6(3):145-160.

Webb, J. and K. McEnerney . 1997. "Implementing Peer Review Programs: A Twelve Step Model.." Pp. 295-316 in *To Improve the Academy*, edited by D. DeZure. Vol. 16. Stillwater, OK: New Forums Press.

Webb, W.B. 1995. "The Problem of Obtaining Negative Nominations in Peer Ratings." *Personnel Psychology* 8:61-63.

Weimer, M. 1987. "Translating Evaluation Results into Teaching Improvements." *AAHE Bulletin* 39(8):8-11.

Weimer, M. J. L. Parrett, and M. Kerns. 1988. *How Am I Teaching?* Madison, WI: Magna.

Weimer, M., M.M. Kerns, and J.L. Parrett. 1988. "Instructional Observation: Caveats, Concerns, and Ways to Compensate." *Studies in Higher Education.* 13:285-93.

Weimer, M. 1990. *Improving College Teaching: Strategies for Developing Instructional Effectiveness.* San Francisco: Jossey-Bass.

Weimer, M. 1991. "Colleagues Assisting Colleagues." *Improving College Teaching.* San Francisco: Jossey-Bass Publishers: 111-29.

Weimer, M. 1993. "The Disciplinary Journals on Pedagogy." *Change* 25 (6):44-51.

Weinbach, R.W., and J.L. Randolph. 1984. "Peer Review for Tenure and Promotion in Professional Schools." *Improving College and University Teaching* 32:81-86.

Weiner, Harvey S. 1986. "Collaborative Learning in the Classroom: Guide to Evaluation." College English January.

Wergin, Jon F. 1994. *The Collaborative Department: How Five Campuses Are Inching Toward Cultures of Collective Responsibility.* Washington, DC: American Association for Higher Education.

Weshah, H.A. 2010. "Issues of Developing a Professional Teaching Portfolio in Jordan." *European Journal of Social Science* 15(1):97-114.

Wherry, R.J., and D.H. Fryer. 1945. "Buddy Ratings: Popularity Contest or Leadership Criteria?" *Personnel Psychology* 2:147-59.

White, K.E. 1991. "Mid-Course Adjustments: Using Small Group Instructional Diagnosis to Improve Teaching and Learning." *Washington Center News* 6(1):20-22.

Wiedmer, T.L. 1998. "Portfolios: A Means for Documenting Professional Development." *Journal of Staff, Program, and Organization Development* 16:21-37.

Wiggins, Grant. 1993. *Assessing Student Performance, Exploring the Purpose and Limits of Testing.* San Francisco: Jossey-Bass.

Wilkerson, LuAnn. 1988. "Classroom Observation: The Observer as Collaborator." In *Professional & Organizational Development in Higher Education: A Handbook for New Practitioners,* edited by Emily C. Wadsworth.

Wilkinson, J. 1991. "Helping Students Write About History." Pp 37-39 in *The Teaching Portfolio,* edited by R. Edgerton, P. Hutchings, and K. Quinlan. Washington, DC: American Association for Higher Education.

Wilson, Kenneth and Bennet Davis. 1994. *Redesigning Education.* Henry Holt.

Wilson, R.C., E.R. Dienst, and N.L. Watson. 1973. "Characteristics of Effective College Teachers as Perceived by Their Colleagues." *Journal of Educational Measurement.* 10:31-37.

Wilson, S. and S. Wineburg. 1993. "Wrinkles in Time and Place: Using Performance Assessment to Understand the Knowledge of History Teachers." *American Educational Research Journal* Winter.

Wolansky, W.D. 1976. "A Multiple Approach to Faculty Evaluation." *Education.* 97: 81-96.

Wolf, K. 1991. "The Schoolteacher's Portfolio: Issues in Design, Implementation, and Evaluation." *Phi Delta Kappan* 73:129-136.

Wolverton, M. 1996. "Teaching Portfolios: The Experience at Miami-Dade Community College." *The Journal of General Education* 45:295-305.

Wotruba, T. R., and P. L. Wright. 1975: "How to Develop a Teacher Rating Instrument: A Research Approach." *Journal of Higher Education.* 46: 653-663.

Wright, G. 2008. "The Use of Digital Video to Increase Teacher Reflection for Action Aptitude and Ability." In J. Luca & E. Weippl (Eds.), *Proceedings of World Conference on Educational Multimedia, Hypermedia and Telecommunications 2008* (pp. 3341-3347). Chesapeake, VA: AACE.

Wright, M.C. 2000. "Getting More Out of Less: The Benefits of Short-Term Experiential Learning in Undergraduate Sociology Courses." *Teaching Sociology* 28:116-126.

--------. 2008. *Always at Odds? Creating Alignment Between Faculty and Administrative Values.* Albany: SUNY Press.

Wright, M. C., et al. 2004. "Greedy Institutions: The Importance of Institutional Context for Teaching in Higher Education." *Teaching Sociology* 32(2): 144-159.

Wright, W.A., & Associates. 1995. *Teaching improvement practices: Successful strategies for higher education.* Bolton, MA: Anker.

Wright, W.A., Peter T. Knight, and Natalie Pomerleau. 1999. "Portfolio People: Teaching and Learning Dossiers and Innovation in Higher Education." *Innovative Higher Education* 24(2):89-103.

Wunsch, Marie A., ed. 1994. *Mentoring Revisited: Making and Impact on Individuals and Institutions.* New Directions for Teaching and Learning, no. 57. San Francisco: Jossey-Bass.

Yon, Maria 2001. "Peer Observation: A Process of Critical Reflection and Self-Evaluation," *The Department Chair* Winter: p.9,12.

Young, J.R. 2001. Professors Publish Teaching Portfolios Online." *Chronicle of Higher Education* August 17:A31.

Zubizarreta, J. 1994. "Teaching Portfolios and the Beginning Teacher." *Phi Delta Kappan* 76:323-326.

----------. 1999. "Evaluating Teaching Through Portfolios." Pp. 162-182 in *Changing Practices in Evaluating Teaching,* edited by Peter Seldin. Bolton, MA: Anker Publishing.

List of Contributors

Carla Beth Howery (1950-2009)
Carla Howery was the former Deputy Executive Officer of the American Sociological Association. During her 25 year career with the ASA, she also directed the Academic and Professional Affairs Program and was a tireless speaker, author, and spokesperson for sociology. She is widely credited with building the institutional supports that have promoted quality teaching and curriculum in sociology at all levels. She was also Director of the ASA Teaching Resources Center, co-director of the ASA's Minority Opportunities through School Transformation (MOST) Program, and helped create the Department Resources Group Carla was a past president of Sociologists for Women in Society and the District of Columbia Sociological Society, served on the board of the National Association of Social Workers, and is the recipient of over a dozen awards for her service to the profession, including the prestigious Distinguished Contributions to Teaching Award of the American Sociological Association, awarded posthumously in 2009.

Thomas L. Van Valey, Western Michigan University
Tom Van Valey received his BA from Hanover College, his MA from the University of Washington, and his PhD from the University of North Carolina at Chapel Hill (1971). Having previously served on the faculties of Colorado State University, the University of Massachusetts, and the University of Virginia, he is currently a Professor Emeritus of Sociology and former Chair of the Department at Western Michigan University. He has more than 50 publications to his credit, and has made over 100 presentations at regional, national, and international meetings and workshops. Tom was the recipient of the North Central Sociological Association=s Award for Distinguished Contributions to Teaching in 1995, and the Section on Undergraduate Education - Hans O. Mauksch Award for Distinguished Contributions to Undergraduate Education in 1999. He is currently one of the directors of an NSF-funded project on ethical decision-making.

Theodore A. Wagenaar, Miami University
Ted Wagenaar is Professor of Sociology at Miami University (Ohio) and is a Carnegie Scholar. He received his A.B. degree from Calvin College and the masters and PhD from the Ohio State University. He has led over a hundred workshops on the evaluation of

teaching, teaching methods, and curriculum development. He served as the inaugural editor of Teaching Sociology and has served on the editorial boards of The Teaching Professor and the Journal of Excellence in College Teaching. He has received numerous teaching awards from local, regional, and national professional associations. He has served as a Research Fellow at the National Center for Education Statistics and has received several grants from NCES. His publications include study guides to accompany leading introductory and methods texts, several volumes published by the Teaching Resources Center of the ASA on the capstone course and other courses, several articles in Teaching Sociology on student journals, study in depth, outcomes assessment, and evaluating teaching, and several articles in various journals on youth and the transition to adulthood. His most recent publication centers on student entitlement and was published in College Teaching.

Vaneeta-marie D'Andrea,
Global Higher Education Consulting
Vaneeta D'Andrea is currently an Associate of Global Higher Education Consulting. She has been a consultant to universities, independent agencies and governments in Africa, Central Asia, Europe, the Gulf States, and North America. Her latest publications include articles ranging from quality enhancement in higher education, to educational research methods and national programmes to promote excellence in teaching, and a book, *Improving Teaching and Learning in Higher Education: a whole institution approach.* Vaneeta received her PhD from the University of Connecticut in 1986, and has held academic posts at the University of Connecticut and Guilford College in the USA, and Oxford Brookes University, Roehampton University, City University, Oxford University, and the University of the Arts in the UK. She is a Carnegie Scholar, and has received numerous awards for her work, including the ASA's Distinguished Contributions to Teaching Award.

Beth Rushing, University of Washington, Tacoma
Beth Rushing is the Vice Chancellor for Academic Affairs at the University of Washington, Tacoma. Prior to her appointment there, she served as Dean of the School of Liberal Arts & Sciences at Georgia College & State University, chaired the Department of Sociology, Anthropology, Social Work and Criminal Justice at the University of Tennessee, Martin, and taught at Kent State University, Wake Forest University, and Meredith College. She has

a B.A. in Sociology from Carson-Newman College, and MA and PhDs from Duke University. Her scholarly interests focus on work and life issues for contemporary families, and particularly on the work/life balance for faculty.

Carol Bailey, Virginia Polytechnic Institute and State University

Carol Bailey is an Associate Professor in the Department of Sociology at Virginia Tech. She is the author of A Guide to Qualitative Field Research, 2nd Edition (2007) published by Sage/Pine Forge Press. She specializes in evaluation research, primarily of programs that serve youth with serious emotional problems, and outreach activities that provide science education for underserved youth. In addition to teaching undergraduate and graduate research methods, Bailey teaches a graduate course on college pedagogy. She has received 17 teaching awards, including the university-wide Alumni Award for Teaching Excellence and the William E. Wine Award, the most prestigious award given at Virginia Tech for faculty with a long history of teaching excellence. She is also a member and past-chair of the Academy of Teaching Excellence, and past director of the University Writing Program.

John DeLamater, University of Wisconsin

John DeLamater was named the Conway Bascom Professor of Sociology at the University of Wisconsin in 2010. He received his PhD at the University of Michigan in 1969. In addition to teaching, his areas of interest include social psychology, human sexuality, gender, life course, and deviance, law and social control. His research interests include sexuality across the life course, intimate relationships, health promotion, and survey research methodology. In addition to many publications, he has received the UW Chancellor's Distinguished Teaching Award. He has just published two new books, *Understanding Human Sexuality* (11th edition, with Janet Hyde) and *Social Psychology* (7th edition, with Daniel Myers).

Keith A. Roberts, Hanover College

Keith Roberts has served on the faculty at Hanover College in Indiana for nineteen years, and currently is a Professor of Sociology. He received his BA from Muskingum College, and his ThM (1972) and PhD (1976) from Boston University. His areas of expertise include religion, family, race and ethnic relations, and social psychology, and his *Religion in Sociological Perspective* is now in its fourth edition. For the past 18 years he has also organized and lead workshops for high school sociology teachers.

Before going to Hanover, he taught at a two-year regional campus of Bowling Green State University for 15 years. He is a member of the ASA's Departmental Resources Group and has won several awards-at local, regional, and national levels-for his distinguished contributions to teaching, including the Hans O. Mauksch award.

Hans O. Mauksch (1917-1993)
Hans Mauksch has been credited with initiating the institutionalization of teaching within the American Sociological Association. He received his PhD from the University of Chicago in 1960, and was appointed to the Presbyterian-St. Lukes School of Nursing until 1962 when he became the Dean of Liberal Arts and Sciences at the Illinois Institute of Technology until 1968. From there, he went to the University of Missouri until he retired from full-time academic positions in 1983. He was the author of the FIPSE proposal that funded the Projects on Teaching Undergraduate Sociology, the first chair of the Section on Undergraduate Education, and he started the Teaching Resources Group and the Teaching Resources Center at the ASA. He was the recipient of numerous awards for contributions to teaching, including several that were subsequently named after him.

Brent Bruton, Iowa State University
Brent Bruton is currently a Professor Emeritus at Iowa State University. He received his BA, MA, and PhD (1971) from the University of Missouri. His areas of interest include the introductory course, youth culture, inequality, student behavior, and teaching effectiveness. He has received a number of awards for his contributions to teaching at the local, state, and regional levels, and was one of the early members of the Teaching Resources Group (now called the Department Resources Group). Brent was active in the Section on Undergraduate Education and retired in 2004.

Maxine P. Atkinson, North Carolina State University
Maxine Atkinson is a Professor and Head of the Department of Sociology and Anthropology at North Carolina State University. She is a member of ASA's Departmental Resources Group and the Atlantic Coast Conference Academy of Teacher-Scholars. She is the recipient of numerous teaching awards including the ASA's Hans O. Mauksch Award for Distinguished Contributions to Undergraduate Education and the Southern Sociological Society's Distinguished Contributions to Teaching Award. In 2009, she became the first woman from NC State ever to receive University of North Carolina's

Board of Governor's Teaching Excellence Award. Maxine conducts teaching workshops focusing on inquiry-guided learning and critical thinking. Her teaching interests are primarily teaching introductory sociology courses to first year students and preparing graduate students to teach. Her research focuses on the scholarship of teaching and learning and has appeared in the *Journal of Marriage and Family, Social Forces, and Teaching Sociology.*

Andrea N. Hunt, North Carolina State University
Andrea Hunt is a doctoral candidate in the Department of Sociology and Anthropology at North Carolina State University. Her work in the scholarship of teaching and learning includes implementing problem-based learning in introductory courses, teaching first year students to do research, and the pedagogical effectiveness of distance education. She is currently examining how graduate students are trained to teach distance education and is developing a series of distance education modules for introductory sociology courses. Andrea's substantive interests in sociology include family and inequality, and her dissertation research focuses on the effects that raising a child with disabilities has on parental employment over time.

Edward L. Kain, Southwestern University
Ed Kain received his B.A. from Alma College in Michigan and his PhD in sociology at the University of North Carolina at Chapel Hill in 1980. After starting his career in the Department of Human Development and Family Studies at Cornell University, he moved to Southwestern University, where he is Professor of Sociology and University Scholar. He has published over 40 articles, chapters, and books in his two major areas of research, families and social change, and the scholarship of teaching and learning. He has also edited/co-edited over half a dozen volumes on teaching-related topics for the ASA Teaching Resources Center. As a member of the ASA Department Resources Group he regularly serves as an external reviewer for sociology programs, and has led/co-led dozens of teaching and professional workshops. His work has been recognized with a number of awards, including the 1997 Hans Mauksch Award from the ASA Section on Teaching and Learning in Sociology, the 2007 ASA Award for Distinguished Contributions to Teaching, and the 2010 Distinguished Teaching Award from the Southern Sociological Society.

J. Michael Brooks, South University

Mike Brooks serves as the Dean of the College of Arts and Sciences at South University. He received his BA and MA from Texas Tech University and the PhD from the Ohio State University. He joined South University in January, 2009 after serving as department head at Valdosta State University. Previously, Mike served in faculty or administrative roles at Washington State University, Texas Christian University, The University of Kentucky, and the University of Tennessee at Knoxville. He specializes in applied sociology with a special interest in urban studies. He has done work with a number of cities and local organizations in identifying and developing programs to deal with substandard housing and related problems. Recognition includes the Hans O. Mauksch Award for Distinguished Contributions to Undergraduate Education from the Section on Teaching and Learning of the American Sociological Association. He is also a member of the Department Resources Group.